The Road Winds Uphill
All the Way

The Road Winds Uphill
All the Way

Gender, Work, and Family in
the United States and Japan

Myra H. Strober and
Agnes Miling Kaneko Chan

The MIT Press
Cambridge, Massachusetts
London England

241805

DEC 0 8 1999

This book was set in Palatino by Asco Typesetters, Hong Kong, and was printed and bound in the United States of America.

Library of Congress Cataloging-in-Publication Data

Strober, Myra H.
  The road winds uphill all the way: gender, work, and family in the United States and Japan / Myra H. Strober and Agnes Miling Kaneko Chan.
    p.   cm.
  Includes bibliographical references (p.   ) and index.
  ISBN 0-262-19415-5 (hc: alk. paper)
    1. Work and family—United States. 2. Work and family—Japan. 3. Sexual division of labor—United States. 4. Sexual division of labor—Japan. 5. College graduates—United States—Social conditions. 6. College graduates—Japan—Social conditions. I. Chan, Agnes Miling Kaneko. II. Title.
  HD4904.25.S87   1999
  306.3'6—dc21   98-41545
                                                                                                          CIP

To our families, the graduates, and the millions of parents in the United States and Japan who seek to combine work and family in nontraditional ways

Contents

Preface

For Agnes, this book started on February 8, 1987. It was a sunny, crisp day in Tokyo, and Agnes was returning to work after the birth of her first child, Arthur. She bundled him up and, together with her manager, took the baby to work. Arthur was three months old and still nursing. Agnes was going to make a comeback appearance on a TV show of which she used to be a regular member. Reporters were ready with cameras to catch a photo of Agnes with Arthur.

The baby never cried and stayed comfortably in the arms of Nana in the dressing room during the recording. Everything went so well that Agnes decided to bring Arthur to work whenever circumstances permitted. She never imagined that by keeping her child close to her at work she would raise the "Agnes Controversy," the most contentious Japanese dispute about work and family in recent times.

The question was "Should a working mother bring her child to work?" For most the answer was "no": "The workplace is a publicly shared space, and private matters like children should not be allowed to intrude." "If every working mother behaves like Agnes, nobody will hire women anymore." "Companies cannot afford to accommodate children in the workplace." "If her behavior is hailed, very soon people will start dragging their disabled elderly to work."

Some people applauded her effort: "Nursing babies have the right to be with their natural mothers and natural mothers have the right to be with their offspring." "Society should be more supportive. Companies should build on-site child care centers to raise the loyalty and diligence of their workers." "It's about time that we deal with the problems of working mothers."

Still others had mixed feelings: "Although Agnes made society aware that there's a crying baby on the back of every working parent, her actions demonstrated that child rearing is still a woman's job. She should let her husband bring the baby to work."

The controversy received even more attention when the upper house of the Diet invited Agnes to discuss the topic before a committee investigating the declining fertility rate in Japan. Agnes suggested that raising the desire of young couples to have children requires increased governmental, company, and societal accommodation for mothers with young children. She recommended the passage of a parental leave law, the development of nurseries within companies employing large numbers of young women, and more public understanding and support for young families.

Mothers started to write letters to newspapers and magazines expressing their experiences and hopes: "I was forced to leave my job when children came." "I had to leave my children at home when they were babies." "I hope my daughters will lead a life with better choices."

Soon, a group of writers banded together to condemn Agnes's position, accusing her of trying to mess up society with ideas of the privileged class. Feminist scholars, in turn, tried to pull the controversy back to the core question of women's position in society. The controversy became a struggle between people who preferred women to stay in their traditional role and those who wanted more choices for women.

After a while, Agnes started to receive hate mail and threats against her child's life. Letters making false accusations against her started to appear in magazines. At that time Agnes realized how politically and emotionally explosive the issue was.

By doing what she thought was right as a mother, she opened a well-covered, but festering, sore in modern Japanese society. She began to feel a pull to learn more about women and society, work and family, child care and marriage—issues that she had taken for granted for most of her life.

In 1989, nine months pregnant with her second child, Agnes went back to school to obtain her doctoral degree. She came to Stanford to study with Myra, who not only wrote about these issues from an economist's point of view but also was a feminist and a mother.

Myra's introduction to work and family issues began on a sweltering August day in 1967, just outside of Washington, DC, some 20 years before Agnes brought Arthur to her TV studio. Jason, Myra's son, was about one month old. Myra was soon to begin her first job as a faculty member in the Department of Economics at the University of Maryland. She began to look for child care for Jason.

Myra and her husband had recently moved to the Washington, DC, area. They had no relatives there and knew only a few couples, who had moved there at the same time. They were only beginning to meet their neighbors. Child care centers were unheard-of in Maryland in 1967, although nursery schools for toddlers were becoming popular. Care for an infant would have to be provided by a nanny. How to find one—that was the question.

For Myra, finding that nanny was the single scariest thing she has ever done in her life. Having just finished graduate school, she had never hired anyone. What questions should she ask? How could she trust the references? Her baby couldn't "report back." How could she be sure he would be getting good care?

Myra put an ad in the local paper. Only Jean responded. The interview seemed to go well, and Myra got a positive response from Jean's only reference. So Myra held her breath and made the hire. For a week Myra and Jean worked together, caring for Jason. Finally, the big day came and Myra left Jean alone with the baby. It seemed all right (but how could she really know?).

After a few weeks Myra breathed more easily. And as time went on, it became clear that Jean was providing reliable and loving care. But Myra never forgot the trauma of selection.

Like Agnes, Myra's own experience propelled her to look at work–family issues not simply as a personal problem but as a matter for scholarly analysis and societal remedy. She began to do research on the economics of child care. From an economic point of view, almost nothing was being written on the topic. President Nixon's 1971 veto of a child care bill had virtually ended scholarly discussion of child care among economists.

In September 1972, Myra began a new job as an assistant professor at Stanford's Graduate School of Business (GSB). The GSB had never before had a woman on its faculty. When she had been there for a few weeks, Myra was asked to give a seminar for other faculty. She decided to present the work she had been doing on the economics of child care. Myra argued that because child care is a service that provides "externalities," benefits beyond those going to children and parents, there is an economic rationale for government to pay for some of its costs.

The reaction of Myra's economics colleagues was strongly negative. The arguments they made were similar to those that surfaced in the "Agnes Controversy" in Japan 15 years later: "Child care is a private matter. Government should keep its hands off." "It is dangerous to have

government, and especially the federal government, involved in the curriculum and funding of child care." "If people want to have children, they
should care for them themselves. It is not the government's responsibility
to help them care for their children."

In 1970, almost two-thirds of American women with children under the
age of six were in the labor force. How were these children being cared
for? How did their parents, and especially their mothers, balance work and
family? Very few people asked these questions, and even fewer were
interested in the answers. Most economists insisted that the continuing
rise in the labor force participation of young mothers "proved" that the
market for child care was working "just fine."

Finding little support for her research on work and family at the
Graduate School of Business, Myra went on to found and direct Stanford's Center for Research on Women (now the Institute for Research on
Women and Gender). In addition to studying child care, she looked at
the effects of wives' income on family spending and at the ways in which
women with MBAs balanced work and family.

As part of her studies on work and family, Myra became interested in
how graduates of Stanford were balancing their lives. In the spring of
1990, she designed several questions on work and family for a survey of
the Stanford class of 1981. Agnes became one of the primary assistants
working with Myra to analyze the data from the Stanford survey.

When it came time for Agnes to choose a dissertation topic, it seemed
natural to both Myra and Agnes that she should repeat the Stanford
survey for the graduates of a Japanese university. And so this book was
conceived.

Japan and the United States, the two largest industrial economies in the
world, have markedly different histories and cultures, different ideologies
about gender, and different systems of education and employment. Yet,
the similarity in Agnes's and Myra's stories suggested to us that despite
all of these cross-national differences, highly educated women in both
countries might be having similar experiences in combining career and
family.

In fact, our study does find important similarities in the two countries.
Although much of what has been written about the Japanese and American economies and societies has stressed the differences between the two
nations and the tensions resulting from those differences, this book dem-
onstrates that with respect to combining career and family in nontraditional ways, many of the difficulties that highly educated women and men

face are the same in the United States and Japan. The pioneers from Todai and Stanford portrayed in this book have much in common, and we write in the spirit of contributing in both countries to a better understanding of these commonalities.

Agnes has learned a great deal from working on this book. She has seen that gender discrimination is real and sometimes cruel in Japan, even at the highest levels of education. Understanding its reality has helped her to plan her steps carefully and to work toward her goals persistently and realistically. She has found that building networks is important, not only with people who share her feelings and ideas but also with those who respect her opinions and are willing to listen—her students, politicians, writers, actors, farmers, people from all walks of life.

The experiences Agnes had as a student in the United States taught her that it is all right for a woman to speak up, but that she must respect other people's opinions no matter how different they are from hers. She feels proud to be a woman and has found an identity as a bridge builder between East and West, older and younger generations, and women and men. She knows now, more than ever, that to make the kinds of changes she works for, she cannot go it alone. She seeks to make as many friends as she can and to work with them for social change.

Having talked frequently over the past twenty years with former Stanford students, and with other young women and men in professional and management positions, about their struggles to combine work and family, Myra was not surprised by the findings in this book. Nonetheless, the problems graphically portrayed in the book have led her to redouble her efforts to work for a better child care system and more flexibility in the employment system, particularly through her work on the board of directors of the NOW Legal Defense Fund. In her teaching, advising, consulting, and lecturing, she encourages young people to discuss the knotty issues of two-career marriages with potential spouses before making marital commitments and before making decisions to limit careers, and works with managers and policy makers to implement innovative solutions to the balancing of work and family.

Like Agnes, Myra knows the importance of creating supportive networks. In the last few years, she has been closely involved with building a new international organization, the International Association for Feminist Economics (IAFFE), of which she is now president. Working with hundreds of young women economists from all over the world to reform the practice of economics and to elevate women's education and economic condition has been invigorating.

Myra receives tremendous support from her two children and her husband. Her son, Jason, whom she so fearfully left with a baby-sitter almost 30 years ago, is now married and talking with his wife, Joanna, about their own plans for combining careers and family. Liz, Myra's daughter, is fighting for a more egalitarian world in her own work. Myra was divorced in 1982 and in 1990 married Dr. Jay Jackman, a psychiatrist. Myra and Jay share their household tasks equally, something Myra did not do in her first marriage, and they also consult together for corporations interested in better utilizing women in management and the professions.

In the final months of completing this book, both Agnes and Myra had significant family changes. Agnes gave birth to her third son, Apollo, and Myra became a grandmother with the birth of Sarah Frances Strober. Also Myra's mother, Regina Hoffenberg, who taught her to aspire to have both career and family, and who fought for women's rights in her own life, passed away at the age of 91. May Apollo and Sarah Frances carry on the struggle for gender equity that Myra's mother began so many years ago.

Acknowledgments

We begin by thanking (in alphabetical order) the Stanford University team that designed the questionnaire for Stanford graduates: John Boli, Herant Katchadourian, Sally Mahoney, and William F. Massy. We also appreciate the research assistance of Henry Banks, Christine Golde, Cassandra Guarino, Douglas Jackson, Lisa Petrides, and Maureen Porter. At an early stage of the research, Thomas Rohlen and Franscisco Ramirez were helpful, as were the members of the Japan Seminar at Stanford University. At Tokyo University, Ikuo Amano provided valuable information and assistance. For assistance with the tables and bibliography we thank Terry Jo Alter, Janet Rutherford, and Ani Shastri.

Papers based on this work were presented to the Fifteenth Arne Ryde Symposium, "The Economics of Gender and the Family," in honor of Anna Bugge and Knut Wicksell, August 18–19, 1995, in Rungstedgaard, Denmark, and at the annual meetings of the Allied Social Sciences Association, January 4–7, 1996, in San Francisco. Helpful comments were received at those conferences from Clair Brown, Lawrence Kahn, Katarina Katz, and Michael Reich. Francine Blau, Yoshio Higuchi, Thomas MaCurdy, and especially Julie Schaffner also provided assistance concerning sample selection bias. Takashi Hikino provided assistance in locating Japanese data.

Special thanks to Clair Brown, Suzanne Greenberg, Cassie Guarino, Takashi Hikino, Yoko Kawashima, Tom Rohlen, Elizabeth Strober, and Aya Yoshida, who carefully read the full manuscript and provided many helpful suggestions.

Financial support by the Associates of the Stanford University Institute for Research on Women and Gender and the Stanford School of Education is gratefully acknowledged.

Our families and friends have been understanding, patient, and unfailingly supportive. We thank especially our husbands, Jay Jackman and

Tsutomu (Thomas) Kaneko; our children, Jason Strober, Elizabeth Strober, Joanna Aptekar Strober, Tenaya Jackman, and Rashi Jackman, and Arthur Kaneko and Alexander Kaneko; and Myra's sister, Alice Amsden.

The Road Winds Uphill All the Way

1　　Introduction

Does the road wind uphill all the way?
Yes, to the very end.
Will the day's journey take the whole long day?
From morn to night, my friend.

Christina Georgina Rossetti, "Up-Hill," 1861

Work and family are two of the most important ingredients in a meaningful adult life. The breadwinner/homemaker system encourages men to pursue both, through paid employment, and marriage and fatherhood, but to "specialize" and get acknowledgment and a sense of accomplishment mainly from paid work; however, it steers women toward working only in the home and obtaining gratification mainly from forming and maintaining that home and raising children.

In both Japan and the United States (two highly industrialized countries with very different histories and cultures), the traditional breadwinner/homemaker system is in transition.[1] No single new system has firmly supplanted it, but the old system is beginning to break down. And the labor market institutions, social norms, individual ideology, and gender division of labor at home, all of which used to fully support the breadwinner/homemaker system, are also experiencing major alteration.[2]

This book is about the efforts of highly educated young women and men, graduates of two elite and prestigious universities, to combine work and family in a time of societal transition. In an era where the breadwinner/homemaker model is dying, but no single nontraditional model has taken its place, the class of 1981 graduates of Stanford University and Tokyo University (Todai) are seeking to build satisfying adult lives. We surveyed these women and men in 1990–91, about a decade after their graduation.

Born in the early 1960s, the graduates were toddlers when the 1963 Equal Pay Act and the 1964 Civil Rights Act passed in the United States, mass higher education became established in Japan,[3] and Betty Friedan's 1963 book, *The Feminine Mystique,* sparked a new wave of feminism. Their work and family lives provide a measure of the extraordinary social and economic transformations of the past 30 years. But they also illustrate how far we still have to travel before less traditional work and family roles for women and men become realities in the United States and Japan.

Highly educated women and men have been at the forefront of many of the changes in work and family. For example, in both Japan and the United States, although the workforce as a whole has remained segregated by gender, many highly educated women have entered jobs and earn salaries that were once the exclusive preserve of men. Also, at least in the United States, highly educated husbands are more likely to share household tasks than are other husbands.[4]

Nonetheless, the women and men graduates of Stanford and Todai were far from having fully shed traditional specializations in homemaking and breadwinning. Both in the labor market and at home, many of the traditional modes of combining career and family were very much alive.

Even though the graduates had come to maturity during a period when their countries seemed to want increased gender equity in the labor market, they found that the structure of the labor market constrained their choices. Employers generally provided little flexibility in hours of employment, leaves, and career tracks. Moreover, they often insisted on frequent geographic transfers in order to secure promotions, and reserved the best jobs for men. Even when women were employed full-time, their earnings were only 80 percent of those of their full-time-employed male classmates. And many women were not employed full-time; despite the major investment they had made in their education, they were employed part-time or were full-time homemakers.

In part because of employers' policies, women often had low bargaining power at home vis-à-vis their husbands and partners. Most husbands were still unlikely to share equally with their wives in doing household tasks and managing the household. Men who had children were even less likely to share household tasks than other men. And most fathers continued to leave most of the work of child rearing to their wives, even when these wives were employed full-time.

Gender ideology at both the societal and the individual level has changed more in the United States than in Japan. As Bina Agarwal has argued, societal-level ideology determines the acceptable scope of bargaining and what must remain in the realm of uncontested tradition.[5] At the national level, in the United States the legacy of the civil rights movement and the emergence of a strong women's movement made it possible to bargain in the legislature for strong equal employment legislation for women. Also, the U.S. women's movement has led to widespread discussion in the public arena of a new egalitarian ideology of sharing household tasks. All of this has resulted in some loosening of the traditional gender ideology on the part of individuals, particularly more educated individuals, and has made it possible for wives with bargaining power to negotiate with their husbands for a more equal division of household tasks.

In Japan, on the other hand, equal opportunity legislation came more than 20 years after its introduction in the United States, and in the absence of a strong women's movement there has been much less talk in the media or in educational institutions of egalitarian sharing of household tasks. As a result, even when their earnings in the labor market gave women bargaining power vis-à-vis their husbands, they generally had a traditional division of labor at home, in part because bargaining for a more egalitarian division of household tasks was not within the acceptable range of negotiable topics.

Commenting on the difficulties women have faced in combining career and family in the past, Claudia Goldin noted that in the United States only about 20 to 25 percent of women who graduated from college between 1966 and 1979 had both a career and children by the time they were 40.[6] In our samples, of course, the men and women had not yet reached 40. Still, only 15 percent of the Stanford women and 23 percent of the Todai women had both full-time employment and children.

Among mothers, only 40 percent in both samples combined caring for young children with a full-time job.[7] And while Goldin concentrated on the difficulties of combining career and family only for women, we also saw difficulties for men. Only 13 percent of Todai fathers and 18 percent of Stanford fathers took an active role in their children's care.

Clearly, the road to more egalitarian work and family roles winds uphill all the way, even for graduates of two of the most highly respected universities. How did labor market institutions constrain the development of more egalitarian modes of combining work and family? How did bargaining power and social norms affect the division of household tasks? How did the graduates who were parents care for their children? What do the graduates' predictions about their future portend for the development of more egalitarian work/family roles as the graduates grow older? And what strategies and public policies are necessary to foster more egalitarian systems of combining work and family? These are the key questions we address.

The book has four major themes. The first is that in many respects (but not all) Stanford and Todai graduates are at the vanguard of social change in forging more egalitarian ways of combining work and family. The second theme is that even this vanguard continues to face major difficulties in developing more egalitarian alternatives to the breadwinner/homemaker model. Of course, some of the graduates do not appear to be seeking more egalitarian alternatives. They have opted for the breadwinner/homemaker model, or some close cousin to it. With respect to them, it is not *their* road that winds uphill, but rather the road of those who would like to see the development of more egalitarian alternatives to the breadwinner/homemaker model.

The third theme is that while conventional wisdom views the United States as "far ahead" of Japan with respect to the development of gender equity in the workplace and in the home, in many respects the graduates in the two countries found it equally difficult to achieve such equity. In both countries, improved public and business policies, as well as improved individual strategies and collective action, are needed if we wish to enable couples to combine work and family in more egalitarian ways.

The fourth theme is that what happens at the workplace affects what happens at home, that the two sectors are connected because those with higher wages in the workplace have more bargaining power at home and because labor market structures constrain couples' choices. Thus, for example, discrimination against women affects them negatively not only in the workplace, by lowering their wages, but also at home, by diminishing their bargaining power. Similarly, employers' lack of flexibility with respect to hours of work for many jobs, particularly for men, constrains men's ability to be active fathers. These kinds of interconnections between work and family mean that policies aimed at changing the labor market (for example, reducing discrimination or providing for more flexibility in careers) also have an important effect on the degree of egalitarianism likely to exist in the home.

The book also has two secondary themes. The first is that there is greater earnings equality in Japan as a whole and among the Todai graduates, compared with the United States and the Stanford graduates. The second is that coming from the upper class still plays an important role in shaping aspirations for Stanford women and men, and earnings and nonwage income for Stanford men.

At the same time that the book is a study of pioneers of social change, it is also an in-depth examination of the lives of elites. While in many respects the Stanford and Todai graduates' experiences are at the forefront of social change in their respective countries, in other respects (economic and social backgrounds, types and levels of jobs, aspirations) their lives are not likely to be emulated by others, even other college graduates, either now or in the future. Some of the careers the Stanford and Todai graduates pursue have more intense time, travel, and transfer requirements than most jobs, making it more difficult for them to create egalitarian marriages than would be the case for those in less demanding careers. Moreover, some of the graduates of Stanford and Todai, particularly the men, are in jobs that will take them to the highest levels of leadership in their societies. The difficulties they and their spouses face in combining career and family are not those that will be braved by others.

With respect to gender equality, being elite cuts two ways. For example, it is easier for elites with very high incomes to hire help, which reduces the amount of housework left to be shared, and thereby makes an egalitarian relationship easier to achieve. On the other hand, if only one member of a married couple (generally the husband) is earning a very high income and has unrelenting demands on his time, and the other partner (generally the wife) has relatively low bargaining power as she devotes her time and energy to fostering his extremely demanding career and raising their children,[8] elite status may make gender equality less easy to achieve than it is for the average married couple.

It is important to note that nonwhites are underrepresented in the Stanford sample. As a result, we do not analyze the data by race and do not make any claims that our conclusions generalize to nonwhites in the United States.

Organization of the Book

The book is organized into seven chapters. This introductory chapter provides a brief account of some of the characteristics of labor markets and public policies affecting women's employment in the two countries and background on the education systems in the United States and Japan, including specific information about higher education for women. It also provides information about Todai and Stanford, particularly concerning women at those institutions.

In chapter 2, we explain our survey procedures and discuss the demographics, educational attainment, occupations, and employment of the women and men in the two samples. In chapter 3, we examine the ways in which the labor market constrains the development of a more egalitarian work/family system. Chapter 4 looks at the division of household responsibilities among married graduates, and chapter 5 analyzes the ways in which the parents in our sample provided care for their children. In chapter 6, we look toward the future, analyzing the graduates' hopes and expectations. Chapter 7 summarizes our major findings and examines policy proposals for assisting women and men to combine work and family.

The Stanford–Todai Comparison

Once we decided to use the Stanford questionnaire to survey a sample of graduates from a Japanese university, we had numerous discussions about *which* Japanese university's graduates would be best to compare with Stanford's. We chose Todai because we wanted a university that was comparable in academic rigor and prestige with Stanford. But, in fact, the Todai–Stanford comparison is far from perfect.

First, among U.S. universities, Stanford is not as extraordinary as Todai is among Japanese universities. Stanford is one of several of the top U.S. universities; Todai, on the other hand, is in a class by itself. No other Japanese university rivals Todai for academic rigor and prestige.[9] Moreover, the differences in the American and Japanese labor markets, discussed below, work to make the Todai degree more valuable than the Stanford degree.

Second, Todai women graduates are much more unusual in Japanese society than Stanford women graduates are in American society. In 1980, women were only 22.4 percent of those enrolled in four-year colleges and universities in Japan,[10] whereas women were half of all those graduating from colleges and universities in the United States.[11] Moreover, women were much less numerous at Todai than they were at Stanford. In the Stanford class of 1981, women were 43 percent of the graduates; in the Todai class of 1981, women were 6 percent of the graduates. Women who went to Stanford in the late 1970s were highly talented, but they were not necessarily front-runners of social change; women who went to Todai in the late 1970s were exceptional pioneers.[12]

Of course, only time will tell to what extent the current arrangements at home and in the labor market will change as the graduates' labor market experience increases, their family responsibilities change with age, and the economies in the two countries struggle with global competition and structural realignments. At the time of our survey, the Japanese economy was extremely strong. (Some observers call the economy during the late 1980s and early 1990s the "bubble economy.") Subsequently, as the economy weakened, women had less labor market success relative to men. For example, between 1991 and 1993 the percentage of women graduates hired by large companies (1,000 or more employees) declined 41 percent, compared with 17 percent for men graduates.[13] It may be that we caught the Todai graduates at the height of gender equality in job opportunities and earnings.

Japanese and U.S. Labor Markets for University Graduates

In Japan, a diploma from an elite university provides a substantial advantage for initial placement on the higher managerial career track. This is especially true of large corporations and government institutions. In turn, such placement offers better opportunities for future prestige and security, including a "good" marriage. For example, 80 percent of the Todai men graduates in our sample were employed in either a large corporation of more than 1,000 employees (63 percent) or in government service (17 percent).

In this "primary" labor market, the Todai degree is not only a ticket to enter but also a ticket to stay (for one's entire employment career), with opportunities for firm-specific on-the-job training, frequent job rotation, and promotions and wage increases based on age and length of service.[14]

The process of moving from school to work is much more regularized for Japanese university graduates than for their American counterparts. For example, graduation from Todai takes place at the end of March, and graduates generally start work at the beginning of April. Most of them began searching for a job in May of their senior year, almost a year before graduation. They get informal decisions from private companies around August and formal decisions at the beginning of October, a full six months before they expect to enter employment.

It is much harder and takes much more time for women students to get formal decisions from private companies. This was particularly true before 1986, when employers could indicate that certain jobs were reserved for men. One Todai graduate from the early 1980s reminisced that while Todai male seniors received boxes of mail from potential employers, Todai women seniors received none.

But not all employment is in the primary market, which consists of large and medium-size firms and public employment. The secondary labor market consists of small companies and doing part-time, temporary, casual, or contract work (including assembly work in the home). Women in general are much more likely to be in the secondary market than are men.[15] Indeed, between 1981 and 1990, the proportion of employed women in the secondary labor market increased from 26 percent to 36 percent. For men, during that same period, the proportion in the secondary market went from 6 percent to 8 percent.[16]

In most industries, it is difficult for women to work in the primary labor market. (Banking and electronics tend to be exceptions to this generalization.) Even among Todai graduates, women were much less likely to work in the primary market than men, and about half of those who worked in the primary market were employed by government organizations. Only 27 percent of the Todai women in our sample were employed in firms with more than 1,000 employees (compared with 63 percent of the men graduates). Another 24 percent of Todai women were employed by the government (compared with 17 percent of Todai men).

Women who are interested in working for companies in the primary labor market often find that they are not welcome or, if they are hired, that they do not receive much on-the-job training (because employers expect women to leave when they marry or have a child).[17] In addition, professional and technical employment in the primary labor market often requires long overtime and weekend hours, and a willingness to take frequent job rotations that often involve geographic relocation. Both pose very real hardships for married women and particularly for married women with children.

Women who wish to balance career and family by working part-time while they raise their children are unable to work for large firms as "regular" employees with union membership and job security. Working part-time means giving up the benefits of the permanent employment system in the primary labor market. Moreover, if a woman seeks to balance work and family by leaving full-time employment in the primary labor market for even a short time—for example, to be a full-time homemaker for a while or to take a temporary leave to accompany her husband when he is transferred—she cannot return to her position and its benefits. Nor can she find a similar job elsewhere. Large firms and government agencies in this market recruit only young people, not middle-aged women returning to the labor force.

For women, government agencies are important sources of employment in the primary labor market. Not only do many women start their primary labor market careers working for the government, but women who work for the government are less likely to leave the labor market when they marry.[18] Still, women are somewhat less well represented than men in government employment. In 1990, when women represented 38 percent of the Japanese labor force, they were only 34 percent of employees in the public sector.[19]

In the early 1980s, at the time the Todai women in our sample entered the labor market, there was widespread exclusion of women from more lucrative and responsible jobs and job ladders. According to a 1981 Ministry of Labor survey of firms that recruited graduates, 83 percent had jobs from which women were excluded, 50 percent did not offer women job rotation, and 45 percent did not offer women opportunities for promotion to supervisory positions.[20] Women who did manage to find employment in these jobs often were refused promotions or, once they married, faced informal pressures to quit. Japanese employers seemed to find many ways of discouraging married women from staying in good jobs.

In the United States, the transition from school to work is much less formalized than it is in Japan. Most graduates receive their degrees in May or June. Those who will be going on to graduate school the following September generally work during the intervening months to provide funds for tuition and living expenses while they are in school, and some may take some time to travel. For those who are not going on to graduate school, their job search depends very much on the subject in which they have majored, whether they want to work for one of the large companies or government agencies who recruit and interview on campus, and in what geographical area of the country (and the world) they wish to locate.

Although many seniors look for jobs while they are still in school, others wait to search seriously until school is over, especially if they know that they would prefer to work in a particular location and employers from that location do not come to their campus to interview. Those in technical fields tend to search while they are still in school, receive multiple job offers, and agree to take one by the time they graduate. Those in the humanities have a more difficult time. Some enter employment (sometimes in a formal training program for a large company) right after graduation, but many continue to search long after they have graduated.

Like their Japanese sisters, but not to the same degree, women who graduated in the early 1980s in the United States also faced job discrimination. However, the most important type of labor market distinction by gender in the United States has not been so much the primary versus secondary labor market distinction, but rather occupational segregation; women are far less likely than men to be in the relatively lucrative occupations or subfields of occupations.[21]

The index of segregation gives the percentage of women (or men) that would have to change their occupation in order for the distribution across occupations to be the same for women and men. In the United States in 1980, using the most detailed occupational categories available, the index of segregation was about 60 percent. By the late 1980s, the index was about 57 percent.[22]

The index of segregation in Japan is lower than in the United States. If we compare the segregation indices in the United States and Japan in the early 1980s, using 89 occupations common to both countries, we find a U.S. index of 56 percent and a Japanese index of 48 percent.[23]

However, within the occupations generally held by Stanford and Todai graduates, there was *more* gender segregation in Japan. Across 24 professional and technical occupations, the index in the United States was 54 percent, while in Japan it was 61 percent. Across seven managerial and administrative occupations, it was 16 percent in the United States and 34 percent in Japan.[24]

A second major reason why women in the United States have lower wages than men is the penalty that women pay when they take time out from the workforce to raise their children. Although the penalty is not as formal as in Japan, where women who have left full-time jobs in the primary labor market cannot reenter it, American women nonetheless pay an earnings penalty when they return to work, in part because they have lost work experience and in part because they cannot get back onto the main promotion tracks because employers see them as "less committed" to an exclusive focus on work.[25]

Earnings discrimination, paying women and men with the same productivity differentially, is also part of the explanation for women's lower earnings compared with their male classmates. For college and university graduates in the United States during the mid-1980s, after accounting for number of hours of employment, possible productivity differences resulting from gender differences in education, length of work experience, the gender composition of their occupations, and other characteristics including size of firm, marital status, and presence of children, about a third of the gender earnings difference remains unexplained. This unexplained difference is generally used as a measure of employer earnings discrimination against women.[26]

For Japanese women, employer earnings discrimination (above and beyond the discrimination involved in excluding women from certain kinds of firms and promotion ladders) is also an important component of the gender earnings differential. For the late 1970s, it is estimated that in small firms about 75 percent of white-collar women's lower earnings was due to lower levels of education and length of work experience, and about 25 percent to earnings discrimination by employers. However, in large firms the results were the reverse, with only about 25 percent of white-collar women's lower earnings due to lower levels of education and work experience, and about 75 percent due to earnings discrimination by employers.[27] In large firms, older women are not employed, so all seniority and promotion gains go to men.

Legal Commitments to Gender Equity in the U.S. and Japanese Labor Markets

In recent years, both the United States and Japan have sought to increase gender equity in the labor market, but U.S. efforts began some 20 years earlier than Japan's. At the time of their graduation, the Stanford women and men entered a labor market that had been influenced by a more equitable public policy for more than 10 years. For the Todai women and men, changes in the law did not affect the labor market until five years *after* their graduation.

In the United States, two major pieces of federal legislation as well as federal executive orders have been important. In addition, there has been equal rights legislation in several states. In 1963, the Equal Pay Act provided that women and men should receive equal pay for work that involved equal skill, effort, and responsibility in the same establishment.

In 1964, Title VII of the Civil Rights Act outlawed discrimination in employment based on sex as well as race, religion, and national origin (and, as later amended, on age or physical disability). This law covered discrimination in all aspects of employment, including wages, salaries, and benefits; hiring and firing; training; and promotion.[28]

In 1967, President Johnson signed an executive order preventing employment discrimination based on sex by any employer with a federal contract or subcontract. This order also required affirmative action (the setting of goals and timetables to increase the employment of women in any occupational categories in which they were underrepresented, compared with the labor force as a whole) and an obligation to recruit in a way that would attract women into the pool of potential hires.

The Equal Pay Act is enforced by the Department of Labor; Title VII of the Civil Rights Act, by the Equal Employment Opportunity Commission (EEOC); and the executive orders, by the Office of Federal Contract Compliance (OFCC). The major form of enforcement of the legislation is through lawsuits against employers, of which there have been many. The major sanctions for violation of the Equal Pay Act and Title VII are monetary. The major sanction for violation of the executive order is cancellation of government contracts. This has occurred in only a very few instances and for only a short period of time.

In general, these antidiscrimination and affirmative action policies were enforced more rigorously during the 1970s than during the 1980s. Although women's and men's earnings and occupational distributions have become more equal in the United States since these policies were enacted, how much of the improvement was due to them is unclear.[29] Certainly, most companies, governmental agencies, and other nonprofit institutions have far more "open" systems of hiring and promotion than they did prior to the 1970s. However, women are still very poorly represented in the upper levels of management, especially in large corporations.[30]

In Japan, the Equal Employment Opportunity (EEO) law was passed in 1985 and amended in 1998. The amendments will take effect in April 1999. The original legislation prohibited sex discrimination in only a very few activities (vocational training, benefits, retirement, and dismissal) and was mostly hortatory, using "administrative guidance" to "encourage" employers to treat people equally in regard to recruitment, hiring, job assignment, and promotion.[31] This type of hortatory legislation is not unusual in the Japanese context, and it may be that it had some salutary effects on the behavior of firms.[32]

Nevertheless, the legislation probably had very little effect on the Todai women in our sample. For many of them, the damage may have already been done, so to speak, at the time of their graduation, when they were unable to find employment in a large firm or to participate in job training and job rotation. Recall that in 1981, 83 percent of firms that recruited graduates had jobs from which women were excluded, 50 percent did not offer them job rotation, and 45 percent did not offer them promotion to supervisory positions. Because the law did nothing to change the Japanese employment system, where employees are hired into the primary labor market only at the point of leaving school, the change in the law did not open up new employment opportunities for the Todai women graduates of the early 1980s.

Since large firms hire only new entrants to the labor market and the Todai women graduates in our sample had been out of school for four to six years at the time the EEO law went into effect in April 1986, the law could not help them get into large firms. The one area in which the Todai women in our sample might have been helped by the new legislation was with respect to promotion. Unfortunately, all of the evidence indicates that promotion has been the one aspect of employment that has been least affected by the EEO legislation.

In fact, for some Todai women, the law may have had a negative influence on promotion prospects. It appears that, as a reaction to the law, more firms have developed a two-track system of promotion to management (similar to what has been called the "mommy track" in the United States).[33] Those on this secondary, *ippanshoku* track, have jobs that are less complicated, have lower mobility requirements (they need to rotate only among jobs in their local geographic area), and can attain only lower-level management positions. A 1987 survey of large firms found that while 97 percent of men were on the "main" track, *sogoshoku*, 96 percent of the women were on the *ippanshoku* track.[34] And a 1993 survey found that less than 5 percent of employed women were on the *sogoshoku* track and only about 7 percent of new women graduates had been offered such positions in that year.[35]

The amendments to the law *prohibit* rather than discourage discrimination and, in particular, prohibit gender discrimination in assignment to tracks. The penalty for noncompliance is that the company's failure is to be made public through the media.

Higher Education in Japan and the United States

Preparing for Entry to University in Japan

While some private schools in Japan are connected to famous private universities or even offer a straight promotion system from kindergarten to university, this is not true for the elite national universities, such as Todai. For students who aspire to them, as well as for students who do not go to private schools directly affiliated with universities, the route to higher education is arduous.

In addition to studying in school and taking rigorous entry examinations, preparing for university entry often involves many years of attendance at "cram" schools (*yobiko*, cram schools specifically for university exams, or *juku*, more generic cram schools). These private, for-profit schools have the latest technology and marketing strategies, and use excellent teachers (often from universities) to prepare students for exams. At the time the 1981 graduates of Tokyo University were high school students (1976), about 37 percent of high school students attended *jukus*. By 1993, that percentage had increased to 67 percent. In addition, younger children also attend *jukus*. In 1976, about 10 percent of elementary school students and just under 40 percent of middle school students attended. By 1993, those numbers had increased to about 20 percent and about 60 percent, respectively.[36] Students who fail to pass the entry exam on the first try may become *ronin*, undertaking additional years of study and preparation to take it again.

In the immediate post–World War II period, American psychometricians were influential in getting Japanese educators to develop an IQ test to be used as an entry examination for national universities. Later it was adopted by all universities. This test, *Shingaku Tekisei Kensa*, often translated as "Scholastic Aptitude Test," but correctly translated as "Scholastic Adaptability Test," had three categories: general, human science, and natural science. However, for a number of reasons the test was not supported by the educational community, and when the American occupation ended in 1955, it was abolished.

At the time the graduates in our sample applied to Tokyo University, there were no national examinations, and each university gave its own entry exam. In 1979, the National University Association instituted a new uniform exam for national universities, the Joint First-Stage Achievement Test (JFSAT), which examined students in foreign language, mathematics, Japanese philology, science, and social studies. However, the second stage of the exam, which could be taken only after the first stage was passed, was not uniform; it was created, administered, and evaluated by the particular faculty of the particular university to which the student applied. In 1990, the JFSAT was revised and renamed. It is now called the National Center Test (NCT). Students who have passed the NCT take "second stage" exams written, administered, and graded by the particular faculties at the particular universities to which they apply.[37]

Preparing for Entry to University in the United States

In the United States, there are no entry examinations given by individual colleges and universities, and certainly none given by departments within those institutions. Students who apply to four-year colleges and universities take the Scholastic Aptitude Test (SAT), generally at the beginning of their senior year.[38] This is a test in English and mathematics that is created, administered, and graded by the Educational Testing Service, a private organization, under the auspices of the College Board, also a private organization. More selective colleges and universities generally require that students also take achievement tests in three subjects. These achievement tests are also created, administered, and graded by the Educational Testing Service.

For American students aspiring to college or university, performance on the SAT is only one of the factors in admissions decisions. Essays written by the student, the student's high school transcript (the record of courses taken and grades received), and letters of recommendation from high school teachers are also important.[39] As a result, although American students study for the standardized college admissions tests, and there are cram courses that many take, there is much less emphasis on these examinations than on Japanese university examinations.

Women in Higher Education

Japan
The history of women in Japanese higher education started in 1900, when Umeko Tsuda, who had been educated in the United States at Bryn Mawr, established the Women's English College (later Tsuda College) in Tokyo.[40] Tsuda's aim was to train women to become teachers of English. Also in 1900, a medical school for women and a school of fine arts for women were opened in Tokyo. In 1901, Nihon Joshi Daigaku (Japan Women's College), was privately founded to prepare women for teaching.

As late as 1918, the members of a special committee on education concluded that there was no need to build public higher education facilities for women.[41] Women who wanted to further their education had two choices: they could enter a national teachers' college for women or they could enroll in a *joshi senmongakko*, a school that taught only women. In 1920, there were 10 institutions of higher education for women; by 1935, there were 46 (6 publicly financed teachers' colleges, 28 private general schools, and 12 private schools for medicine, dentistry, and pharmacy).[42]

In 1935, less than 1 percent of college-age women were attending institutions of higher education, compared with about 5 percent of men.[43] However, women's education was given a strong boost during the Allied occupation following World War II, and women increased their attendance at institutions of higher education throughout the postwar period.[44] By 1989, women surpassed men in their attendance at institutions of higher education.

But it is important to note that women and men attend quite different types of institutions. In 1990, 39 percent of college-age men, but only 15 percent of college-age women, attended a four-year university.[45] In 1991, while 39 percent of women high school graduates entered higher education, compared with 36 percent of men, almost all of the men went to four-year universities, while only 41 percent of women did so. The other 59 percent of women entered two-year colleges. These junior colleges offered curricula that often prepared women only for occupations that are predominantly female. Very few women who attended junior college saw it as a bridge to a four-year university.[46]

The United States
Like Japanese institutions, colleges in the United States initially were not open to women. In the words of M. Carey Thomas, who graduated from Cornell in 1877 and was later president of Bryn Mawr, a woman's college: "No woman who was not born before the Civil War [1861–1865] knows out of what Egyptian darkness women came into the promised land of political and educational opportunity."[47] Although occasionally a woman attempted to enroll in one of the seven men's colleges founded before 1770, it was not until the opening of female seminaries, in the 1820s and 1830s, that women gained a foothold in higher education. Many of these seminaries later evolved into women's colleges.[48]

The first coeducational college was Oberlin, which admitted women in 1837.[49] Two other private colleges that were open to women before the Civil War were Hillsdale (Michigan) and Antioch. Three state universities also opened their doors to women before 1865: the universities of Iowa, Utah, and Wisconsin.[50]

After the Civil War, opportunities for women began to expand. Several women's colleges were separately endowed (Vassar, 1865; Smith and Wellesley, 1875; and Bryn Mawr, 1884).[51] The Morrill Act of 1862 provided for the founding of land-grant universities, which were open to women. Several private universities were founded as coeducational institutions, including Cornell University in 1865,[52] and the University of Chicago and Stanford University in 1891.[53] Thus, by the turn of the century, women were in American colleges and universities to stay. This contrasts sharply with the experience of women in higher education in Japan, where acceptance into higher education came much later.

By 1900 almost 20 percent of American bachelor's degree recipients were women, and by 1930 that proportion was nearly 40 percent. However, the post–World War II influx of veterans lowered the proportion of degrees going to women in the 1950s to 20–30 percent. By the early 1980s women had become the majority of undergraduates, and they now earn over half of the bachelor's degrees awarded annually.[54]

Tokyo University and Stanford University

Tokyo University

As noted earlier, Tokyo University (Todai) is the most prestigious Japanese university. Its status was high from the time of its founding, and entry to its faculties has always been difficult. Todai opened its doors in the 1870s, when the Japanese government decided it wanted to emulate Western universities. Without a clear idea of what a system of higher education should look like, the government established several institutions to train high-ranking civil servants. These included the faculties of law, science, and letters at Tokyo University.[55]

The teachers in these faculties were mainly foreigners brought from England, France, Germany, Scotland, and the United States. As a result, knowing foreign languages was prerequisite for entering students. The process was time-consuming (it generally took students three years to learn the requisite languages), and very few students succeeded in gaining admission.

By 1992, it was felt that the representation of Todai graduates in ministry jobs was too high; Prime Minister Kiichi Miyazawa requested that government agencies ensure that no more than 50 percent of the managerial class of the bureaucracy were graduates of Todai. The aim was to help reduce the overheated examination fever in the education system. The Ministry of Foreign Affairs, the Ministry of Finance, and the Ministry of International Trade and Industry cited difficulties in reducing their percentages of Todai graduates. Representatives of the Ministry of Finance pointed out that 22 of the 24 accepted applicants in 1992 were graduates of Tokyo University, and that for the past ten years the percentage of Todai graduates had been around 90 percent.[56] However, it appears that government bureaucracies are beginning to meet the prime minister's goal. In late 1997, *Shinbun* reported that in April 1998, at the end of the school term, half of the 207 new college graduates who would begin jobs as elite government officers (not including scientists and engineers) would be Todai graduates.[57]

Corporations also have a preferred list of universities when they recruit employees.[58] The most preferred national universities are Tokyo University, Kyoto University, and Hitotsubashi University. Within the last several years, some large companies, such as Sony, Toyota, and Hitachi, have announced that they will not consider the university of the applicant as a recruiting factor, and the Ministry of Labor is trying to convince other companies to follow suit. Nonetheless, it is unlikely that the labor market advantages given to Todai graduates will be seriously eroded any time soon.

Most Todai men did not answer the open-ended question at the end of the survey inviting comment on their college education and its effect on their life.[59] One man who did write about his Todai experience said:

Todai tested my confidence in myself because it showed me the ability of top-class individuals. This led to a new development in myself.

Another young man pointed out that under some circumstances an outstanding Todai education could be a somewhat negative factor:

The education at Todai gave me a wide perspective on life, and I was taught by great educators and people with character. However, since I am now in a rural area, I sometimes encounter discrimination based on my education background and feel mental anguish because of it.

Stanford University

Stanford University is a highly prestigious and selective institution, one of the top five or six private research universities in the United States. It was founded in 1891, later than most of its peer institutions, and came to the front ranks of prestige fairly recently.[60] Nonetheless, since the late 1970s, Stanford has been acknowledged as one of the premier universities in the world. In the spring of 1977, when Stanford's class of 1981 was admitted to the university, only one out of four applicants was offered admission.[61]

A degree from Stanford helps in the American job market, but not to the extent that a degree from Todai helps in Japan. Some of the following comments on the open-ended question at the end of the survey about the effects of the Stanford degree give a flavor of the value of a Stanford degree in the job market.

From a man:

My Stanford education has opened many doors, or at least oiled their hinges.

From a woman:

Owning a Stanford degree seems to impress your basic 55-year-old chauvinistic businessman, and consequently does open certain doors.

Interestingly, one male graduate thought his Stanford degree was most helpful when dealing with Japanese. After noting that in some American settings the Stanford degree could actually be detrimental (by raising expectations), he said:

On the other hand, I found that almost universally foreign business people (primarily Japanese real estate business people) wanted to know my educational background, and seemed pleased with and familiar with the Stanford name.

However, most of the Stanford graduates who wrote comments on their survey about their Stanford education did not look upon their college years simply as a ticket to a better job.

One man said:

I don't use the Stanford name on the diploma as much as I could to improve my financial condition. I don't view Stanford that way. I view Stanford as the catalyst or turning point that put me on the road to becoming a whole and happy person.

And another man:

People often remark about my having gone to Stanford and what that implies. I guess it is supposed to mean that you're smart or something. All I know is that it makes me feel humble. Waking up in the morning and realizing that I have a Stanford education just reminds me that I'm very fortunate and I should do something positive for someone, anyone.

Women at Tokyo and Stanford Universities

Women at Tokyo University

The first women entered Tokyo University in 1946. Throughout the next thirty years, the percentage of women students at Todai inched up from less than 2 percent in the late 1940s to slightly under 6 percent in the late 1970s. Intelligent women's confidence in applying to Todai was buoyed by the implementation of the 1979 JFSAT examination for national universities. In addition, *juku*s began to give "mock" exams so that students knew where they stood relative to other students in the *juku*. Once all students applying for entry to national universities took a common exam, women students could more easily compare their academic abilities against those of men. Although the common examination and "mock" examinations in the *juku* were criticized for fanning the heat of the entrance examination "fires," the new system helped many women candidates to realize that they ranked fairly high academically, and brought more women candidates to the doors of Todai and other elite national universities.

Applying to Todai requires cooperation from one's family, and particularly from one's mother, who plays a major role in children's education. Girls who apply to Todai generally have their mothers' encouragement to concentrate their time and efforts on academic studies, as well as their mothers' assent to pay for a *juku*. In addition, they generally have considerable encouragement from their teachers. The growth in this encouragement, together with Todai's efforts to open more courses to women, led in 1992 to women making up 14 percent of the student body. (In the class of 1981, women were only 6.6 percent of the graduates.)

Some Todai women who wrote comments on their surveys in response to the question about their Todai education and its effects said that their alma mater had provided them with an excellent education and a sense of confidence in their own abilities. However, many of them felt that Todai had not prepared them for the tremendous difficulties they found in the work world and in their own families. At times, some viewed their Todai degree as a negative, but thought it might help them to return to the workforce when their children were grown. One woman thought that given the labor market constraints she had faced, her Todai education would be more important to her effectiveness as a mother than as a worker.

I did receive rigorous training at Todai like no other Japanese university can offer. From that I have confidence. And I was supposed to be on the elite track ... so it seems I got into a very well-known big company after my master's degree. But once I started to have children, a chorus of "quit! quit!" started. This came from my own parents and my partner's parents, too. In the end, not even a Todai degree helped.

Unless you want to be a public servant, or take the bar exam, or become a doctor, being a graduate of Todai is a disadvantage for women. What I learned by myself or in other schools is more useful now than the things I learned from Todai.

Because all my high school classmates took the entrance exam [for Todai], I took it, too. At first I hated to be called a Todai student. Now, I try to hide my Todai degree from the mothers of my children's friends, because I do not want to be looked upon as special or different. In a sense, the Todai degree is a handicap for me right now. But I had a good time at Todai, and in the future, if I go back to the workforce, it may be useful.

Being a graduate of Todai, the world sees you as a super first-class individual, and this oftentimes made me feel proud, although I don't think my three years at work allowed me to express all the education. But now I am a mother of two and a full-time homemaker, so I will give all the things I have learned at Todai to my children.

Women at Stanford University
Stanford accepted women students from the start. According to its charter, Stanford was founded "to afford equal facilities and give equal advantages in the University to both sexes."[62] In its first year, women were
roughly one-quarter of the students. However, by the end of the decade,
women were about 40 percent of the students and Mrs. Stanford (who
was the surviving founder, and thus leader of the institution) became
apprehensive.[63] In 1899, she declared that there should be no more than
500 women students, explaining:

I have watched with interest the large growth in the attendance of female students, and if this growth continues in the future at the same rate, the number of
women students will before long greatly exceed the number of men, and thereby
have it regarded by the public as a university for females instead of for males. This
was not my husband's wish, nor is it mine, nor would it have been my son's.[64]

Mrs. Stanford strongly refused administrative suggestions that her cap
on women students be flexibly interpreted, or be replaced with a proportional cap. The limit of 500 women per class was reached in 1903, and
soon caused difficulties. Women were no longer admitted under various
special categories, and the Rule of 500 was interpreted to include female
graduate students.[65]

As time went on, the Rule of 500 became an increasing problem. The
number of women applicants far exceeded the number of slots available,
and friends and alumni who had financially supported the university were
irate that their daughters were not offered admission.[66] By 1933, the
number of men had increased to 2,800, but the number of women
remained at 500. In that year, the Stanford trustees changed the rule,
deciding that the proportion of women students should be 40 percent, the
proportion that had been in place in 1899, when the cap was enacted.[67]

By the 1970s, the enrollment cap again began to chafe. In June 1972,
the Stanford Academic Senate's Committee on Undergraduate Admissions and Financial Aid issued a report recommending that both the Rule
of 500 and the 1933 amendment be rescinded,[68] and in September 1972
the Stanford trustees voted to change the founding grant to remove any
quotas on women.[69] This change was approved by the Santa Clara
County Superior Court in California in March 1973.[70]

Slowly, the number of women students began to equal the number of
men students. In the class of 1981, 42.8 percent of the graduates were
women. By September 1994, the incoming first-year class had slightly
more women than men; women were 50.5 percent of entering students. In
September 1995, women were 53 percent of the entering class.

By and large, Stanford women were satisfied with their education, although, as we shall see in chapter 4, some women who were full-time homemakers felt pressure to hide their Stanford degree or to use it more fully. This comment was typical of most Stanford women's feelings.

Stanford taught me an important lesson: anything is possible.... This type of environment gave me the confidence to say things and do things which were "a little different." When you feel that your voice is important and that you can make a difference, you take chances.

2

The Women and Men of Stanford and Todai: Survey Procedures, Demographics, Educational Attainment, Occupations, and Employment

This chapter explains our survey procedures and discusses the graduates' demographics, educational attainment, occupations, employment, and commitment to paid work. In the chapter's conclusion, we highlight some of our major findings on these matters.

Surveying the Graduates

In the spring of 1990, Stanford University began preparing for a self-study for the Accrediting Commission for Senior Colleges and Universities of the Western Association of Schools and Colleges. As part of that self-study, Stanford wished to survey some of its graduates. Because the class of 1981 had been extensively surveyed while they were students, as part of an ongoing research project by Professor Herant Katchadourian, Stanford decided to use that class for its survey of graduates. Myra was asked to participate in the survey design, to frame questions about work and family.

In May 1990, Stanford sent 1,600 surveys to all members of the Stanford class of 1981.[1] All respondents were guaranteed anonymity.[2] Responses were received from 404 men and 330 women. The 46 percent response rate (48 percent for women and 44 percent for men) is standard in the United States for this type of survey work.[3]

While we cannot know with certainty that the sample precisely mirrors the Stanford class as a whole in terms of such items as marital status, job status, or the sharing of household tasks, the fact that the distribution of majors for both women and men in the sample so closely parallels the distribution of majors for the class as a whole, gives us confidence in the representativeness of the sample. Table 2A.1 shows the undergraduate majors of the Stanford sample compared with the undergraduate majors of the entire Stanford class of 1981.[4]

In September 1991, Agnes sent the graduates of Tokyo University (Todai) class of 1981 the same survey, translated into Japanese, that the graduates of Stanford had received in May 1990.[5] As at Stanford, all respondents were guaranteed anonymity. There were 388 men and 190 women respondents. The total response rate, 46 percent, was exactly the same as the Stanford response rate.[6] However, while the Stanford response rate was about the same for women and men, the Todai men had a much larger response rate (54 percent) than the Todai women (35 percent).

A comparison of the departments (called faculties) of the Todai sample and the entire class of 1981 (for men) and classes of 1980–82 (for women) is in table 2A.2. Compared with the Todai class(es) as a whole, the Todai sample has a small underrepresentation of men in law and a somewhat larger underrepresentation of women in law. There is a small over-representation of men in engineering and of women in humanities and in science. In general, the Todai sample has more engineers and scientists and fewer lawyers, compared with the class(es) as a whole.[7]

Demographics of the Graduates

This section looks at the demographics of the graduates: their gender and race; their marital and parental status; their social class backgrounds, current social class, and social class mobility; and their education and occupations.

Gender and Race

In the Stanford sample, 404 of the respondents (55 percent) were men and 330 (45 percent) were women. Almost 90 percent of the men and women were Caucasian; about 5 percent of the sample were Asian American, about 4 percent were Hispanic, about 2 percent were African American, about 2 percent were other (including those with more than one racial background), and less than 1 percent were Native American.[8] The number of people of color in each of these groups was too small for us to ana-lyze the data by race. Nonetheless, a few comments written on surveys indicated that some respondents from racial minorities had experienced discrimination.

An Asian-American man in the computer field who finally became a systems manager said he encountered "cultural discrimination (not severe, but noticeable)." Another man, who did not specify his race, said that the main problems he has faced in pursuing his career are "racism and hetero-

Table 2.1
Marital and Parental Status of Graduates, by Gender
(percentages)

	Stanford Sample		Todai Sample	
	Men (N = 401)	Women (N = 329)	Men (N = 365)	Women (N = 177)
Marital status				
Married	63.6	62.3	73.2	73.5
Living with partner	7.7	7.6	0.3	1.7
Never married	26.4	26.4	23.8	19.8
Separated	0.5	0.3	0.6	1.7
Divorced	1.8	3.0	2.2	3.4
Widowed	0.0	0.3	0.0	0.0
Total[a]	100.0	99.9	100.1	100.0
Parental status				
Has children[b]	37.1	37.6	52.6	59.8
Has child 6 or over	7.5	4.9	9.9	26.8
Has child 3–5	17.3	17.3	29.3	36.9
Has child ≤2	19.1	22.1	27.1	26.3

[a] In the Stanford sample 3 men and 1 woman did not give their marital status. In the Todai sample, 2 women did not give their marital status.
[b] 32 respondents in the Stanford sample and 3 in the Todai sample told us they had at least 1 child but did not give child(ren)'s age(s).

sexism." Interestingly, a Todai woman said that when she worked in the United States, she found racial discrimination: "In Japan there was discrimination against women. In the U.S., there was racial discrimination."

In the Todai sample there were 365 men (67 percent) and 179 women (33 percent). The racial composition of the Todai sample was 99.8 percent Japanese and 0.2 percent Korean. (There was one Korean in the sample.)

Marital and Parental Status

Stanford women and men were quite different from the Todai women and men in terms of marital and parental status. (See table 2.1.) However, within each of the samples, the women and men were similar on these dimensions.

Among the Stanford graduates, almost two-thirds were married: 64 percent of the men and 62 percent of women. An additional 8 percent of women and 8 percent of men were living with a partner. About one-fourth (26 percent) of the men and women had never been married. Two percent of the men and 3 percent of the women were divorced, and a few women and men were separated. One woman was a widow.

Thirty-seven percent of Stanford men and 38 percent of Stanford women had at least one child, and about 60 percent of the married graduates had children.[9]

Todai graduates were much more likely to be married than their Stanford counterparts. Almost three-fourths of the Todai alums were married (73 percent of men and 74 percent of women). Living with a partner was rare: only one man and three women reported doing so. The divorce and separation rates were low, about the same as for the Stanford sample. A smaller percentage of Todai graduates had never been married, compared with their Stanford counterparts. The percentage of men who had never been married (24 percent) was slightly less than the percentage for Stanford men, but the percentage of Todai women who had never been married (20 percent) was six percentage points lower than the percentage for Stanford women.

As in the case of marriage, a higher percentage of the Todai graduates had children, compared with the Stanford graduates. Slightly over a half of the Todai men and about 60 percent of the Todai women had children. Once married, Todai graduates were much more likely to have children than Stanford graduates; 72 percent of the married men and 82 percent of the married women had children.

Todai graduates had children earlier than Stanford graduates. This was particularly true among the women. Twenty-seven percent of the Todai women, but only 5 percent of the Stanford women, had a child six or over. Among the Todai graduates, a smaller percentage of men than of women (10 percent versus 27 percent) had a child six or over. Among the Stanford graduates, a slightly higher percentage of men (8 percent) than women (5) had children six or over. Stanford women waited the longest before they began to have children.[10]

Some of the graduates indicated that they intended to remain single or childless, others hoped they would not, and still others were ambivalent or had not yet made up their mind. In some cases, they wanted children but their spouse did not.

From the Stanford sample:

A single woman photographer:

I travel constantly and it wreaks havoc on my personal life. But, I love what I do, and my personal life takes a back seat.

A married woman finishing a Ph.D.:

I am *passionately* committed to my work and unwilling to make sacrifices to have children. [The decision] is right for me, and a smart decision. In the pro-family 90s, however, I feel a lot of pressure to reproduce.

A male research engineer:

I have delayed marriage and children in order to obtain a Ph.D. I feel like I am missing something, incomplete.

A woman lawyer:

I'd give up my career in a second and have children immediately if I could find a husband. Help!

And finally, a married woman in marketing:

My achievement orientation has led to delaying having family, maybe permanently. But I had my first mid-life crisis two days ago when I had a blinding thought that I'm leading a mediocre life. Happy, but I'm exploring the possibilities for a big change.

From the Todai sample:

A married woman with no children who worked fifty hours a week and ate dinner away from home seven nights a week:

I am too busy to have children. No intention to have children right now.

A man who wanted children but whose wife did not:

Because my wife works and it is difficult to find child care during the day, she has no intention of having children.

Social Class Background

Social class background, which is determined by such factors as parents' income, parents' occupation, family wealth, and family culture, often affects one's outlook on life as well as one's connections. These, in turn, may affect earnings, earnings aspirations, and, in the case of women who are mothers, the decision to be a full-time homemaker or to be employed. Rather than ask the graduates to provide information about all the elements of social class background, we asked them to circle one of six categories that best represented their parents' social class "when you were in college." (See table 2.2.) Compared with the Stanford sample, the Todai sample had a larger percentage of both women and men from the lower middle class and working class, and a smaller percentage from the upper class.

Table 2.2
Social Class of Graduates' Parents, by Gender
(percentages)

	Stanford Sample		Todai Sample	
	Men (N = 398)	Women (N = 327)	Men (N = 354)	Women (N = 167)
Class				
Lower	0.3	0.9	0.6	0
Working	2.5	5.8	13.3	7.8
Lower middle	5.8	6.1	24.9	15.6
Middle	32.7	23.6	37.0	46.7
Upper middle	51.3	52.0	23.2	28.1
Upper	7.5	11.6	1.1	1.8
Total[a]	100.1	100.0	100.1	100.0

The survey question about parents' social class was worded as follows: "Now we would like for you to circle the number that best describes the social class of your parents when you were in college." Respondents were then given the 6 options listed in the table.
[a] In the Stanford sample, 6 men and 3 women did not respond to the question. In the Todai sample, 13 men and 12 women did not respond.

In the Stanford sample, about half of the women and half of the men came from the upper middle class. About one-fourth of the women and one-third of the men came from the middle class. In general, the women's social class backgrounds were more diverse than the men's, with a higher percentage of women than men coming from both working-class and upper-class families.

About 8 percent of the men and 12 percent of the women come from upper-class families. We shall see in later chapters that these graduates from upper-class families are different from their fellow graduates in some important ways.

Relatively few graduates were from the three lower social class groups (9 percent of men and 13 percent of women). The following comment from a woman who came from the lower middle class indicates both her awareness at Stanford of her class background and her sense of opportunity:

I cried the day I last hurried across campus to class, seeing the Balkan dancers in the Quad, being struck with the profound awareness of what a privilege this was for a child of a large Irish family barely clinging to the bottom rung of the middle class ladder.

In the Todai sample, almost one-fourth of the women and almost 40 percent of the men came from the three lower social class groups, com-

Table 2.3
Social Class of Graduates, by Gender
(percentages)

	Stanford Sample		Todai Sample	
	Men (N = 397)	Women (N = 323)	Men (N = 353)	Women (N = 168)
Class				
Lower	0.0	0.0	1.1	0.0
Working	0.8	0.6	7.7	6.6
Lower middle	3.5	3.4	25.8	17.9
Middle	29.2	30.3	44.2	50.6
Upper middle	59.7	59.1	19.8	23.8
Upper	6.8	6.5	1.4	1.2
Total[a]	100.0	99.9	100.0	100.1

The survey question about social class was worded as follows: "The list below is often used to describe social classes that exist in the United States (Japan). Circle the number that best characterizes *your own* social class." Respondents were then given the 6 options listed in the table.
[a] In the Stanford sample, 7 men and 7 women did not respond to the question. In the Todai sample, 14 men and 11 women did not respond.

pared with about 10 percent of the Stanford women and men. However, at the other end of the spectrum, only 1 or 2 percent of Todai graduates said their parents had been in the upper class, a much smaller percentage than in the Stanford sample.

The women in the Todai sample had a higher class background than the men. Almost three-fourths of the women were from the middle class and upper middle class, compared with about 60 percent of the men. This relatively high class background of the Todai women was also found in the 1977 survey of Todai women graduates.

It is important to note that Stanford is a private institution and Todai is a public institution. Although the Todai sample has a much greater representation from the lower middle class and working class than does the Stanford sample, in Japan there are some who think that given its public character, Todai should have still greater representation from the lower social classes.[11]

Current Social Class

The survey also asked respondents to circle their current social class, and again they were given six choices.[12] As shown in table 2.3, the distribu-

Table 2.4
Summary of Social Mobility of Graduates, by Gender

	Percentages of Graduates Whose Social Class		
	Rose	Stayed Same	Fell
Stanford			
Men	26	59	15
Women	24	56	20
Todai			
Men	25	51	24
Women	19	57	24

tion across social classes was virtually identical for Stanford women and men, with 60 percent in the upper middle class, 30 percent in the middle class, 7 percent in the upper class, 4 percent in the lower middle class and working class and no one in the lower class.

Compared with the Stanford graduates, the Todai graduates listed lower social class standings. This may reflect the generally lower social class backgrounds from which the Todai sample came, compared with the Stanford sample. It may also reflect the fact that the monetary and accompanying social class rewards of graduation from Todai tend to come later in life than in the American case. Or it may reflect the greater income equality in Japan.[13]

Social Mobility of the Graduates

As shown in table 2.4, the patterns of social mobility for the Todai and Stanford graduates were similar: the majority stayed in the same social class.

In the Stanford sample, the mobility pattern was about the same for the women and the men, with about 56 to 59 percent remaining in the same social class over the nine-year period.[14] However, about one-fourth of the women and one-fourth of the men rose in social class in the years following college graduation, and about 15 percent of the men and 20 percent of the women fell in social class.

Starting out in the upper class was no guarantee of staying there. Among the Stanford men, of the 30 who had been in the upper class in college, half remained there. Among the 37 women starting out in the upper class, 40 percent remained there. On the other hand, winding up in the upper class was greatly facilitated by having started out fairly high in the social class strata. Of the 27 men and 21 women who were in the upper class nine years after graduation, almost all had been in either the upper class or the upper middle class in college.

In the Todai sample, half of the men and almost three-fifths of the women stayed in the same social class. About one-fourth of the women and men fell in social class; about one-fourth of the men and about one-fifth of the women rose in social class.

Education

Major or Faculty

Tokyo University is divided into 10 faculties (corresponding to schools or colleges within larger U.S. universities).[15] Student selection of faculties at Todai is different from the system at most other universities in Japan. At the time of application, applicants choose one of six broad areas of study: Humanities 1, Humanities 2, Humanities 3, Science 1, Science 2, or Science 3. They belong to these broad areas for their first two years of undergraduate education. The broad areas of study are not equally competitive. For example, Sciences 3 is a particularly competitive area. A student might decide to apply to an easier faculty in order to enter Tokyo University. However, if he or she did so, then certain opportunities, like becoming a student in the medical faculty, would be foreclosed. To be a student in the medical faculty, one must have first been in the Sciences 3 area.

After about 18 months at Todai, students apply to enter one of the faculties. As noted, their choices depend on their initial broad area. Decisions about their acceptance into a particular faculty depend upon their exam scores at Todai.[16]

The faculty to which a graduate belonged does not necessarily determine his or her career. For example, not all graduates from the faculty of law will pursue a legal career, and not all engineering graduates will become engineers. Unless the student aims to be a specialist in a particular field, a certificate from Tokyo University, no matter from which faculty, is good enough for him or her to compete for a good job.

The faculty composition of the Todai graduates is presented in table 2.5. Thirty percent of the men graduated from the faculty of engineering. It is one of the most popular and strongest faculties within the university. Twenty-three percent of the men came from the faculty of law,[17] and about 20 percent from sciences and humanities. Women graduates received

Table 2.5
Undergraduate Majors of Stanford Graduates and Faculty of Todai Graduates, by Gender
(percentages)

	Stanford Sample	
Major	Men (N = 404)	Women (N = 330)
Engineering	21.0	10.3
Human biology	7.7	15.5
Humanities	15.6	18.5
Individually designed	0.5	0.9
Interdisciplinary	0.5	0.9
Natural sciences and math	20.0	15.2
None specified	3.0	3.9
Social sciences	31.7	34.9
Total	100.1	100.1
	Todai Sample	
Faculty	Men (N = 365)	Women (N = 178)[a]
Agriculture	8.0	9.6
Arts and sciences	3.9	11.8
Economics	6.9	4.5
Education	3.0	6.7
Engineering	29.9	2.8
Humanities	9.6	28.1
Law	22.5	9.6
Medicine	2.2	6.7
Pharmacy	3.0	8.4
Sciences	11.0	11.8
Others	0.3	0.0
Total	100.3	100

[a] One woman graduate did not answer the question.

degrees mostly from the faculties of the humanities (28 percent) and were relatively equally spread across the other faculties, except for engineering, which accounted for only 3 percent of the women graduates.[18]

Unlike Todai students, Stanford students do not choose a major until after they have arrived, often not until their second year. But, like Todai graduates, Stanford graduates often have careers bearing little relation to their undergraduate major.[19] Generally, students stick with a major once they have chosen it, though some students switch majors and a few switch more than once.[20]

As shown in table 2.5, among the Stanford graduates, social sciences (anthropology, economics, political science, psychology, sociology) was the most popular major for both the women (35 percent) and the men (32 percent).[21] For Stanford men, the next most popular major was engineering (21 percent). Among the Stanford women, only 10 percent were in engineering.

Among Stanford graduates, men were somewhat more likely to major in science and math than women (20 percent versus 15 percent), and women were somewhat more likely to major in the humanities than men (19 and 16 percent, respectively). Stanford has a unique interdisciplinary major called human biology, which combines biology and social sciences. Human biology was (and still is) a popular major for women.[22] In our sample, 16 percent of women, but only 8 percent of men, majored in human biology.

Compared with the Todai men graduates, a smaller percentage of the Stanford men graduates were in engineering (21 percent of the Stanford men graduates versus 30 percent of the Todai men graduates). But a much larger fraction of the Stanford women graduates were engineers, compared with their Todai sisters (10 percent versus 3 percent).[23]

Graduate Work

In the Stanford sample, the majority of respondents went on to graduate school, but men were much more likely to obtain an advanced degree than women. (See table 2.6.) About three-fourths of the men and about three-fifths of the women obtained a graduate degree.[24] The most common advanced degree was an M.B.A. (18 percent of men and 16 percent of women). The M.D. was earned by 18 percent of the men and 13 percent of the women, and the J.D. was earned by 16 percent of the men and 10 percent of the women. About 5 percent of both the women and the men earned the Ph.D.[25]

Table 2.6
Highest Advanced Degree Obtained by Graduates, by Gender
(percentages)

	Stanford Sample		Todai Sample	
	Men (N = 404)	Women (N = 330)	Men (N = 365)	Women (N = 179)
Bachelor	24.0	38.5	60.6	66.5
J.D.	16.1	10.0	1.1	2.2
M.A.	7.4	8.8	7.1	15.1
M.B.A.	18.1	15.5	2.2	0.6
M.D.	17.6	13.3	1.1	2.2
M.S.	12.1	9.4	17.5	7.8
Ph.D.	4.7	4.6	10.4	5.6
Total	100.0	100.1	100.0	100.0

Todai graduates were much less likely than Stanford graduates to obtain advanced degrees. About 40 percent of the men and about one-third of the women in the Todai sample earned an advanced degree. Most of the Todai men who attended graduate school received an M.S. degree, whereas most of the Todai women received an M.A. The percentage of men who received the Ph.D. (10 percent) was double the percentage for men in the Stanford sample. For women the percentage receiving the Ph.D. (6 percent) was similar to the percentage for women in the Stanford sample. Unlike the Stanford graduates, very few Todai graduates obtained the M.B.A., the M.D., or the J.D.

Certificates

In addition to graduate degrees, the survey asked about other qualifications or certificates that the graduates had acquired. For the Todai sample, these qualifications and professional certificates were closely tied to the jobs and professions of the graduates. Most of the certificates were proof that the graduates had passed certain tests and had the qualifications to pursue a special career. Some of the technical qualifications were necessary for specific professions. These qualifications could be obtained while working full-time and taking examinations on the side.

In Japan, such qualifications are at times more useful in helping people to pursue a particular career than are graduate degrees. Sometimes they are essential as prerequisites for promotion. In many corporations and within the government, promotion comes after some kind of qualification test or training. Employees are urged to continue learning even on the job. Forty-five percent of the respondents had one or more qualifications. The qualifications attained by the Todai sample are shown in table 2A.3.

Sixty-five percent of the women graduates reported having at least one certification, compared with 35 percent of the men graduates. This seems to support the belief that women need extra certifications to compete in the workforce. However, within our sample, half of the qualifications acquired by women were teaching certificates. These include certifications as schoolteachers, flower arrangement teachers, and handwriting teachers.[26]

For the Stanford respondents, and in U.S. society, certificates played a much less important role. Six men and nine women said they had obtained certificates, but these were unspecified. Thirteen men and two women indicated that they were board-certified in a particular medical specialty.

Occupations of the Graduates

The occupations of the Stanford and Todai graduates, by gender, are in table 2.7. The most popular occupations for Stanford men were medical doctor (17 percent) and nontechnical manager (17 percent). An additional 8 percent of the men were technical managers. About 15 percent of the men were lawyers and about 13 percent were engineers.

Among the Stanford women, 18 percent were managers and 17 percent listed their occupation as homemaker. Of those 56 women who designated their occupation as homemaker, 15 worked more than 10 hours per week and earned more than $5,000. We defined them as part-time homemakers;[27] the 41 other women homemakers we designated as full-time homemakers.[28] In chapter 5, we discuss the lives of the homemakers in our samples more fully.

A substantial number of women were in traditionally male occupations. Thirteen percent of the Stanford women graduates were medical doctors, 8 percent were lawyers, and 8 percent were engineers and scientists.

Among the Todai men, almost one-third fell into the category "salaryman (no title)." These are white-collar workers who have not been promoted. They are sales workers, office workers, bankers, insurance sales workers, or government employees. Managers are in these same occupations, but they have been promoted to section chief or group leader. The occupational category "manager" has quite different meanings in the United States and Japan, with the Japanese term being more narrowly

Table 2.7
Occupations of Graduates, by Gender (percentages)

	Stanford Sample			Todai Sample	
	Men (N = 404)	Women (N = 330)		Men (N = 365)	Women (N = 179)
Artist or writer[a]	1.7	3.3	Artist or writer	0.6	3.9
Editor or reporter	1.2	1.2	Business owner	0.3	1.7
Engineer, scientist[b]	13.1	8.2	Editor or reporter	2.5	3.9
Finance[c]	9.7	7.0	Government manager	2.7	1.7
Health practitioner[d]	1.0	1.8	Homemaker	0.0	17.9
Homemaker	0.3	1.8	Lawyer	2.2	4.5
Lawyer[e]	14.6	17.0	Manager	14.8	2.2
Manager[f]	16.6	7.6	Medical Doctor	1.4	1.7
Medical doctor	16.6	17.9	Misc. professional	2.7	3.9
Misc. professional	0.5	13.3	Professor (lecturer)	11.2	8.9
Nontechnical consultant	3.0	1.2	Researcher	11.8	12.3
Professor	1.0	3.3	Salaryman (no title)	31.5	14.0
Sales	3.0	1.8	Student	1.9	4.5
Student[g]	4.7	1.0	Teacher	4.9	7.3
Teacher	2.2	6.1	Technical professional	6.3	3.4
Technical manager	7.9	5.5	Top management	2.5	0.6

Unspecified / Unspecified/other	2.2	1.5	1.9	5.6
Unemployed	0.7	0.3	0.8	2.2
Total	100.0	100.1	100.0	100.2

[a] Includes actors, designers, and photographers.
[b] Includes technicians, technical consultants, and pilots.
[c] Includes accountants and bookkeepers.
[d] Includes social workers.
[e] Includes 1 judge.
[f] Includes 1 legislator.
[g] 3 men students are employed full-time, as are 6 women students.

defined and applied to such jobs as chief of a section or director of a division. Fifteen percent of the Todai men graduates were managers. Twelve percent of the men were researchers, and 11 percent were professors and lecturers.

For the Todai women, the most popular occupation was homemaker, with 18 percent of the women falling into this category. This is almost the same as the percentage for the Stanford women graduates (17 percent), but all of the Todai women who said they were homemakers met the criteria for full-time homemaker, while only 73 percent of the Stanford women who listed themselves as homemakers in fact met these criteria.[29] Fourteen percent of the Todai women fell into the category "salaryman (no title)." Perhaps the category will soon be renamed "salaryperson." Also, about 12 percent of the Todai women were researchers.

In the Stanford sample, the percentages of women and men in the manager category were about equal, 17–18 percent. In the Todai sample, this was not the case. About 15 percent of the men graduates were managers, but only 2 percent of the women graduates were in that category.[30]

The percentage of the Todai sample that were professors and lecturers (11 percent of men and 9 percent of women) was much greater than in the Stanford sample (1 percent of men and 2 percent of women).[31] On the other hand, the percentages of Stanford graduates in law (15 percent of men and 8 percent of women) and medicine (17 percent of men and 13 percent of women) were much higher than the percentages of Todai graduates in those fields (2 percent of men and 5 percent of women in law, and 1 percent of men and 2 percent of women in medicine). The prestige accorded to lawyers and physicians in the United States is much greater than in Japan. Moreover, per capita, Japan has far fewer lawyers than the United States.

The index of segregation, interpreted as the percentage of women (or men) in each of the samples that would have to change their occupation in order for there to be parity of women and men in that sample across occupations, indicates that there was more occupational segregation among the Todai graduates than among the Stanford graduates. For the occupations listed in table 2.7, the index of segregation was 37.6 for the Todai sample; for the Stanford sample, it was 26.9.[32]

Employment Status

The vast majority of the Todai and Stanford graduates were employed (or self-employed)[33] nine years after graduation.[34] (See table 2.8.) Among the

Table 2.8
Employment Status of Graduates, by Gender
(percentages)

	Stanford Sample		Todai Sample	
	Men (N = 404)	Women (N = 330)	Men (N = 365)	Women (N = 179)
Employed	96.3	83.6	97.5	74.3
Full-time	88.4	67.3	86.0	48.6
Part-time	4.2	14.8	7.4	21.8
Not clear	3.7	1.5	4.1	3.9
Unemployed	0.7	0.3	0.8	2.2
Not employed	2.7	15.7	1.4	21.8
Students	2.5	3.3	1.4	3.9
Full-time Homemakers	0.2	12.4	0.0	17.9
Missing	0.2	0.3	0.3	1.7
Total	99.9	99.9	100.0	100.0

men, as expected, the employment rate was exceedingly high: 96 percent of the Stanford men and 98 percent of the Todai men were employed. Among the women, 84 percent of the Stanford women and 74 percent of the Todai women were employed.

The unemployment rate (the percentage of those in the labor force who were actively seeking paid work) was very low in both samples, as is generally the case with highly educated people in the two countries. Less than 1 percent of the Stanford men and women and the Todai men were unemployed; for the Todai women, the unemployment rate was 2 percent.

The labor force participation rate (the number employed plus the number unemployed, divided by the total in the sample) was 83.9 percent for the Stanford women and 76.5 percent for the Todai women. Although these rates were lower than the rates for the men in the sample (97 percent for Stanford men and 98 percent for Todai men), they were *much* higher than the labor force participation rates for women in this age group in the respective countries. In the United States, the labor force participation rate in 1990 for women 25–34 was about 73.6 percent, about ten percentage points lower than the rate for the Stanford women.[35] In Japan, in 1990, the labor force participation rate for women 25–34 was 56.6 percent, 20 percentage points lower than the rate for the Todai women.[36]

Part-time work (less than 35 hours per week) was rare among the men, but more common among the women. Only 4 percent of the Stanford men and 7 percent of the Todai men were employed part-time, whereas among Stanford women 15 percent of the sample was employed part-time, and among Todai women 22 percent were employed part-time.

Among employed Stanford women, about 18 percent worked part-time; among employed Todai women, almost 30 percent worked part-time. In the United States in 1990, 20 percent of employed women aged 25 to 54 were employed part-time. The percentage of women who were employed part-time in the Stanford sample was only two percentage points lower than that for all women in this age range.[37] This is surprising, given the higher education level of Stanford graduates.

Stanford women's reasons for having part-time employment were varied. Some were employed part-time as a way of accommodating their career to their husband's career. For others, spending fewer hours at the job was a strategy to combine paid work with having a child or raising a child.

This is a comment from a woman who was employed 25 hours a week, earned $24,000 a year, and planned to pursue a Ph.D. in the future:

Relocations for my husband's upward mobility left long gaps while job hunting and caused discontinuity. Family is my chosen priority. My turn to delve into a full-time career will come. In the meantime, I pursue part-time endeavors that I can build on in the future and have started my own business to provide more flexibility.

A woman who left law in order to work 20 hours a week in business:

It has been one of the most difficult times, trying to work and raise an infant.

Some men who were employed part-time also were trying to spend more time with their children. The following comment is from a male physician who was earning $150,000, had two children (and wanted a third), and had an employed wife with whom he shared (equally) household management, household tasks, and child care during nonwork hours:

I am currently changing my practice to part-time, to spend more time with my children.

In addition to using part-time work to balance employment and family, Todai women sometimes worked part-time when they could not find suitable full-time work.

From a mother who worked part-time at home as a translator:

I was not able to balance between work and child care, so I chose to work from home. Now I can work only when my children are sleeping. I hope, say for every other day, maybe just in the morning, I can send them to a public nursery.

In Japan, where the progression from school to lifetime, full-time employment is much more "lockstep," opportunities for women to reenter the labor market in excellent jobs do not exist. Todai women who have left full-time employment (or never were employed full-time) face closed doors that probably can never be reopened.

A degree from Todai is a prized possession in Japan. For a man, such a degree is a ticket that offers a lifetime of employment in well-paying jobs with good promotion opportunities. In the next several chapters we will see some of the reasons why half of the Todai women did not cash in on this prized possession.

Given the heavy investment the women in our samples (or their parents) made in their education, and given the earnings penalties in both countries for women who take a break in their employment and then return to the labor market, we did not expect to find as many full-time homemakers as we did.[38] However, as we shall see in subsequent chapters, for many of these women, full-time homemaking was not their first choice; they became full-time homemakers because they were unable to balance a career with raising young children.[39]

Commitment to Paid Work

Our questionnaire asked a standard question used on surveys to test commitment to the paid workforce: "If by some chance you were to get enough money to live comfortably without working for pay, do you think you would work anyway?" (See table 2.9.)

About 80 percent of Stanford and Todai women said they would continue to work even if they did not need the income. This kind of commitment to paid work among women usually characterized as in the "prime" childbearing and child-rearing age group is quite remarkable. Among the men, the rate of commitment to paid work was a bit higher, 85 percent.

Twenty percent of the women and 15 percent of the men said they would not work for pay if they didn't have to. The following comments give a sense of the views of those not committed to work.

A Stanford woman who earned $7,000 a year working 20 hours a week:

I never wanted a career. I wanted a well-rounded life instead. Got married to a man who pays the mortgage, got a part-time job to pay for the horse. [I] take piano lessons.

A Stanford man who worked 50+ hours a week and earned $80,000 a year:

Table 2.9
How Committed to Working for Pay Are the Graduates? Proportions of Graduates, by Gender, Who Would Work for Pay Even if They Had Enough Money to Live Comfortably Without Doing So[a]

	Stanford Sample	
	Men (N = 398)	Women (N = 319)
Would work for pay	85.4	78.4
Would not work for pay	14.6	21.6
Total[b]	100.0	100.0
	Todai Sample	
	Men (N = 348)	Women (N = 170)
Would work for pay	85.1	80.6
Would not work for pay	14.9	19.4
Total[b]	100.0	100.0

[a] "If by some chance you were to get enough money to live comfortably without working for pay, do you think you would work anyway?"
[b] 6 Stanford men, 11 Stanford women, 17 Todai men, and 9 Todai women did not answer this question.

I would not work if I didn't have to. I would volunteer or do other nonpaid work in the gay community.

In both the Stanford and Todai samples, there was very little difference in work commitment between women who were employed full-time and women who were employed part-time. However, women who were full-time homemakers had a much lower commitment to work. Only about 40 percent of the full-time homemakers in each sample were committed to work. Among Stanford women, physicians had the highest commitment to work (97 percent)—not surprising, given the investment these women have made in their education and work experience. In the Todai sample, women professionals and managers had virtually 100 percent commitment to work.

Among both Stanford and Todai women, social class origin was related to work commitment, but the relationship was somewhat different for the two groups. Stanford women were less committed to work if they came from the working class (50 percent committed) or the upper class (65 percent committed). (We will see in chapter 4 that Stanford women homemakers came disproportionately from the upper class.) Todai women from both the working class and the lower middle class were less committed to work (69 percent and 64 percent, respectively). We have no ready explanation for these findings but present them in the event that other studies of highly educated women wish to investigate the relationship between social class origin and work commitment.

Summary of Major Findings

The response rates to the Stanford and Todai surveys were both fairly standard for social science research of this type. The response rates for the Stanford women and men were about the same, but the Todai women had a lower response rate than the Todai men.

The samples are generally representative of those surveyed, although, compared with the Todai class(es) as a whole, the Todai sample has a small underrepresentation of men in law and a somewhat larger underrepresentation of women in law. There is also a small overrepresentation of men in engineering and of women in humanities and in science.

The graduates in the Todai sample were much more likely to be married and to have children than the graduates in the Stanford sample. But, interestingly, within each of the samples marital status and parental status were generally similar for women and men, although Todai women were slightly more likely to have children than Todai men. Of the four groups, Stanford women waited the longest before beginning to have children.

With respect to social class origin, Todai graduates were more diverse than Stanford graduates. A higher percentage of Todai men and women came from the lower middle and working classes, compared with Stanford men and women. Todai women had higher social class backgrounds than Todai men. Among Stanford graduates, the women had a more diverse class background; compared with the men, a higher percentage of women came from both the top and the bottom of the social class hierarchy.

The women and men from Stanford reported higher current social class status than the women and men from Todai. Interestingly, the differences between Stanford women and men in social class origin were no longer present in current social class: women and men from Stanford had the same distribution across the social class hierarchy. Within the Todai sample, the women retained the higher social class standings that they had during their college years.

The social class mobility of the four groups was similar, although not precisely the same. The majority of graduates had stayed in the same social class over the nine years since graduation. Approximately one-fourth rose in social class and about one-fourth fell. The notion that attending a high-prestige university raises one's social class does not seem to hold for these samples, or at least not for the first decade after graduation. It will be interesting to repeat these analyses after another decade or so has elapsed.

Engineering was the most popular major among Todai men, and humanities was most popular among Todai women, reinforcing the stereotype about men's and women's subject preferences. However, Todai women were much less likely to be humanities or education majors, and more likely to be engineering majors, than women graduating from other Japanese colleges and universities in 1980.

Among the Stanford graduates, the most popular subject was the same for women and men: social sciences. However, within that category, women were less likely to major in economics than men. Like Todai women, Stanford women were less likely to major in the humanities and more likely to major in engineering, compared with women graduating from other colleges and universities at that time.

Stanford graduates were much more likely than Todai graduates to obtain advanced degrees. In both samples, the women were less likely to have advanced degrees than the men. The kinds of advanced degrees earned differed by country, and for Todai graduates they also differed by gender. Stanford graduates were much more likely than Todai graduates to obtain the M.B.A., the J.D., and the M.D.; Todai women were more likely to obtain the M.A., while Todai men were more likely to obtain the M.S.

Reflecting their choices of degrees, the occupations of the graduates differed by country and by gender. Among Todai men, the vast majority were either white-collar workers ("salarymen") or managers in the public or private sector. Stanford men, on the other hand, were more likely to be doctors and lawyers as well as managers.

Gender differences in occupation were greater in the Todai sample than in the Stanford sample, and Stanford women were more likely than Todai women to be in occupations traditionally considered male. In particular, relatively few women in the Todai sample were white-collar workers ("salarypeople") and relatively few were in management positions.

Almost all the men in the two samples were employed. Among the women, the employment rates were lower, but still higher than those for all women in the same age range in the two countries. Women in both samples were more likely to work part-time and to be full-time homemakers than were men. The vast majority of men and women in both samples were highly committed to paid work, indicating in the survey that they would work for pay even if they did not need the money.

Appendix

Table 2A.1
Undergraduate Majors of Stanford Sample Compared with Undergraduate Majors of Entire Stanford Class of 1981
(percentages)

	Men		Women	
	Stanford Sample (N = 392)	Entire Class (N = 915)	Stanford Sample (N = 317)	Entire Class (N = 685)
Major				
Engineering	21.7	21.3	10.7	9.1
Human biology	7.9	7.1	16.1	15.3
Humanities	15.1	16.9	16.7	22.8
Individually designed	0.5	0.3	0.9	1.0
Interdisciplinary	1.5	1.0	3.5	3.4
Natural sciences and math	20.7	20.9	15.8	13.6
Social sciences	32.7	32.5	35.6	34.9
Total	100.1	100.0	99.3	100.1

Twelve men and 13 women did not specify their major. They are not included in the table.

Table 2A.2
Faculties of Todai Sample Compared with Faculties of Men (Class of 1981) and Women (Classes of 1980–82)
(percentage)

	Men		Women	
Faculty	Sample	Class of 81	Sample	Classes of 80–82
Agriculture	8.0	6.9	9.6	6.7
Arts and science	3.9	3.8	11.8	12.9
Economics	6.9	9.9	4.5	4.8
Education	3.0	2.7	6.7	9.0
Engineering	29.9	25.3	2.8	4.6
Humanities	9.6	10.1	28.1	24.5
Law	22.5	28.9	9.6	19.0
Medicine	2.2	3.3	6.7	5.2
Pharmacy	3.0	1.5	8.4	5.1
Science	10.1	7.6	11.2	4.6
Total	99.1	100.0	99.4	100.0

Table 2A.3
Certificates Attained by Graduates, by Gender: Todai Sample (percentages)

Certificates	Men (N = 365)	Women (N = 179)
Accounting	0.0	0.6
Architect	1.9	0.0
Financial	0.6	0.0
Language	1.4	5.6
Law	1.9	5.6
Medical doctor	1.9	3.9
Real estate	2.7	0.6
Religion	0.3	0.0
Social science	1.6	1.7
Teacher	9.9	32.4
Technical	12.3	13.4
Veterinarian	0.8	1.7
No certificate	64.7	34.6
Total	100.0	100.1

3   What Influences the
Earnings of the Graduates?

Todai married woman with no children:

I changed my job from the private sector to a public facility, thinking there would
be less gender discrimination in promotion opportunities. However, I was wrong.
I do not have hopes for the future. I can just hope for good luck to get a very low-
level management post after all the men have been promoted.

Todai married man who works for a large company:

Because of Todai, I gained valuable connections ... that have helped me in my
career.

Stanford single woman:

Being a Stanford engineer and also having an MBA have still not given me the
professional credibility I thought they would.

Stanford married man, physician:

I didn't realize when I was in college how the Stanford name would have such
lasting beneficial ramifications, both socially and professionally.

These quotations highlight the differences in men's and women's labor
market experiences. While many men stressed the importance of their
Stanford and Todai connections, many women found they lacked professional credibility despite these connections. While some men were trou-
bled by long hours and long commutes (particularly in the Todai sample),
many women in both samples were experiencing gender discrimination
and were paying a financial penalty for attempting to coordinate their
careers with those of their husbands. Those who argue that all women
have to do to succeed in the job market is to get the "right" human capital
are mistaken.

This chapter uses regression analysis to understand the earnings discrimination faced by women graduates of both Stanford and Todai. This

earnings discrimination has several negative effects. First, it is inequitable, in that it deprives the women of the kind of return on their educational investment that their male classmates get. Second, it results in a waste of human resources; it doesn't permit the economy to make full use of the women graduates' skills and talents. Third, as we will see in chapter 4, earnings are an important determinant of bargaining power in a marriage, so that another negative result of earnings discrimination is that women have lower bargaining power in their families and wind up doing more of the household tasks than they otherwise might. Finally, as we shall see in chapter 6, those with lower current earnings have lower earnings aspirations; earnings discrimination can be dispiriting for women, acting to dampen their labor market motivation.

This chapter also examines two of the book's secondary themes: that there is greater equality of earnings in the Todai sample than in the Stanford sample, and that for men in the Stanford sample, coming from the upper class has a large positive effect on earnings, even when other variables are held constant.

Theories About Earnings

Why do some people earn more than others? Although social scientists agree about which factors affect earnings (education, work experience, hours of work, size of company, occupation, gender, race, marital status, having children, and social class), there are sharp differences among them about *how* these factors come to influence affect earnings.

Human capital theorists believe that in capitalist societies such as the United States and Japan, people are paid according to their contribution to productivity, the value of their output per hour of work. The greater their contribution to productivity, the higher their earnings. Education (which provides formal training) and work experience (which is said to provide on-the-job training) are seen as increasing productivity: people with more and higher-quality education and with more work experience are said to have more skills, which makes them more productive; their higher productivity, in turn, gives them higher wages and salaries.[1]

There are numerous critics of the notion that increases in education and work experience increase productivity.[2] Some argue that people with high levels of education are more productive than others because they were smarter to begin with (which is why they were successful in the education system), not because education *made* them more productive. They contend that very little of what is learned in school contributes directly to productivity at work; most of what affects productivity is taught to people on the job. Thus, they conclude, education does not *cause* higher productivity, but is simply a signal to employers that the individual is trainable. These critics argue that what produces high productivity is the combination of a trainable person, appropriate technology and high-quality machinery and facilities, and excellent management.[3]

The link between work experience and earnings is sometimes thought to depend less on productivity and more on wage-setting customs. Some argue that shared worker and employer beliefs about "just" compensation (for example, that older workers *should* be paid more) may result in older workers' being paid more even when they are not more productive than younger workers.[4]

Some economists think that it is the link between higher productivity and higher earnings that is weak; that even if work experience does increase productivity, that higher productivity may not be translated into higher earnings. In particular, efficiency wage theorists argue that many profit-maximizing employers purposely decouple productivity from earnings; in order to induce workers to remain attached to a particular employer, the employer will pay new workers less than their productivity would suggest and hold out the promise that if they remain on the job, in later years their earnings will exceed their productivity.[5]

In the human capital view, not only years of education but also subject matter affects productivity. Engineering, science, law, medicine, and economics are said to make people more productive than the more traditionally female majors of education, the humanities, and such "soft" social sciences as psychology. Human capital theory teaches that women choose fields of study that are less productivity-enhancing, and therefore less lucrative, than men's fields because women are primarily interested in becoming mothers, and that women's fields are more compatible with taking time out from employment to have a family and then returning to the labor market after one's children have grown.[6] Human capital theorists also argue that women choose less lucrative fields than men because women are more interested than men in pleasant working conditions.[7] However, these arguments are highly contested and are not confirmed by research findings.[8]

According to human capital theorists, only worker productivity affects earnings. Therefore, in their view, if other variables (such as gender) seem to have an effect on earnings, it must be because these variables are somehow proxies for productivity. Thus, for example, Becker, a chief proponent (indeed, an architect) of the human capital theory of earnings has suggested that women earn less than men because they exert less effort at work, since they need to save their energy for their home "duties."[9] These speculations also have been contested by empirical work.[10]

To critics, human capital theory often seems tautologous, simply *assuming* that those who are more highly paid are more productive. These critics ask whether the earnings difference between high-paid men and low-paid women is truly a reflection of the difference in their respective productivities. They wonder aloud: "Is the value of the hourly 'output' of an investment banker *really* ten times higher than the value of the hourly 'output' of a nurse? Or is the difference in earnings in these two occupations reflective of sexism rather than differential productivity?"[11]

The major alternatives to human capital theory for explaining gender differences in earnings are discrimination theory and institutional theory, both of which challenge the notion that earnings are based on merit or productivity. Where human capital theory stresses the education and employment choices of *workers* in determining their productivity, discrimination theory and institutional theory emphasize the prejudices and choices of *employers*.

Employment discrimination by gender is said to occur when women and men have the same productivity but do not have the same chance of being hired and, if hired, are not paid the same wage. In the economics literature, discrimination is divided into two types, taste discrimination and statistical discrimination, although in the end they often both boil down to just plain prejudice.

Taste discrimination occurs when employers have a distaste for hiring women into certain occupations and will do so only if they can compensate themselves for their "pain" by paying women less than men, even though the two groups' productivity is equal. If there is no reasonable amount of compensation that employers can pay to themselves for hiring women into the occupation, then they will exclude women from the occupation altogether. In paying lower wages to women or excluding them, the employer may be acting out his or her own prejudices, or those of employees or customers.[12]

Statistical discrimination is said to occur when employers believe that on average women are less productive than men and it is too expensive to get information about the future productivity of particular prospective employees. Instead, employers simply assume that all women have the presumed lower productivity of the average woman, and either pay all women less than men or exclude women entirely from a particular job or occupation.[13] This theory attributes no ill motives to employers; their behavior is seen as stemming from "rational" choice in the face of uncertainty. Nonetheless, when employers persist in believing that on average, women are less productive than men, even when there is no evidence for this belief, or perhaps even when there is evidence to the contrary, then statistical discrimination becomes tantamount to taste discrimination.

Institutional theories (theories about internal labor markets, segmented labor markets, and occupational segregation) all debunk the notion that pay is determined strictly in accordance with worker productivity, and instead examine employers' power to set wages based on other factors, including the propensity to discriminate. Internal labor market theory is particularly important to our discussion because the Japanese employment system relies so heavily on internal labor markets.

While external labor markets set wages based on supply and demand, internal labor markets set wages based on administrative rules and procedures. The two labor markets are seen as connected through certain jobs that provide ports of entry to the internal labor market. Other jobs in the internal market are thought of as being on job ladders that rise from the jobs at the ports of entry.[14]

The existence of internal labor markets give employers wide scope for decision-making (and hence for discrimination). They decide not only how much on-the-job training to provide to whom, and how to share training costs with workers (the narrow range of decision-making power accorded to employers in human capital theory), but also which jobs are assigned to which job ladders, how wide or narrow the earnings differentials are between job ladder "rungs," and how much, if any, crossover there is among job ladders.[15]

In an internal labor market, unless the employer provides for crossover among ladders, the decisions made at the time of hiring affect not only the initial job and wage level of the employee, but also his or her entire career at the firm. And, as in the Japanese case, when internal labor markets are combined with a system of lifetime employment for the most favored employees, the decisions made at the time of initial hiring reverberate throughout employees' work lives. In particular, if only men are placed on ladders that lead to management positions, employers will have little opportunity even to become aware of women's potential to perform managerial tasks.

A second aspect of institutional theory is segmented labor market theory, which emphasizes the labor force's division into two noncompeting segments: primary and secondary. The primary sector provides jobs with high wages, job security, and mobility on promotion ladders—jobs that pay a return to educational attainment. The secondary segment has low wages, poor promotion opportunities, little job security, and no return to educational investments.[16]

For Japan, the primary/secondary dichotomy is particularly useful in explaining the gender difference in earnings, since until recently, women were segregated into the secondary labor market and rarely found in the primary labor market. In the United States the primary/secondary distinction has been less important in explaining the female/male earnings ratio, since women and men are employed in both segments of the labor market. Rather, it has been occupational segregation that has characterized the division of labor by gender in the United States, with jobs reserved for men paying more than women's jobs at any given level of educational attainment.

Occupational segregation theory argues that occupational segregation by gender operates on both the supply side and the demand side of the market, and includes both ideological and economic factors. The argument is as follows: On the demand side, because of widespread societal belief that men should provide financial support for their families, employers, until quite recently, have given men first choice of occupations.[17] To do otherwise would have been to court costly disapproval from colleagues, family, community, customers, and male employees. For their part, on the supply side of the market, given the opportunity to choose first, men have chosen those occupations that are relatively more attractive, where attractiveness is measured by income, working conditions, and opportunities for advancement. While women have also chosen occupations, they have been able to choose only among those occupations that remained open after men's choices were made. Because men have chosen first and have preferred higher-paying occupations, inequality in women's and men's earnings emerges directly from the process of occupational segregation.[18]

Since the mid-1970s in the United States and the late 1980s in Japan, the notion that men should have primary responsibility for supporting their families has probably weakened somewhat. At the same time, affirmative action and other legal remedies have led more women to be employed in what used to be exclusively male occupations. However, in many cases, those occupations that women have been allowed to enter have themselves been decreasing in attractiveness (for example, medicine),[19] and in other cases women have not made significant inroads into the most attractive male specialties within occupations or into the upper reaches of those occupations. So, while occupational segregation has been lessening, it remains strong and continues to be a factor in producing differences between women's and men's earnings.[20]

Human capital theory stresses supply-side factors in determining earnings (particularly employee choices about education and work experience), while discrimination and institutional theories emphasize the demand side of the market (employer prejudice and power to determine institutional arrangements for the setting of earnings). But, in fact, both supply and demand factors affect earnings. As Alfred Marshall suggested, just as one needs both blades of a pair of scissors to cut, so one needs both supply and demand to determine a price (or a wage). Our analyses will allow us to examine the extent to which both supply and demand factors produce earnings inequality by gender.

The Graduates' Earnings Compared with Those of Their Contemporaries

The female/male earnings ratio for the Stanford and Todai graduates employed full-time was about 80 percent.[21] How did this compare with the gender earnings ratio of other women and men in the two countries?

As shown in table 3.1, Stanford women and men had earnings that were more similar than women and men in other groups. In the U.S. economy as a whole, women earned only 69 percent of what men earned.[22] Among young workers (25–34) and college-educated young workers (25–34) women earned 76 percent of what men earned. The greater similarity in earnings among the Stanford women and men is to be expected, since they were a more homogeneous group with respect to ability and quality of education than were all women and men 25–34 or all women and men college graduates in that age group. Indeed, given the similar backgrounds of the women and men, it is surprising that their earnings ratio was as low (unequal) as it turned out to be.

Table 3.1 also gives the Japanese earnings ratios.[23] For all Japanese full-time workers in 1990, the gender earnings ratio was 55 percent, one of the lowest gender earnings ratios in industrialized countries. For younger workers, 25–34, the gender earnings ratio was *much* higher, 71 percent. For all college and university graduates aged 25–34, the group most similar to Todai graduates, we had to estimate women's and men's earnings.[24] Our estimate yielded a female/male earnings ratio of 79 percent, precisely the same gender earnings ratio as for the Todai graduates. This was surprising. As in the case of the American comparisons, we expected

Table 3.1
Average Annual Earnings for Full-Time Employed Stanford and Todai Graduates, Compared with Average Annual Earnings for Full-Time Earners in Their Own Country, by Gender

	U.S. 1989			Japan 1990		
	Men	Women	Ratio Women/Men	Men	Women	Ratio Women/Men
All workers	$28,605[a]	$19,643[a]	0.687[a]	¥5,068,600[c]	¥2,800,300[c]	0.552[c]
All 25–34	$27,350[b]	$20,774[b]	0.760[b]	¥4,247,944[c]	¥3,020,586[c]	0.711[c]
All college- and university-educated	$49,020[b]	$30,107[b]	0.614[b]	¥6,121,200[d]	¥3,836,800[d]	0.627[d]
College- and university-educated 25–34	$36,432[b]	$27,559[b]	0.756[b]	[¥4,485,445[e]]	¥3,545,188[e]	[0.790][e]
Stanford graduates	$67,085	$53,972	0.804	—	—	—
Todai graduates	—	—	—	¥7,088,658	¥5,628,611	0.794

[a] Median income of all full-time, year-round workers in 1989. U.S. Dept. of Commerce, Bureau of the Census, Current Population Reports, Consumer Income, Series P-60, *Money Income of Households, Families and Persons in the United States: 1988 and 1989* (Washington, DC: Bureau of the Census, 1991), table 24, pp. 102–03.
[b] Mean income of full-time, year-round workers. Ibid., table 29, pp. 124–39.
[c] Monthly contract earnings (×12) plus annual special earnings for all regular employees in all sizes of enterprises, as of June 1990. Japanese Ministry of Labour, Minister's Secretariat, Policy Planning and Research Department, *Year Book of Labour Statistics, 1990* (Tokyo, 1991), table 96, p. 146.
[d] Ibid.
[e] Estimated. Average monthly scheduled earnings from ibid., table 97, p. 166. Then, men's earnings were multiplied by 1.07927 to obtain total contract earnings and then by 1.362 to obtain total earnings, including annual special earnings. For women, the multiplicative factors were obtained from the published data on all college and university graduates.

Table 3.2
Ratios of Full-Time Employed Graduates' Average Earnings to Average Earnings of Full-Time Earners in Their Own Country, by Gender

	U.S.		Japan	
	Men	Women	Men	Women
Graduates/all	1.95[a]	2.29[a]	1.40	2.01
Graduates/all 25–34	2.45	2.60	1.67	1.86
Graduates/all college and university	1.37	1.79	1.16	1.32
Graduates/college- and university-educated 25–34	1.84	1.96	[1.58][b]	[1.58][b]

[a] Ratios based on median earnings. Median earnings for Stanford women were $45,000, and for Stanford men, $56,000.
[b] Estimated. Average monthly scheduled earnings from ibid., table 97, p. 166. Then, men's earnings were multiplied by 1.07927 to obtain total contract earnings and then by 1.362 to obtain total earnings, including annual special earnings. For women, the multiplicative factors were obtained from the published data on all college and university graduates.

that because the Todai graduates were more homogeneous with respect to ability and quality of education, their gender earnings ratio would have been higher (more equal) than the ratio for all young college and university graduates.

How did the graduates' earnings compare with the earnings of other young college graduates in the two countries? As one might expect, the graduates of two of the most prestigious universities in the world have done well in the workplace. As indicated in table 3.2, Stanford men and women both earned about two and a half times what their same-sex contemporaries 25–34 earned, and almost double what college graduates aged 25–34 earned.[25]

The ratios of Todai men graduates' earnings to other Japanese earnings were much smaller (more equal) than the ratios of Stanford earnings to other Americans' earnings. The relatively low earnings dispersion (relatively high equality) in the Japanese wage structure is mirrored in our findings for Todai men who earned about 1.4 times the earnings of all men, 1.7 times the earnings of all men 25–34 and 1.16 times the earnings of men college and university graduates.[26] However, in many of the comparisons, the ratio of Todai women's earnings to the earnings of other women were similar to the ratio of Stanford men's earnings to other men.

The Graduates' Earnings and Hours Employed

Table 3.3 provides information on the mean earnings and mean hours of all earners and full-time earners. It is not possible to compare the Stanford

Table 3.3
Mean Earnings and Mean Hours Employed for All Earners and Full-Time Earners, by Gender

| | Mean Earnings | | | | | |
| | Stanford Sample | | | Todai Sample | | |
	Men	Women	Ratio	Men	Women	Ratio
All earners	$64,228	$49,114	0.76	¥7,053,262	¥5,056,465	0.72
	($52,343)	($48,078)		(¥3,003,339)	(¥2,394,617)	
Coeff. of var.	0.81	0.98		0.43	0.47	
N	377	273		328	99	
Full-time earners	$67,085	$53,972	0.80	¥7,088,658	¥5,628,611	0.79
	($53,101)	($48,526)		(¥2,932,260)	(¥2,307,219)	
Coeff. of var.	0.79	0.90		0.41	0.41	
N	342	215		298	72	

| | Mean Hours | | | | | |
| | Stanford Sample | | | Todai Sample | | |
	Men	Women	Ratio	Men	Women	Ratio
All earners	54.06	47.58	0.88	49.92	40.79	0.82
	(15.14)	(17.35)		12.75	(17.41)	
Coeff. of var.	0.28	0.36		0.26	0.42	
N	359	259		319	96	
Full-time earners	55.73	53.00	0.95	52.12	48.25	0.93
	(13.39)	(13.38)		(9.74)	(11.96)	
Coeff. of var.	0.24	0.25		0.19	0.25	
N	342	215		298	72	

Standard deviations are in parentheses.

and Todai earnings directly from table 3.3, but the appendix for this chapter does provide a cross-country comparison of earnings.

The ratio of women's earnings to men's was lower (more unequal) for all earners than for full-time earners. This is in part because among all workers, a higher proportion of women than men worked part-time.

The coefficients of variation show that full-time earnings had less dispersion than all earnings, and that Todai earnings dispersion was about half that of Stanford. Although Todai women and men had rather similar earnings dispersion, in the Stanford sample, women's earnings had more dispersion than men's. Stanford women's earnings had the greatest inequality of all four groups.[27]

Gender differences in hours employed were much smaller than gender differences in earnings. Among all earners, dispersion in women's hours of employment was higher than for men, but among full-time earners, dispersion in women's and men's hours of employment was about the same.

The mean number of hours employed per week for all men in the Stanford sample who reported any hours of employment was 54. For women it was about 48. Women were employed about 88 percent of the hours that men were employed. Among full-time earners (those who were employed for at least 35 hours a week), men were employed an average of about 56 hours per week and women an average of 53, a ratio of 95 percent. In other words, among full-time earners, men's and women's involvement in work was much more similar than their earnings.

All employed Todai men averaged about 50 hours per week in the labor market, while all employed Todai women averaged 41 hours, a ratio of 82 percent. Among those employed full-time, Todai men averaged about 52 hours per week and Todai women averaged about 48 hours a week, a ratio of 93 percent. It is interesting to note that despite the prevailing notion that women and men are more equal in the United States than in Japan, the ratio of hours the full-time men were employed to the hours the full-time women were employed was almost the same in the Stanford and Todai samples.

It is also noteworthy that for both women and men who were employed full-time, Stanford graduates worked about four hours *more* per week than their Todai counterparts. This finding is in contrast to the usual statistics that show Japanese employed for many more hours per week than American workers.[28]

It may be that the Todai graduates underreported their hours, possibly because their companies must pay them overtime until they are out of the union and they are allowed only a certain amount of overtime.[29] It may also be that Todai graduates did not report after-hours socializing as work hours, while Stanford graduates did. In addition, it is important to remember that Japanese workers generally have longer commute times than American workers. It is possible that if all of these factors were taken into account, the hours worked, including commute time, in the two samples might well have been more equal.

Complaints about long hours of work came from both Stanford and Todai respondents. In the Stanford sample, the complaints were mostly from medical residents (and physicians who remembered their residencies), from lawyers, and from men who wanted to spend more time with their children. In the Todai sample, the complaints were mainly from those who worked in large companies.

Determinants of Earnings

Based on the theory we have discussed, our statistical work looks at the contribution to earnings of years of work experience, hours of employment, occupation, being married, and being a parent. For the Todai sample we also look at the effect on earnings of company size, and for Stanford men we look at the effect on earnings of coming from an upper-class background. To understand and interpret our results, the reader does not need a high level of economic or statistical sophistication. Our intent is to make our findings easily understandable. A brief discussion of the interpretation of regression coefficients and the meaning of statistical significance is in the appendix to this chapter.

The variables used in our earnings regressions are listed in table 3.4, along with their means and standard deviations.[30] The sample sizes are smaller than the sample sizes reported in table 3.3 because the regression samples are restricted to those who provided information on all of the variables in the regressions, were employed for at least one hour a week, and had earnings greater than zero; those in the samples of full-time earners also had to have been employed for at least thirty-five hours per week.[31]

Table 3.5 tells us the size of the effect on earnings of each of the variables we shall consider. Because the dependent variable in all of the regressions is the natural logarithm of annual earnings (rather than annual earnings themselves), the coefficients on the independent variables may be interpreted as the percentage increase or decrease in income associated with a one-unit change in that variable.[32] For example, in the Todai regression for all women earners, the coefficient on number of years of full-time work experience is 0.06. That means that, *all other things held constant*, an additional year of full-time employment increases earnings by 6 percent. The "other things held constant" are all of the other variables in the regression.

As the adjusted R-squares at the bottom of table 3.5 indicate, the regressions explained between 21 and 46 percent of the variance in the log of earnings. In all eight regressions, the F-values were statistically significant at the 1 percent level.

Work Experience

Work experience is measured by number of years of full-time employment and number of years of part-time employment. Although the Stanford survey took place 16 months before the Todai one, the Stanford men and women had 1.7 to 2.7 fewer years of full-time work experience than their Todai counterparts.[33] This is largely because a smaller percentage of Todai graduates had undertaken graduate work.

Among all earners, full-time work experience was about the same for the Stanford men and women, about 6.5 years, but, among the Todai earners, women had about a year less full-time work experience than men (eight versus nine). On the other hand, Todai women had about a half-year more part-time work experience than Todai men. Stanford women also had about a half-year more part-time work experience than Stanford men.

Among full-time earners, there were only slight gender differences in full-time and part-time work experience in the two samples. Todai women and men had a little over nine years of full-time work experience, and Stanford women and men had about 6.5 years of full-time work experience.

Additional years of full-time experience generally paid off in terms of earnings. Todai women in the all-earners sample had the largest payoff, 6 percent. In the other cases where the full-time experience variable was significant, the payoff was a more modest 2 or 3 percent. Part-time experience, however, was generally not significantly related to earnings, and for Stanford men, part-time work experience negatively affected earnings.

Hours of Employment

In the regressions for full-time earners, we measured hours employed with a single variable: number of hours employed per week. In the regressions for all workers, we used three different variables to measure hours of employment. The first was a so-called dummy variable equal to 1 if the respondent worked part-time and 0 if the respondent worked full-time. The second was the part-time dummy variable multiplied by hours worked per week; and the third was a full-time dummy variable (equal to 1 if the respondent worked full-time and equal to 0 if the respondent worked part-time) multiplied by hours employed per week.[34]

In the all-earner regressions, part-time workers were only 4 and 7 percent of the Stanford and Todai men, respectively, but 16 and 25 percent of the Stanford and Todai women, respectively. Working part-time had a very large negative effect for Stanford women, although for every additional hour per week employed, the earnings of Stanford women who were employed part-time increased by 5 percent.

Table 3.4
Means (and Standard Deviations) of Variables in Regressions to Predict Annual Earnings of All Earners and Full-time Earners, by Gender

| | All Earners | | | | Full-Time Earners | | | |
| | Stanford | | Todai | | Stanford | | Todai | |
Variables	Men (N = 365)	Women (N = 258)	Men (N = 318)	Women (N = 95)	Men (N = 350)	Women (N = 217)	Men (N = 297)	Women (N = 71)
Ln earnings	3.9921609 (0.5856191)	3.6205654 (0.7302229)	6.4856748 (0.3482351)	6.0940042 (0.6487514)	4.0323494 (0.5421231)	3.7959412 (0.5411156)	6.4980466 (0.3201680)	6.2707241 (0.3711002)
# Yrs. F.T. employment	6.50 (2.74)	6.26 (2.63)	9.03 (2.91)	7.96 (3.77)	6.62 (2.68)	6.53 (2.64)	9.28 (2.62)	9.24 (2.81)
# Yrs. P.T. employment	0.62 (1.32)	1.13 (1.91)	0.86 (2.28)	1.41 (2.57)	0.51 (1.08)	0.82 (1.64)	0.61 (1.74)	0.51 (1.27)
# Hrs. empl/week	—	—	—	—	55.9 (13.6)	53.1 (13.5)	52.1 (9.75)	47.2 (8.14)
Percent employed part-time	0.04 (0.20)	0.16 (0.37)	0.07 (0.25)	0.25 (0.43)	—	—	—	—
Number of hrs. empl/week × part-time	0.89 (4.57)	3.40 (8.29)	1.24 (5.19)	4.65 (9.62)	—	—	—	—
Number of hrs. empl/week × full-time	53.7 (17.3)	44.6 (23.0)	48.7 (16.0)	35.28 (21.79)	—	—	—	—
Percent financial manager	0.08 (0.28)	0.07 (0.26)	—	—	0.09 (0.29)	0.09 (0.28)	—	—
Percent lawyer	0.14 (0.36)	0.10 (0.30)	—	—	0.15 (0.36)	0.10 (0.30)	—	—

Percent marketing manager	0.07 (0.25)	0.10 (0.30)	—	—	0.07 (0.25)	0.12 (0.33)	—	—
Percent medical doctor	0.15 (0.36)	0.13 (0.33)	—	—	0.15 (0.36)	0.14 (0.35)	—	—
Percent misc. manager	0.09 (0.29)	0.10 (0.30)	—	—	0.09 (0.29)	0.10 (0.30)	—	—
Percent technical manager	0.08 (0.28)	0.03 (0.16)	—	—	0.09 (0.28)	0.03 (0.18)	—	—
Percent technical professional	0.14 (0.34)	0.10 (0.30)	0.07 (0.25)	0.04 (0.21)	0.14 (0.35)	0.11 (0.31)	0.07 (0.26)	0.06 (0.23)
Percent manager	—	—	0.07 (0.25)	0.04 (0.21)	—	—	0.16 (0.37)	0.06 (0.23)
Percent professor	—	—	0.11 (0.31)	0.18 (0.36)	—	—	0.09 (0.29)	0.08 (0.28)
Percent researcher	—	—	0.13 (0.34)	0.16 (0.37)	—	—	0.14 (0.35)	0.20 (0.40)
Percent teacher	—	—	0.04 (0.21)	0.08 (0.28)	—	—	0.03 (0.18)	0.07 (0.26)
Percent in co. ≥ 1000 employees	—	—	0.61 (0.49)	0.23 (0.42)	—	—	0.64 (0.48)	0.28 (0.45)
Percent government employee	—	—	0.17 (0.38)	0.23 (0.42)	—	—	0.18 (0.39)	0.30 (0.46)
Percent married	0.64 (0.48)	0.56 (0.50)	0.75 (0.43)	0.69 (0.46)	0.66 (0.47)	0.51 (0.50)	0.75 (0.44)	0.66 (0.48)
Percent parent	0.37 (0.49)	0.28 (0.45)	0.53 (0.50)	0.55 (0.50)	0.38 (0.49)	0.22 (0.41)	0.53 (0.50)	0.49 (0.50)

Table 3.5
Determinants of Earnings for All Earners and Full-Time Earners: Parameter Estimates from OLS Regression Analysis Predicting Natural Log of All Earnings and Full-Time Earnings, by Gender

	All Earners				Full-Time Earners			
	Stanford		Todai		Stanford		Todai	
	Men (N = 358)	Women (N = 258)	Men (N = 318)	Women (N = 95)	Men (N = 341)	Women (N = 214)	Men (N = 297)	Women (N = 71)
Intercept	3.38**	3.55**	5.95**	5.53**	3.44**	3.46**	6.07**	5.67**
Number of yrs. F.T. employment	0.03*	0.01	0.02*	0.06**	0.03*	0.02	0.01	0.03^
Number of yrs. P.T. employment	−0.05*	−0.04	0.003	−0.02	−0.05*	−0.03	0.01	−0.04
Number of hrs. empl/week	—	—	—	—	−0.0005	−0.001	0.003*	0.01^
Employed part-time	−0.49	−1.79**	0.29^	−0.44	—	—	—	—
Number of hrs. empl/week × part-time	0.01	0.05**	−0.01	0.03**	—	—	—	—
Number of hrs. empl/week × full-time	0.00008	−0.002	0.004*	0.01	—	—	—	—
Financial manager	0.67**	0.65**	—	—	0.63**	0.60**	—	—
Lawyer	0.76**	0.73**	—	—	0.70**	0.71**	—	—
Marketing manager	0.53**	0.47**	—	—	0.49**	0.45**	—	—
Medical doctor	0.36**	0.60**	—	—	0.30**	0.49**	—	—
Misc. manager	0.55**	0.36**	—	—	0.51**	0.26*	—	—
Technical manager	0.49**	0.49**	—	—	0.46**	0.44*	—	—
Technical professional	0.36**	0.32*	−0.20**	−0.28	0.30**	0.29*	−0.21**	−0.30^
Manager	—	—	−0.09^	0.13	—	—	−0.08^	0.15

Professor	—	—	0.00	0.26^	—	—	-0.07	-0.27^
Researcher	—	—	-0.18**	-0.21	—	—	-0.20**	-0.27**
Teacher	—	—	-0.16^	-0.63**	—	—	-0.22*	-0.22
Married	0.08	0.05	0.05	-0.07	0.07	0.05	0.07	0.04
Parent	0.07	-0.08	0.09*	-0.14	0.08	-0.10	0.06	-0.11
Employed in co. ≥ 1000	—	—	0.26**	0.03	—	—	0.23**	0.07
Employed in government	—	—	-0.09^	-0.17	—	—	-0.12*	-0.19*
Adjusted R²	0.31	0.38	0.33	0.46	0.23	0.21	0.32	0.31
F	12.5**	12.3**	12.2**	6.6**	9.6**	5.7**	12.8**	3.7**

** Significant at 1% level.
* Significant at 5% level.
^ Significant at 10% level.

Todai women who worked part-time increased their earnings by 4 percent for every additional hour per week they were employed. But their penalty for part-time work was smaller than that for Stanford women. Although the coefficient, -0.44, on the dummy variable for working part-time was not significant in the Todai regression for women, its size was about what we expected. In the Japanese economy as a whole, the average earnings of women part-time workers, including bonuses, is about 30 to 40 percent less than the average earnings of women who are full-time workers.[35]

Occupation

Table 3.4 gives the percentages of the respondents in each regression sample who were in the various occupations listed. The occupations listed for the Todai and Stanford graduates are different, reflecting the differences in the importance of particular occupations in the two samples, and as a result, the reference group is different for each sample.[36]

In the Stanford samples, several of the occupations were associated with higher earnings for both women and men. Being a lawyer was extremely lucrative for all four Stanford samples, as was being a financial manager. Lawyers earned 70–76 percent more than the reference groups, and financial managers earned 60–67 percent more. For Stanford women in the all-earners group, being a physician also yielded a very high return, 60 percent higher than the earnings of those in the reference group.

The largest (negative) effect of an occupation for the Todai sample was for women teachers in the all-earners sample, who earned 63 percent less than those in the reference group. Otherwise, the coefficients, while largely negative, were fairly small.

Two sets of occupational coefficients for the Todai sample merit particular comment. Surprisingly, Todai men who were managers earned 8 to 9 percent less than men in the reference group. It may be that the men who were promoted to manager early were in types of employment where status was high but pay was not. It is also interesting that among full-time earners, the six women who were professors or lecturers suffered an earnings penalty, but that among all workers, the seventeen women who were professors or lecturers received an earnings premium. Perhaps post-secondary teaching is a relatively more attractive occupation for women when it is part-time (and compared with other part-time work) than when it is full-time (and compared with other full-time work).

Marital Status and Parental Status

As we have seen, there is contention among economists about whether or not work experience, occupation, and size of company affect worker earnings because they affect worker productivity. There is similar contention about the reasons why marital status and parental status affect earnings. Some argue that being married and having children have opposite effects on men's and women's earnings. Having in mind the traditional homemaker/breadwinner family, they contend that for men, marriage and fatherhood increase their need for income, and therefore make them work harder and/or seek out opportunities where their productivity is maximized, whereas for women, being a wife and mother leads to being more tired, more distracted at work (and therefore less productive), and less interested in maximizing work productivity (for example, by taking a job that would require a long commute or a lot of travel).[37]

Others argue that marital status or parental status variables in an earnings regression are not proxies for productivity but, rather, measure employer discrimination. They believe that employers pay married men and fathers more, and married women and mothers less, not because of actual productivity differences by gender, but because of feared or assumed productivity differences or because they think that married men and fathers need the earnings more while married women and mothers need the earnings less.[38]

Marital status and parental status were insignificantly related to earnings in all of the samples, except that for Todai men in the all-earners regression, holding all else constant, being a parent was associated with a 9 percent earnings increase. This result for Todai men is not surprising, since earnings supplements for men (but not for women) who are parents are built into the wage structure in many Japanese companies.[39]

Size and Type of Employer

For the Todai sample, information about the size of the company the graduate worked for and whether or not he or she worked for the government is in table 3A.3.[40] This information was not solicited on the questionnaire sent to Stanford graduates.

Some argue that large firms pay more to workers because workers are more productive in these firms, the higher productivity stemming from higher capital/labor ratios (more capital per worker) and from economies of scale in the product market.[41] Others argue that the causality runs the other way: that large employers use higher wages to increase worker effort, reduce turnover, and reduce "shirking" by employees. Still others contend that productivity has little to do with the correlation between firm size and earnings: that large firms simply have more monopoly power and higher profitability, and hence more ability to pay than small firms, and that (often pressured by unions) they pass on some of the fruits of this economic power to their workers in the form of higher-than-average wages.[42]

In the Japanese context, as discussed in chapter 1, employment in a large firm (at least 1,000 employees) and government employment are quite important for on-the-job training, job rotation, lockstep promotions and wage increases, and job security. Government employment has been a particularly valuable career path for women. It has also been significant for Todai graduates; indeed, as mentioned in chapter 1, in some government ministries, Todai graduates are a majority of nonclerical employees.

As shown in table 3.4, Todai men were much more likely than Todai women to work for a large firm: 61 percent in the all-earner sample and 64 percent in the full-time-earner sample. Among Todai women, only 23 percent of all earners and 28 percent of full-time earners were employed in a large company.

Only 17–18 percent of Todai men worked for a government agency. People who think of Todai graduates as synonymous with government workers may be surprised by this result. In fact, a higher proportion of Todai women than Todai men were government employees: 23 percent in the all-earner sample and 30 percent in the full-time-earner sample.

Those employed in large firms and in the government accounted for about 80 percent of the employment of Todai men. Among Todai women, however, these two types of employers accounted for only 46 percent of all earners and 58 percent of full-time earners.

Table 3.5 tells us that even when women did work in a large firm, they did not benefit financially to the same extent men as men. Holding all else constant, men who worked in large firms had earnings that were 23–26 percent higher than those of other men. Women who worked in large firms, on the other hand, had small and insignificant additional earnings.

For Todai men, the earnings penalty for working in government was 9 to 12 percent; for Todai women it was 17 to 19 percent. Given the prestige of government employment for Todai graduates, and the fact that many women see government employment as their entry ticket into an internal labor market, we were surprised to find that such employment was associated with lower earnings. Perhaps financial rewards for government service will occur later in the graduates' careers.

Upper-Class Background

At an early stage of our work, we noticed that almost 20 percent of Stanford men who were high earners (the top 12 percent of all earners) came from the upper class, and that 40 percent of Stanford men who came from the upper class wound up in the high-earner category. In doing some more systematic investigation of the relationship between social class and earnings, we found, as shown in table 3.6 that Stanford men whose parents were upper class had mean earnings of $88,897, 40 percent higher than the mean earnings for all Stanford men earners ($64,228).

Table 3.5 indicates that among Stanford men who were employed full-time, the 8 percent who had an upper-class background earned 24 percent more than other men, even after holding constant all of the variables listed. In the regression for all earners, the 8 percent of Stanford men from the upper class had an earnings premium of 19 percent, even after holding constant all of the variables listed.

As shown in table 3.6, among Stanford women, it was not those who came from the upper class who had the highest earnings. Rather, women whose origins were in the lower middle class had the highest mean earnings, almost 30 percent higher than the mean earnings for all women, a finding that is intriguing.

Among Todai men, no particular class had a large earnings advantage over others. Among the Todai women, however, those from the lower middle class had earnings that were about 25 percent higher than the mean for all women, similar to the earnings premium of Stanford women from this same social class. Perhaps for women, having a relatively low (but not the lowest) social class background is particularly motivating with regard to seeking (and finding) high-paying employment.[43]

Gender Differences in Earnings

How much did the various determinants of earnings contribute to gender inequality in earnings? Knowing the answer to this question is particularly useful for designing policies to lessen gender earnings inequality. For example, suppose we were to find that a major reason why women in our samples earn less than men is that they have fewer years of work experience or are employed fewer hours per week. We might then conclude that

Table 3.6
Graduates' Earnings by Parents' Social Class, by Gender

| | Stanford Sample | | | |
| | Men | | Women | |
Parents' social class	N	Mean Earnings (Std. Dev.)	N	Mean Earnings (Std. Dev.)
Lower working	9	—	20	$40,700 ($25,848)
Lower middle	21	$66,143 ($53,866)	18	$64,055 ($79,437)
Middle	121	$60,273 ($68,720)	69	$50,812 ($39,211)
Upper middle	193	$62,606 ($35,544)	142	$48,965 ($51,811)
Upper	29	$88,897 ($69,485)	22	$46,818 ($29,563)
Total	373		271	
	Todai Sample			
	Men		Women	
Parents' social class	N	Mean Earnings (Std. Dev.)	N	Mean Earnings (Std. Dev.)
Lower working	42	¥6,725,000 (¥2,270,817)	10	¥5,003,000 (¥1,766,441)
Lower middle	76	¥6,890,000 (¥2,108,918)	12	¥6,265,000 (¥3,178,855)
Middle	120	¥7,169,667 (¥2,904,964)	47	¥4,696,383 (¥1,877,831)
Upper middle	77	¥7,313,844 (¥4,200,093)	22	¥5,361,818 (¥3,027,790)
Upper	3	—	2	—
Total	318		93	

an important route to gaining greater earnings equity is through making it possible for women to participate to a greater extent in labor market work, leading us, possibly, to suggest improvements in the availability and affordability of child care. On the other hand, suppose we found that a major reason why the women in our samples earn less is that they don't get the same return as men for a year of work experience or for working in a large company. We might then conclude, assuming we thought that women and men, on average, had the same productivity, that employers were discriminating against women, and suggest legislation to monitor and penalize it. A technical discussion of the decomposition of the gender earnings differential may be found in the appendix to chapter 3.

As may be seen in table 3A.1, for both sets of Stanford earners, gender differences in occupation accounted for almost one-fourth of the total gender earnings differential. Some of these differences in occupations were the result of individual choice, but some undoubtedly stemmed from employer discrimination.

Interestingly, while gender differences in occupation were an important source of the gender earnings differential, gender differences in *returns* to occupation were not. Rather, the second major source of the difference in earnings by gender in the Stanford sample was the substantial difference in payoff that women and men received for work experience and hours of work, particularly for all earners, but also for full-time earners. Discrimination likely played an important role in these differential returns.

A flavor of the type of discrimination women faced in their jobs and/or their training may be had from some of the women's responses to the questions What kinds of problems, if any, have you faced in pursuing your career? How have you dealt with these problems? The Stanford women whose comments follow were employed in a wide variety of occupations; some were single and others were married.

Bias against women prevented me several times from getting a promotion which I deserved. Bias against being pregnant/being a mother—looked upon as being "limited" in my ability to serve.... I am considering a discrimination suit. I am up for a promotion again. If denied, I may sue.

Prior to working for my current company, I worked for a bank for seven years and ran into the "glass ceiling" syndrome for women.

My gender has been problematic. "I'm not a secretary" is a constant statement for me.... My problems are by no means over. I'll always be a woman in a man's world.

Encountered a fair amount of sexism from clients, judges, and other lawyers. Tried to ignore it and convince people that I was correct on the merits.

I have faced bias against women physicians. (I am frequently called a nurse.) Some attending physicians treated us differently and listened less to suggestions/ comments, etc. I decided to go into a field where being a woman is a *benefit*, not a hindrance (pediatrics).

Although it hasn't prevented my pursuit of surgery, ongoing sexism has been alienating and disconcerting.

A major problem has been gender discrimination @ virtually every level of graduate education.

In the Todai decompositions without type of work organization (Todai I), gender differences in mean characteristics accounted for only 15–16 percent of the difference in earnings by gender, a much smaller proportion than in the Stanford decompositions. However, when type of work organization was included (Todai II), the gender difference in mean characteristics accounted for 34 percent of the earnings difference by gender for all earners and 57 percent of the differential for full-time earners. Gender differences in type of work organization alone accounted for 26 percent of the difference in earnings by gender for all earners and 42 percent of the difference in earnings by gender for full-time earners. Again, while gender differences in type of work organization are partly the result of individual choices, we know that Japanese employer discrimination was an important factor in determining the types of organizations in which women and men were employed.

Some of the comments from Todai women about the problems they faced in their careers show the difficulties they had in working for large companies, and the discrimination they experienced in work assignment as well as pay.

After I graduated, I worked for a big import–export company. The company told me that the terms of employment were that I must work for at least three years, and that once I got married, I must leave the company. In my case, I married my classmate from Todai after working for two years and nine months. I requested to continue working after marriage. My department head said: "You should postpone your wedding to three months later and quit after that." I thought if I cannot work after marriage, I might as well get married as planned, and I quit one month before the wedding.

From a woman who works as a researcher:

The problem with my work is gender discrimination in the workplace. I protested against the discrimination in the kind of work being given to males and females.

After three–four years of effort, the situation became better. But the difference in pay is still present. At first I tried to negotiate through the labor association, but no results. Now I have quit being a member [of the association].

A salarywoman, married with two children, had worked in the same company for 12 years. She had never taken off any time for child rearing, but had never been promoted.

Child care has been my biggest problem. But, somehow, I manage. I want to work as a teacher because there is gender discrimination in the company I work in.

A woman management consultant said that her biggest problem at work was discrimination against women. To remedy the problem she relied on

... proving myself by results and networking with helpful seniors and colleagues.

With regard to payoffs to experience and hours of employment, the Todai decompositions yielded a quite different picture than the Stanford analyses. In the Todai samples, there was no discrimination against women in payoff to experience and hours. Indeed, women received a *higher* return to their experience and hours than men did. (One might say that Todai *men* were discriminated against with regard to payoff to work experience and hours of work, but it is likely that they will recoup their payoff later in their careers when their companies promote them.)[44] Todai women earned less than men because they were not employed in large companies to the same extent as men; because when they were employed in large companies and in government organizations, their payoff was not as large as men's; and because employed women who were wives and mothers were paid less than men who were husbands and fathers.[45]

Compared with its role in explaining differences in earnings by gender for the economy as a whole, occupational segregation played a relatively modest role in explaining the gender earnings differences in the Stanford and Todai samples. This is in part because the degree of occupational segregation in these samples is much smaller than in the Japanese and American economies as a whole. Still, in the Stanford samples, occupational segregation accounted for 23 to 26 percent of the gender earnings differential. Also, it is likely that had salaryman been one of the occupations in the regression, rather than part of the reference group, the contribution of occupational segregation to the Todai gender earnings differential would have been greater.

The results of these earnings decompositions suggest several policy prescriptions. However, we will postpone discussion of them until chapter 7.

Summary of Major Findings

There are three major sets of findings in this chapter. They concern the size of the female/male earnings ratio and its causes; the dispersion of earnings for Todai compared with Stanford graduates; and the effect of upper-class origins on the earnings of Stanford men.

In both the Stanford and the Todai samples, the female/male earnings ratio for those employed full-time was about 80 percent. These were much higher than the gender earnings ratios for the economy as a whole (particularly in Japan), but only slightly higher than the ratios for college-educated 25–34-year-olds.

Although the gender earnings ratios were the same for the two samples, the causes of the differences in women's and men's earnings were not. In the Stanford full-time-earner sample, there were two major causes of the gender earnings differential: women were less likely than men to be in the high-paid occupations, and women had lower returns to labor market experience and hours of employment. The latter is a fancy way of saying that women faced earnings discrimination by employers; for the same labor market experience and hours of employment as men, they were paid less.

In the Stanford sample of all earners (including those who were employed part-time), the gender earnings ratio was 76 percent and five major factors were responsible for women earning less than men: (1) women had less labor market experience and were employed fewer hours than men; (2) women paid a heavy earnings penalty if they were part-time employees; (3) the payoff to women for labor market experience and hours of employment was lower than the payoff to men; (4) women were not in high-paying occupations to the same extent as men; and (5) women who were wives and mothers were paid less than men who were husbands and fathers.

In the Todai full-time-earner sample, there were three major reasons why women earned less than men: (1) women were less likely than men to be employed in large firms, which paid higher-than-average wages and bonuses, and more likely to be employed in the government sector, which paid lower-than-average wages and bonuses; (2) women who were employed in large firms got a smaller payoff than men who were employed in those firms, and women who were employed by the government paid a larger wage penalty than men employed by the government; and (3) women who were wives and mothers were paid less than men who were husbands and fathers.

In the all-earner Todai sample, the female/male earnings ratio was 72 percent. The three factors that explained the gender earnings difference in this sample were the same as those in the all-earner sample, except that the difference in pay for wives and mothers compared with husbands and fathers was an even more important factor in the all-earner sample.

Occupational segregation did not play a major role in generating gender earnings differences in the Todai samples. Also, unlike the Stanford situation, women in the Todai samples got a *larger* payoff to years of labor market experience and hours of employment than did Todai men. We could say that Todai men faced discrimination in this respect, except that we know it is likely that later in their careers they will more than reap the accumulated rewards for experience and long hours on the job.

We were continually brought up short by the large earnings dispersion in the Stanford data compared with the Todai data. We knew, of course, that Japanese earnings as a whole exhibit much less dispersion than U.S. earnings; but to see these national patterns of dispersion reflected so consistently in a sample of rather homogeneous graduates was impressive. The coefficients of variation (the standard deviation divided by the mean) in the Stanford samples were about double those in the Todai samples. Also, except among full-time Todai earners, the coefficients of variation were higher for the women than for the men. Stanford women had the greatest inequality of earnings.

We found a pronounced effect of upper-class social origins on the earnings of Stanford men. (There was no effect of upper-class origins on earnings for Stanford women or for Todai women or men.) Holding constant the usual determinants of earnings, Stanford men from upper-class backgrounds had earnings that were 19 to 24 percent higher than their male classmates'. In chapter 4, we will see that for Stanford women, upper-class social origins were associated with a greater probability of becoming a full-time homemaker. These findings suggest the continuing importance of upper-class origins in the United States.

Appendix

Comparing Stanford and Todai Earnings

In 1990, GDP per capita was $21,961 in the United States. Using the market exchange rate for that year, Japanese GDP per capita was almost the same, $23,734.[1] Were the average earnings of Stanford and Todai graduates about the same?

This question cannot be answered directly from table 3.3 because the Stanford earnings are for 1989 while the Todai earnings are for 1990. Also, the answer depends on whether we use a market exchange rate or a purchasing power parity exchange rate.

To begin the comparison, we need to adjust the earnings of the Stanford graduates by the amount their earnings would have increased between 1989 and 1990. We assume Stanford earnings would have been higher in 1990 than in 1989 because the graduates would have had an additional year of experience and because earnings would have grown to keep pace with inflation.

The regression coefficients in table 3.5 show that for each additional year of full-time work experience, earnings were higher by 2.96 percent for full-time men workers and 1.67 percent for full-time women workers. Assuming that between 1989 and 1990 earnings would have increased for women and men by these amounts, in 1990 full-time men's earnings would have been $69,071 and full-time women's earnings would have been $54,873.

In addition, the Stanford earnings would probably have grown with inflation. If we inflate the earnings of the Stanford graduates by the American inflation rate for 1989, 4.8 percent, then full-time men's earnings in 1990 would have been $72,386 and full-time women's earnings would have been $57,507.

If we next convert the 1990 Todai earnings by the average dollar/yen exchange rate for 1990, 144.79, the dollar equivalents of Todai men's and women's full-time earnings become $48,958 and $38,874, respectively. That is, Todai men who worked full-time earned about 68 percent of what full-time Stanford men earned. Interestingly, the ratio of Todai women's earnings to Stanford women's earnings was the same, 68 percent.

If we use purchasing power parities to convert the Todai earnings, the dollar equivalents of the Todai earnings are even lower than if we use market exchange rates.[2] The purchasing power parity rate for Japan per U.S. dollar in 1990 was 168, making the dollar-equivalent earnings $42,194 for full-time Todai men and $33,504 for full-time Todai women. Using this measure, the ratios of full-time earnings of Todai men to Stanford men and Todai women to Stanford women were 58 percent.[3]

Why, if per capita GDP was about the same in the two countries, were Stanford graduates' earnings so much higher than those of Todai graduates? Part of the reason may be that some of the earnings supplements that Todai graduates received were not fully reflected in their earnings data. In addition, most large companies and the government rent apartments to their workers for a nominal fee. It is highly unlikely that in reporting their earnings, the graduates included the market value of this rental subsidy.

But we think there were two more important reasons for the lower earnings of the Todai graduates compared with the Stanford graduates. First, as we have already seen, there is not as much difference in Japan as in the United States between high earners and low earners. Todai graduates may have been at the top of the earnings distribution in Japan, but relative to average earnings, their earnings were not as high as those of Stanford graduates.

Second, although neither Todai nor Stanford graduates had reached the peak of their earnings capacity at the time we surveyed them, it may be that Stanford graduates' age–earnings curve was steeper than the age–earnings curve for Todai graduates. That is, it may be that Todai graduates have to wait until later in their careers to get the major payoff to their degree.

Interpreting Regression Coefficients

The first variable listed in table 3.5 is the intercept. This is a variable for which we have no data in our samples. Rather, the intercept is calculated in the regression process, in effect, to make both sides of the equation equal. It is the constant term. In the equation for a straight line, $y = mx + b$, b is the intercept or the constant term. In a two-dimensional graph of a straight line, the intercept is where the straight line intersects the y axis. In the regression, the intercept tells us the log of income for those with the mean values of all of the variables in the regression.

Readers will note that some of the regression coefficients in the tables have one or two asterisks or a ^ sign next to them. As the tables' notes indicate, these symbols mean that coefficients are significant at the 1, 5, or 10 percent level. Translated into ordinary English, this means that we are confident that the probability that the coefficient occurred "by chance" is only 1, 5, or 10 percent. That is, if we took repeated samples of the Stanford and Todai graduates, and ran regressions with each sample, only 1, 5, or 10 percent of the time would we get a coefficient much different from the one we report.

By convention, in social science research we call coefficients that are significant at least at the 10 percent level, "significant." Those that have a significance level of less than 10 percent are called insignificant. It is important not to confuse the concept of a coefficient's statistical significance with the size of its effect. A variable can have a small effect and still be significant. To avoid confusion, we often use the terms "statistically significant" or "statistically insignificant" (rather than merely "significant" or "insignificant").

In general, statistically insignificant coefficients are interpreted as "no different from zero." That is, we do not pay attention to their values or compare them with other coefficients. However, a variable that has a statistically insignificant coefficient nonetheless remains in the regression for one or more of several reasons. First, from the standpoint of theory, we think it affects earnings, even if it is not statistically significant; second, it may be important that it be "held constant" when interpreting other variables; third, it may be important in the decomposition of the gender earnings differential.

At the bottom of the regression table, we find two statistics of interest: the adjusted R-squares and the F-values. The adjusted R-squares (adjusted for the number of variables in the regression) tell us the percentage of the variance in the natural log of earnings explained by the variables in the regression. Adjusted R-squares of between 20 and 40 percent are standard for cross-section earnings regressions.

The F-value of a regression is another measure of the regression's statistical power. When we look at the significance of the F-value we are asking, If the regression were repeated numerous times, what is the probability that the findings we got this time would be shown to have occurred by chance? An F-value that is significant at the 1 percent level indicates that in repeated runs, only 1 percent of the time would the findings be likely to happen by chance. In other words, with an F-value significant at the 1 percent or 5 percent level, we can have a high degree of confidence in our regressions.

Sample Selection Bias

The results that we have presented look at the female/male earnings ratios for women and men who are employed. One could ask another, more hypothetical, question: How would the regressions analyzing the determinants of women's and men's earnings be different if we could include in the regression samples not only those who were employed but also those who responded to our survey but were not employed or did not provide information about their earnings, work experience, or hours of employment? In other words, would our regression coefficients generalize to the hypothetical situation where all respondents to the survey were employed? If the coefficients are not generalizable, so-called sample selection bias is said to exist.[4] There are statistical techniques that help us to determine whether sample selection bias exists and, if so, how it changes the regression coefficients.

It is unlikely that there was sample selection bias for the men. Only 4 percent of Stanford men and only 2 percent of Todai men were not employed, and relatively few men failed to provide complete employment information on their surveys.

However, 54 Stanford women (16 percent of all Stanford women) and 46 Todai women (22 percent of all Todai women) were not employed, and 31 employed Todai women (17 percent of all Todai women) failed to provide sufficient information to be included in the regression samples. Therefore, we thought it worthwhile to look at how coefficients in the women's regressions might have been different had these excluded women been included.

To do this, we used a generalized tobit model (the Sampsel procedure in TSP) to calculate new regression coefficients as well as the parameters sigma and rho.[5] In the first stage of the analysis we ran probit regressions to explain labor force participation. Then, using the information from the probit regressions, we estimated the regressions found in table 3A.4.[6]

For both Stanford regressions and for the Todai all-earner regression, rho was significant, indicating that the coefficients in table 3.5 were not necessarily generalizable to the hypothetical situation where all respondents were employed. However, for the two Stanford samples, comparing tables 3A.4 and 3.5, we found only very small differences in the coefficients of a few variables. For the Todai all-earner sample, on the other hand, there were several important differences in coefficients. In the generalized tobit model in table 3A.4, compared with the OLS regression reported in table 3.5, the earnings premium associated with marriage became larger (from 7 percent to 23 percent) and significant; the earnings penalty for being a mother became much larger (from 14 percent to 50 percent); and the earnings penalty for being employed by the government became much larger (from 17 percent to 37 percent).

Decomposition of the Gender Earnings Differential

In economic analysis, the gender earnings differential is generally divided into two parts: that due to the gender difference in the *means* of the variables in the earnings regression (for example, the difference in the number of hours women and men are employed), and that due to the gender difference in the *coefficients* of the variables in the earnings regression (for example, the difference between the return that men get and women get for an hour of employment).

Thus, the decomposition of the gender earnings differential seeks to answer two questions: (1) If women and men both had the men's return (coefficient) to the variables in the earnings regression, how much of the earnings differential would be "explained" (accounted for) by the difference between men's and women's mean characteristics? (2) If women and men both had the women's means for the variables, how much of the earnings differential would be accounted for by the difference between men's and women's coefficients on these variables?[7]

Generally, when social scientists answer these questions, they assume that the difference in coefficients is the result of employer discrimination, but that the difference in mean characteristics is the result of individual choices and is therefore not employer discrimination.[8] We think that such a division is not correct.

For example, suppose women and men have very different distributions across occupations or across various company sizes, so that the women and men have quite different means on the occupation and type of organization variables. These outcomes could be the result simply of individual supply-side choices; but more likely they are the result of a set of complicated interactions among employer discrimination, women's and men's choices, and feedback effects between discrimination and choices.[9]

While it may look to the outside observer like the choice of occupation, or company, or hours worked was solely the woman's, in fact, her choice has often been conditioned by employer behavior. In other words, arguing that none of the gender differences in mean characteristics are due to employer discrimination understates employer discrimination.

On the other hand, attributing all of the gender differences in coefficients to employer discrimination may either overstate or understate employer discrimination. In the first place, there are factors that affect earnings that we have not accounted for—for example, motivation and ability.[10] By excluding these variables from the analysis, we are essentially assuming that on average the motivation and abilities of women and men in the samples were equal. But, in fact, it may be that women had to meet higher standards than men to enter Todai, and that Todai women's ability on average is higher than that of Todai men. If so, then the coefficients will understate gender discrimination. If the reverse is true, then the coefficients will overstate gender discrimination.

Also, economists have recently pointed out that the kind of decomposition of the gender earnings differential that we have carried out cannot accurately distinguish the contribution of noncontinuous variables (so-called dummy variables) to the coefficients' portion of the decomposition.[11] The noncontinuous variables' contribution to the coefficients' portion of the decomposition is sensitive to which category of the variable is omitted, that is, to the reference group. Had we chosen different categories of occupation or company size as the reference group, we would have produced different estimates of the share of the coefficients attributable to occupation and company size.

Given all of these caveats, there is still important information to be gained from a decomposition of earnings differentials, and it is to an examination of those decompositions that we now turn. As can be seen in table 3A.1, in the bottom rows of the two sets of data, in the all-earner samples, Stanford women's earnings were 35 percentage points less than Stanford men's, and Todai women's earnings were 39 percentage points less than Todai men's. In the full-time earner samples, Stanford women's earnings were 23.8 percentage points less than Stanford men's, and Todai women's earnings were 22.7 percentage points less than Todai men's.

Table 3A.1 is based on the means shown in table 3.4 and the regression coefficients shown in table 3.5. The Means column in table 3A.1 is the difference in means weighted by the coefficients from the men's regressions, and the Coefficients column is the difference in coefficients weighted by the means from the women's regressions. The Total column is the sum of the numbers from the means and coefficients columns.[12]

There are two sets of decompositions for the Todai regressions. Todai I, which excludes the variables measuring type of work organization, is meant to be compared with the decomposition of the Stanford regressions. The regression coefficients on which the Todai I decompositions are based are in table 3A.5. Todai II, which includes the variables measuring type of work organization, is a decomposition of the regressions reported in table 3.5.

To obtain a more meaningful understanding of the contributions of means and coefficients to the total gender earnings differential, we have combined a number of variables. The Experience category includes both full-time and part-time work experience, the Hours category in the all-earners decomposition includes all three variables measuring hours of employment, the Occupation category includes all of the occupational dummy variables, the Demographics category includes the two dummy variables measuring marital and parental status, and, in the Todai II regressions, the Work Organization category includes the two dummy variables for being employed in a large company and for being employed by the government.

Table 3.A1
Analysis of Gender Earnings Differentials (Decomposition of Regressions)

All Earners

Variables	Stanford			Todai I			Todai II		
	Means	Coefficients	Total	Means	Coefficients	Total	Means	Coefficients	Total
Experience	0.0343	0.1222	0.1566	0.0319	-0.1503	-0.1184	0.0196	-0.2783	-0.2588
Hours	0.0334	0.1836	0.2170	0.0159	-0.2943	-0.2785	0.0174	-0.1630	-0.1456
Occupation	0.0795	0.0035	0.0830	0.0125	-0.0300	-0.0175	-0.0043	-0.0004	-0.0047
Demographics	0.0126	0.0624	0.0750	0.0007	0.1925	0.1932	0.0006	0.2041	0.2048
Type of work organization	—	—	—	—	—	—	0.1021	0.0698	0.1719
Constant	—	—	-0.1783	—	0.6129	0.6129	—	0.4241	0.4241
Total	0.1599	0.1934	0.3533	0.0609	0.3308	0.3917	0.1350	0.2567	0.3917

Full-time Earners

Variables	Stanford			Todai I			Todai II		
	Means	Coefficients	Total	Means	Coefficients	Total	Means	Coefficients	Total
Experience	0.0193	0.0385	0.0577	0.0023	-0.0229	-0.0206	0.0019	-0.1617	-0.1598
Hours	-0.0001	0.0671	0.0670	0.0118	-0.4710	-0.4592	0.0172	-0.3235	-0.3063
Occupation	0.0549	0.0083	0.0632	0.0165	-0.0077	0.0088	0.0073	0.0241	0.0314
Demographics	0.0225	0.0480	0.0706	0.0067	0.0796	0.0863	0.0078	0.0954	0.1032
Type of work organization	—	—	—	—	—	—	0.0956	0.0697	0.1653
Constant	—	—	-0.0206	—	0.6120	0.6120	—	0.3937	0.3937
Total	0.0966	0.1413	0.2380	0.0373	0.1900	0.2273	0.1298	0.0976	0.2273

Table 3A.2
Graduates' Nonwage Income by Parents' Social Class, by Gender: Stanford Sample

	Men		Women	
Parents' social class	N	Mean Nonwage Income (std. dev.)	N	Mean Nonwage Income (std. dev.)
Lower working	6	—	15	$41,333 ($56,234)
Lower middle	20	$21,150 ($38,331)	14	$51,643 ($95,424)
Middle	104	$35,558 ($72,625)	59	$20,373 ($44,102)
Upper middle	175	$42,051 ($86,169)	122	$34,254 ($68,713)
Upper	24	$66.667 ($78,898)	18	$27,167 ($16,885)
Total	329		228	

Table 3A.3
Size of Institution of Employment of Graduates, by Gender: Todai Sample
(percentages)

Number of Employees	Men (N = 322)	Women (N = 95)
0	0.0	2.1
1–4	1.2	3.2
5–9	0.9	1.1
10–29	3.1	4.2
30–99	4.7	11.6
100–299	3.1	13.7
300–499	1.9	4.2
500–999	3.4	4.2
1000 or more	63.0	27.4
Government	17.4	24.2
Other	1.2	4.2
Total	99.9	100.1

Table 3A.4
Regression Coefficients from Generalized Tobit Model to Examine Possible Sample Selection
Bias
(compare with table 3.5)

	All Earners		Full-Time Earners	
	Stanford Women (N = 258)	Todai Women (N = 95)	Stanford Women (N = 214)	Todai Women (N = 71)
Intercept	3.55**	6.50**	3.47**	5.68**
Number of yrs. F.T. employment	0.01	0.05^	0.03	0.03
Number of yrs. P.T. employment	−0.04	−0.03	−0.03	−0.04
Number of hrs. empl/week	—	—	−0.001	0.01^
Employed part-time	−1.77**	−0.75	—	—
Number of hrs. empl/week × part-time	−0.05*	0.02*	—	—
Number of hrs. empl/week × full-time	−0.002	0.004	—	—
Financial manager	0.65**	—	0.54**	—
Lawyer	0.73**	—	0.68**	—
Marketing manager	0.47**	—	0.38**	—
Medical doctor	0.59**	—	0.46**	—
Misc. manager	0.35*	—	0.20*	—
Technical manager	0.49	—	0.43	—
Technical professional	0.32^	−0.74*	0.28*	−0.30
Manager	—	−0.10	—	0.15
Professor	—	−0.02	—	−0.27*
Researcher	—	−0.39	—	−0.27^
Teacher	—	−0.53**	—	−0.22
Married	0.06	0.23^	0.10	0.05
Parent	−0.04	−0.50**	0.13	−0.10
Employed in co. ≥ 1000	—	−0.15	—	0.07
Employed in government	—	−0.37*	—	−0.19^
Sigma	0.57*	0.58**	0.51**	0.28*
Rho	−0.17**	−0.99**	−0.68**	−0.09

**Significant at 1% level.
*Significant at 5% level.
^ Significant at 10% level.

Table 3A.5
Regression Coefficients Used for Table 3.7 Analysis of Gender Earnings Differentials: Todai Sample

	All Earners		Full-Time Earners	
	Men (N = 318)	Women (N = 95)	Men (N = 297)	Women (N = 71)
Intercept	6.03**	5.41**	6.14**	5.53**
Number of yrs. F.T. employment	0.03**	0.06**	0.02**	0.03 ^
Number of yrs. P.T. employment	−0.01	−0.02	0.01	−0.03
Number of hrs. empl/week	—	—	0.002	0.01*
Employed part-time	0.21	−0.34	—	—
Number of hrs. empl/week × part-time	−0.01	0.03**	—	—
Number of hrs. empl/week × full-time	0.003	0.01	—	—
Financial manager	—	—	—	—
Lawyer	—	—	—	—
Marketing manager	—	—	—	—
Medical doctor	—	—	—	—
Misc. manager	—	—	—	—
Technical manager	—	—	—	—
Technical professional	−0.16*	−0.18	−0.17**	−0.15
Manager	−0.001	0.21	−0.005	0.25
Professor	−0.09	0.29 ^	−0.16	−0.23
Researcher	−0.13*	−0.15	−0.15**	−0.19 ^
Teacher	−0.25**	−0.63**	−0.31**	−0.23
Married	0.04	−0.07	0.05	0.03
Parent	0.08 ^	−0.12	0.05	−0.08
Adjusted R^2	0.19	0.46	0.17	0.26
F	7.3**	7.6**	6.9**	3.5*

**Significant at 1% level.
*Significant at 5% level.
^ Significant at 10% level.

4   How Did the Graduates Combine Career and Marriage?

From a Todai married woman:

Because of my husband's transfer, we live separately now. I want children but cannot make the decision because of my workload. I want to make arrangements so we can live together again.

Stanford married woman:

Moving was a serious career setback for me, but it offered a great opportunity for my husband. There was not freelance work to speak of, so I joined the staff of the local paper at an even lower income level than my previous freelance pay.

Stanford woman, full-time homemaker:

Until last month, my husband and I made a combined income of $145,000. We chose for me to leave my job and for him to take another job at approximately 50 percent less salary so that we could have a better quality family life. So far, it's working out great, although it is financially tight.

Stanford man, wife employed:

It's a tough trade-off between having one parent stay home with the kids versus the higher standard of living afforded by two incomes. But without the two incomes now, how could we afford Stanford in 18 years?

Stanford man, living with partner:

I'm limited geographically to the Los Angeles area by my partner's job.

Todai married woman with no children:

I wish my husband would at least wash the dishes and do some housecleaning.

Stanford married woman:

I would prefer more equal sharing of housework, but based on our interests and preferences. I am happy to do all the cooking, but maybe he should pay the bills.

Combining work and family life in a nontraditional manner was a major challenge for the highly educated women and men in our samples.[1] Those with heavy travel schedules often postponed marriage. Those who were married had to decide where to live and when to favor one spouse's career over the other's. Some women with young children, who could not satisfactorily combine employment and motherhood, decided to become full-time homemakers. All of the married graduates had to work out a division of household tasks and household management, and determine how financial responsibility would be divided in their family.

In developing a theoretical framework for examining the graduates' decisions, we consider four complexly interwoven factors. Using the lens of bargaining power theory, we argue that the graduates' decisions about market and household labor depend on the relative bargaining power of the two spouses, and that bargaining power stems from having resources, in particular, earnings (or potential earnings) and wealth. But bargaining takes place in a context affected by three additional factors: the individual ideology (or tastes) of the two spouses, the institutional arrangements in the labor markets where the spouses work, and the social norms particular to the country in which the couple lives.

This chapter deals with six questions: (1) What sorts of compromises did couples make in seeking to maintain two careers, and why did some women give up on a two-career family and opt to become full-time homemakers? (2) How did the married Stanford and Todai graduates divide their household tasks, and were their arrangements more egalitarian than those of most American and Japanese married couples?[2] (3) How satisfied were the married graduates with their household task arrangements? (4) In two-earner[3] families, how did earnings, relative earnings, and hours of employment affect the division of household tasks? (5) What were the effects on hours of employment and earnings of having an egalitarian, as opposed to a traditional, division of housework? (6) How did graduates in families that divided household tasks, household management, and responsibility for family well-being in traditional fashion differ from those who divided these responsibilities in egalitarian fashion?

Couples' Decisions About Combining Work and Family: A Theoretical Framework

The relative bargaining power of each spouse is a key factor in couples' decisions about combining career and marriage. But equally important in the decision-making process is the context in which the partners bargain, including the individual ideology each holds, the structure of the labor markets in which they are employed, and the social norms of their society. The interaction of these four factors affects couples' decisions about whose career to favor, whether both partners should work for pay, and how to divide household tasks.

Bargaining power theory argues that the more resources, particularly economic resources, a spouse brings to a marriage, the greater is his or her bargaining power. Conversely, economic need reduces bargaining power. The more economic need a spouse has to maintain the marriage (because of his or her own low earnings or potential earnings, or because of his or her partner's high earnings or potential earnings), the lower is his or her bargaining power.

Earnings thus measure both economic resources and economic need. The usual argument is that the higher a wife's earnings (either absolutely or relative to her husband's earnings), the more power she has in a marriage; not only is she bringing in economic resources, but she has less economic fear about the possibility of the marriage ending, and therefore has the ability to drive a tougher bargain. Similarly, the higher the husband's earnings (either absolutely or relative to his wife's earnings), the more bargaining power he has.[4]

In addition to economic resources and needs, marriage partners bring personal resources and needs to the bargaining table. Such factors as relative degree of spousal affection and assessments of relative attraction to other potential partners are likely to affect bargaining power in a marriage. Also, it appears that perceived career importance and self-image (descriptions of oneself as autonomous, dominant, and achievement-oriented, as compared with nurturant and affiliative) are important in determining bargaining power.[5]

The ideology or tastes of the two spouses are also a key factor in determining the division of household labor. Each spouse seeks to bargain to achieve the lifestyle that conforms to his or her taste. Those with relatively egalitarian ideologies will seek to favor both careers (rather than favor one at the expense of the other), to have a dual-career marriage (rather than a breadwinner/homemaker marriage), and to divide household tasks equally; those with more traditional tastes will gravitate toward favoring the husband's career, possibly having the wife leave the labor force entirely for some period of time, and having the wife assume the lion's share of household task responsibility. In those rare situations where both spouses have exactly the same ideology and exactly the same strength of belief in that ideology, bargaining power may be relatively unimportant in their decisions. But in the vast majority of cases, both bargaining power and the degree to which either spouse seeks to *exercise* that power explain couples' decisions about how to combine career and marriage.

Many women (and often their husbands or partners as well) feel strongly that their children should be raised solely by their mothers and that even if the opportunity cost of full-time motherhood is high (with respect to lost income and future career progress), it is best for women to take time out of the labor market to be full-time homemakers.[5] Other women, particularly some feminists, are fervent in the opposite belief: that women, including mothers of young children, should be economically independent, or at least contribute wage income, and that successfully combining career and family is important to adult fulfillment.

Some women develop an ideological commitment to full-time home-making or to combining employment and family early in their lives. These women may make it a high priority to find a partner who is like-minded and supportive of whichever lifestyle they wish to pursue. Other women do not make a particular ideological commitment unless or until they are married or become mothers, and some may change a prior ideological commitment once they become mothers. Still other married women never develop strong feelings one way or the other; their employment decisions are based mostly on economic factors and, in some cases, on the ideological convictions of their husbands.

In addition to ideology, labor market institutions, such as customary hours of employment, the system of career preparation and career mobility, degree of flexibility of employment, occupational segregation, and lower earnings for women relative to men, are also important in determining couples' work/family decisions. In both the United States and Japan, building a professional career is a long-term process that involves earning and successfully negotiating promotions and being perceived as showing commitment to an employer. Couples that make decisions to sacrifice the wife's career in favor of the husband's initiate a cycle of lowered job rewards that reinforces the wife's disadvantage in the labor market relative to her husband and also relative to women whose families did not make such decisions.

Flexibility of employment is important to parents who are active in rearing their children. Women who have put their own careers second may find they have very little power to negotiate flexible employment arrangements when they wish to combine a career with motherhood. Without such power, and with lower earnings and career prospects, they may have an easier time deciding to give up their careers entirely (for the time being) and devoting their full energies to child rearing.

Labor market institutions in Japan and the United States are such that even women who are ideologically committed to combining career and family, and have not sacrificed their career for that of their husband, find formidable problems negotiating for flexibility. With very few exceptions, neither U.S. nor Japanese employers are oriented toward accommodating or fostering dual-career families. "Perks" such as extended maternity leaves, reduced travel schedules, part-time employment, and working from home assist mothers in combining career and family; all are generally difficult to negotiate in the United States, and particularly difficult in Japan.

Moreover, in many managerial and professional careers, particularly for young people, there is a need to put in what is termed "face time." Face time is being personally present on the job (showing one's face), even when that does not result in additional productivity. This may take the form of pressure to come early, to stay at one's desk during lunch, and, most often, to stay later than the boss, often a difficult feat when children need to be picked up at day care and/or dinner for the family needs to be arranged.[6]

Because so many women still find it problematic to enter and succeed in the more lucrative occupations, and because so many men earn more than women even in the same occupation, the chances are that for any given male–female couple, the husband will earn more than the wife. And the husband's career trajectory (future promotions and raises) generally looks more positive than the wife's. Thus, for many couples, it often looks like good family economics to favor the husband's career.[7]

This economic "fact" of family life, combined with the transfer policies that most companies insist upon, particularly in Japan but also in the United States, wreaks havoc for women in dual-earner couples. Until women gain pay equity and success in more lucrative jobs, and until employers begin to moderate their policies requiring mandatory transfers to move up the career ladder, there will remain Herculean obstacles to wives' career development, so that favoring the husband's career, full-time homemaking for the wife, and an unequal distribution of household labor will continue to appear relatively attractive even to some highly educated women.[8]

The final element we need to add to this picture is social norms or societal-level ideology. These norms determine the acceptable scope of bargaining and what must remain in the realm of uncontested tradition.[9]

And, of course, societal ideology very strongly affects individual taste and ideology and labor market institutions. In Japan, at the societal level, egalitarian ideology has been much less discussed and popularized than in the United States. Moreover, relatively few women and men appear to be taking advantage of the slowly emerging new norms by developing a personal or couple ideology in which egalitarian arrangements are a high priority. Thus, although women's increased employment and earnings may have raised their bargaining power vis-à-vis their husbands, most Japanese women have not sought to use this increased power, or have been less successful in using it, to attain a more egalitarian marriage.

Combining Two Careers

Often, the first set of decisions that couples face is how to combine their two careers: which geographic area to live in, which spouse should accommodate the other for further schooling or job opportunities, and in general whose career should be favored at various points. Although many couples protest the notion that they negotiate with one another on these matters ("Negotiation is for business associates," they say. "Lovers don't negotiate"),[10] in fact they do negotiate, and bargaining theory is quite relevant to their decision-making. And they bargain subject to some very real constraints from labor markets.

Husbands, whose earnings or expected earnings are higher than those of their wives, are likely to have more bargaining power. It will often seem sensible to a couple to favor the husband's career if he is to be the primary breadwinner. In a labor market that favors men's careers, even couples who espouse egalitarian ideology can unconsciously or inadvertently make a series of decisions that seriously disadvantages the wife's career. If a couple is trying to maximize joint income, at each juncture it may seem to "make sense" to move to accept the better job offer, which more often than not may turn out to be his offer rather than hers. It is not until several years have gone by that the negative consequences of continually favoring one career over the other become apparent.

To get at some of the dynamics of the process of combining two careers, we asked the graduates: "Have you limited or turned down career opportunities because of your spouse or partner? If yes, explain." Also, the graduates sometimes wrote about matters concerning the coordination of two careers in response to the open-ended question "What kinds of problems, if any, have you faced in pursuing your career?"

Of the four groups of married graduates, Stanford women were most likely to have limited or turned down a career opportunity because of a spouse (43 percent).[11] Todai women were not far behind; their rate was about 38 percent. Stanford men were less likely than Stanford women to have turned down or limited their career for their spouse, but 30 percent of Stanford men answered the question affirmatively. Todai men, however, were *much* less likely than any of the other groups to have sacrificed their career for their spouse. Only 8 percent of Todai men said they had limited their career for their wife.[12]

Of those who explained how they had limited their career, most Stanford graduates said they had restricted their career geographically. Here is a flavor of the Stanford women's stories.

I moved from a job I particularly enjoyed in order for my husband to enter a medical residency program.

I went to a less-good graduate school for my M.A. so I could live with my husband, and I've delayed progress in my Ph.D. program by commuting and by accompanying him to Europe, where he's done research.

I resigned a managing position with a large corporation to marry. My husband's job was in another state at the time, and there were no transfer opportunities available.

I started a company in Boulder [Colorado] with 4 others. Had to leave after 5 months, since the only job my husband could find was in New York City. Following my husband in his career has made my résumé look bad, since it looks like I've changed jobs so many times. (scientist)

Had to give up a great job recently in order to move ... where my husband could find work.

Some couples chose the less-than-satisfactory option of a commuter marriage in order to avoid disfavoring one of their careers.

I would prefer to live with my husband. We now have two households, one in San Francisco and one in L.A. (medical resident)

Others tried to treat their careers with equal seriousness by limiting both partners' geographic mobility.

We limited our job search when leaving graduate school to 3 cities where we felt both of us could find satisfying opportunities.

There were also other types of problems coordinating two careers. One example:

I am married to someone ... in the same business. We have to hunt for jobs as a team with companies that don't have nepotism policies.

Stanford men were much less likely to write their stories on their questionnaires in response to the invitation to explain how their marriage had limited their career. One physician did explain:

Our location must be suitable to her career as an attorney. This has limited both my private practice and academic job locations.

Among those few Todai men who had limited their career for their spouse, most, like the majority of the Stanford graduates, said that the limitation was geographic. However, among the Todai women, although some listed geographic restrictions, half of those who limited their career for their spouse said that they had left a job "for their husband," and about 19 percent said they had left a job for child rearing. Todai women were more likely than their Stanford sisters to have limited their career for child rearing. This is partly because a larger percentage of Todai women had children.

Todai women who commented on their surveys about how their spouse limited their career mentioned geographic restrictions, problems of combining their careers with those of their husbands, and problems combining their careers with children. One woman who worked in a bank had to quit when her first child was born. She then returned to school and obtained a master's degree. At the time of the survey, she was 34 and had two children, 3 and 8.

My husband works in Tokyo. It is very difficult for a relatively older woman to find a position here as a researcher. If I could take up jobs outside of Tokyo, I would have more opportunities.

A Todai woman who had a good job at the beginning of her career:

Because of my husband's transfer I had to leave my job as a government employee. I did not want him to go alone.

Another Todai woman:

I had to give up work, because in the two years between the time I got married and I gave birth to my first child, my husband was moved around by the company 3 times. I could not even hold down a part-time job.

A woman physician, who lives in the United States:

Because of my husband's decision to study overseas, I was not able to do my internship, which means I cannot practice medicine. Now I am doing research, although I want to be a practicing physician. It is too much of a sacrifice for my husband and my child for me to start as a resident now.

A Todai man who had been promoted twice in his job as a government employee noted that the most difficult problem he has had at work is the impossibility for him and his wife both to have careers:

Because my job requires frequent transfers to different provinces, my wife cannot hold down a job.

A few Todai graduates were concerned not only about balancing career and family with respect to their immediate family, but also with respect to their extended family.

A single man said:

Being the oldest son, I feel guilty about leaving my parents and taking up this job.

One married man tried to balance not only his career and his wife's but also his obligations to his extended family. He had worked in Tokyo for five years, but then felt he needed to return to his family in a rural area and assist them with their small business.

I wanted to be a publisher, but due to family reasons I continue my father's business. Because I was not trained in the field of construction, I find myself lacking both technical and management skills. My wife went to graduate school and it was difficult for her to adapt to life in this rural area. I am now learning from scratch to be a good businessman. As for my wife, I talked to her and made her accept my decision to come back, and now I let her travel to Tokyo every month for study groups and scholarly gatherings.

A Todai woman:

I wanted to work in Tokyo, but because my husband's family wants us to live in Kanagawa, I entered my first job in that area.

Transfers of husbands to foreign countries were sometimes viewed negatively by Todai graduates, but they also seemed to present opportunities.

A Todai woman:

I am requesting my husband not to resist being transferred to an overseas position.

Women Who Became Full-Time Homemakers

About one-third of Stanford mothers and 26 percent of Todai mothers were full-time homemakers. Some of these women intended to be "career homemakers."[13] Most, however, expected to return to the labor market when their children were grown

Ideology

In the Stanford sample, several of the full-time homemakers, particularly those who saw themselves remaining in the full-time homemaker role for ten or more years, embraced a strong ideology of motherhood, and some of their written comments on the questionnaire reflected a moralistic stance to validate and legitimate their role. Many were active in Christian service and study groups, and several cited their involvement in religious institutions as highly influential in their lives.

Current social devaluation of the homemaker role in American society may have fueled the apparent perception of several that a defensive position about their role was necessary. For example, one homemaker wrote on her survey that she felt we had given insufficient attention on the questionnaire to matters directly related to homemaking. She argued:

[Homemaking] is not prestigious, but it *is* important. Putting the welfare of one's children before one's own self-aggrandizement is worthwhile and should be recognized.

One measure of ideology with respect to full-time homemaking is commitment to work. As discussed in chapter 2, we asked the graduates: "If, by some chance, you were to get enough money to live comfortably without working for pay, do you think you would work anyway?" Only about 40 percent of full-time homemakers, compared with almost 75 percent of employed mothers, said they would work for pay even if they had enough money to live comfortably without doing so.

Todai full-time homemakers commented much less on the ideology of full-time homemaking than their Stanford counterparts, in part because homemaking has much higher status in Japan than in the United States. Homemakers in Japan are not thought of simply as women who stay at home, take care of children, and cook meals. Homemaking in Japan is treated as a profession.[14] Also, the expectations of mothers of school-age children are much higher in Japan than in the United States,[15] and some teachers and schools in Japan think that mothers cannot possibly do justice to the task of educating their children unless they devote full time to it. This belief is now relatively rare in the United States.

Some Todai women chose to be a full-time homemaker based on their own convictions. But most of those who wrote on their surveys seemed to have made the decision mostly because of their husbands or because of the difficulties they faced in finding employment that they felt they could realistically combine with raising children. Nonetheless, most of those who wrote comments expressed satisfaction with their decision to spend full time raising their children.

The difference in labor market commitment between full-time home-makers and employed mothers was much greater in the Todai sample than in the Stanford sample. About 40 percent of both Stanford and Todai full-time homemakers said they were committed to the labor market, but the percentage of Todai employed mothers who were committed to the labor market was about 16 percentage points higher than for Stanford employed mothers.

Bargaining Power and Resources

Two types of bargaining power are important for a woman seeking to combine a career with raising a young child: bargaining power vis-à-vis her husband and bargaining power vis-à-vis her employer. Both types are dependent in part upon the decisions and possible compromises the woman made earlier in her life: college major, whether or not she obtained graduate training, and the degree to which she limited her career for her husband's. But they are also dependent upon her other economic resources and upon factors stemming from the labor market.

At home, a woman who wants to combine career and family has more bargaining power the higher the opportunity cost of her leaving the labor force is to her family, that is, the higher her current earnings and her prospects for advancement and future earnings. Also, the completion of graduate work is costly; those who have advanced degrees are generally more inclined to seek paid work, in part because they want to reap the financial rewards of time and financial resources invested in obtaining the graduate degree.

At work, the higher the opportunity cost of her leaving is to her employer, that is, the more critical she is to the operation of the business, the greater her bargaining power to negotiate for employment flexibility —maternity leave, more flexible hours or part-time work, less travel, and so on. All other things being equal, having a particular major or a partic-ular graduate degree may make a woman more critical to her employer.

A woman's decision about whether or not to be a full-time homemaker will also be influenced by her other economic resources: her nonwage financial resources; the earnings, labor market prospects, and nonwage financial resources of her husband or partner; and the economic resources of her parents, should she need them in case of divorce or separation.

Ideological predisposition and economic resources are sometimes closely related. For example, if a woman is ideologically committed to raising her own children full-time, she may then be less interested in obtaining a graduate degree before having children because she will be unable to reap its full economic rewards. Moreover, she may seek out a particularly high-earning husband or partner who will be able to support children with a single income, and she may be willing to subordinate her career prospects to those of her partner.

If a woman has a husband or partner with particularly high earnings (whether or not she purposely sought out a high-earning spouse or partner), she will have an easier time deciding to give up her earnings and rely solely on his income. Nonwage income has the same effect; no matter which spouse or partner has the nonwage income, its existence makes a single-earner family economically more feasible.

Having parents with considerable economic means may also facilitate the decision to be a full-time homemaker. In a society like the United States, where the divorce rate is very high and women who take time out for child rearing pay a financial penalty when they return to work, giving up one's own earnings and one's own place on the career ladder to raise children full-time is risky. We would expect that women who can cushion this risk are more likely to become homemakers than are other women.

Undergraduate Major (or Faculty) and Having a Graduate Degree
To what extent were undergraduate major (or faculty) and having a graduate degree related to being a full-time homemaker? Among Stanford women, their choice of major when they were undergraduates was unrelated to whether or not they became full-time homemakers. While full-time homemakers were less likely to have been science or math majors (7.5 percent) compared with employed mothers (16.7 percent), the percentages of full-time homemakers and employed mothers who majored in engineering (12.5 percent and 14.3 percent) and the humanities (10 percent and 11 percent) were virtually identical.

However, full-time homemakers were much less likely than employed mothers to have a graduate degree (42 percent versus 55 percent). Since our data come from a survey at a single point in time, we do not know the direction of causality for this relationship. It may be that some women chose not to get a graduate degree because they expected to be homemakers. On the other hand, it may be that those without a graduate degree simply had less to lose by leaving the labor force.

Like the Stanford full-time homemakers, Todai full-time homemakers were somewhat less likely to have been in the faculty of natural sciences and mathematics (7.1 percent) than employed mothers (12.8 percent).[16] But unlike the Stanford women, where the same percentages of full-time homemakers and employed mothers majored in the humanities, Todai full-time homemakers were somewhat *less* likely to have been in the faculty of arts and humanities (17.9 percent) than employed mothers (24.4). This contradicts the notion that full-time homemakers were in more traditional faculties than employed mothers.

The most interesting difference in faculties between the two groups of mothers in the Todai sample was pharmacy: 20 percent of full-time homemakers but only 3 percent of employed mothers came from the faculty of pharmacy. In Japan, pharmacy has always been a woman's field. Schools for training pharmacists were some of the first higher education institutes for women, and graduates of these schools became the first generations of professional women. Women from this faculty can easily return to the job market with their credentials; perhaps that is why so many of them chose to become full-time homemakers.

The proposition that women are less likely to become full-time home-makers if they have a graduate degree is amply supported by the Todai data. Only 14 percent of full-time homemakers, compared with 34 percent of employed mothers, had a graduate degree. This difference of 20 per-centage points was even larger than in the Stanford sample.

Other Resources

As can be seen in table 4.1, for Stanford women, the evidence does not support the hypothesis that the decision to become a homemaker is more likely in families where husband's earnings and household nonwage income are higher. Husbands of full-time homemakers earned on average only $5,000 a year more than husbands of employed mothers. And household mean non-wage income was only about $10,000 more per year in families with a full-time homemaker compared with families with an employed mother, hardly enough to compensate for the loss of a full-time homemaker's earnings.

Stanford women who became homemakers seem to have done so despite the financial penalties. And, indeed, some said as much, as the following quote indicates:

Table 4.1
Homemakers with Children Compared with Other Women with Children

| | Stanford Women | |
	Homemakers with Children[a]	Nonhomemakers with Children
Graduates' mean earnings	—[b]	$47.431
(Standard deviation)		($40,562)
N		65
Husbands' mean earnings	$68,588	$63,607[c]
(Standard deviation)	($36,770)	($61,243)
N	34	61
Household mean nonwage income[c]	$28,467[c]	$18,966[c]
(Standard deviation)	($37,083)	($26,574)
N	30	60
Percent with graduate degree	22.5	38.6
N[d]	40	70
Percent whose parents were upper class	32.5	11.4
N[d]	40	70
Percent in egalitarian family	12.8	45.3
N[d]	39	64
Percent in traditional family	59.0	35.9
N[d]	39	64
Percent with relative nearby to help in emergency	52.6	47.6
N[d]	38	63

Living on one income in the Bay Area is difficult, but being an at-home mother is my career of choice and top priority in our home. I manage the household budget carefully to allow me to stay at home.

However, it is important when comparing two-earner and full-time homemaker families to remember that two-earner families have substantially higher work-related expenses than full-time homemaker families, including higher taxes, child care expenses, commuting expenses, additional clothing expenses, and so on. Thus, when a mother leaves the labor force to care for a child full-time, the loss in her earnings after additional expenses are accounted for is generally quite a bit less than the loss in her total earnings.

To measure the degree of "insurance" that women could count on from their parents in case of a divorce, we looked at social class origins. Those from the upper class, we reasoned, would have the greatest potential

Table 4.1 (continued)

	Todai Women	
	Homemakers with Children[a]	Nonhomemakers with Children
Graduates' mean earnings	—	¥4,585,556
(Standard deviation)		(¥2,278,515)
N	0	54
Husbands' mean earnings	¥8,226,667	¥6,941,636
(Standard deviation)	(¥2,220,189)	(¥2,314,825)
N	15	55
Percent with graduate degree	14.3	34.2
N[d]	28	79
Percent in egalitarian family	3.6	14.9
N[d]	28	74
Percent in traditional family	46.4	37.8
N[d]	28	74
Percent with relative nearby to help in emergency	47.8	61.3
N[d]	23	75

[a] Homemakers are defined as those who earned no income and were not employed, and who had children. But see b.
[b] Five Stanford homemakers earned ≤ $4,000. Three earned between $30,000 and $68,000 when employed, but were currently on child care leave and not employed.
[c] Calculation includes those who had zero earnings or nonwage income.
[d] N indicates the total number of respondents on which the percentage is based.

resources from their parents. While there was little difference in husbands' income or nonwage income between full-time homemakers and employed mothers, there was considerable difference in social class origin. It is rather striking that almost a third of the full-time homemakers in the Stanford sample had parents who were in the upper class. Among employed mothers, only 11 percent came from such families.

Upper-class origins had very different effects on women and men in the Stanford sample. We have already seen that for men, coming from the upper class was associated with having higher earnings than their classmates. This was true even after other relevant variables were held constant. And in chapter 6 we will see that Stanford men from upper-class families were much more likely than their male classmates to have particularly high earnings aspirations. But for women, coming from an upper-class family had a very different kind of effect: it made them more likely than their classmates to become full-time homemakers.[17]

The theory that women whose husbands have higher earnings are more likely to become full-time homemakers is difficult to test with the Todai data because about half of the homemakers and one-fourth of the non-homemakers did not answer the question about their husband's earnings. Among those who did answer, homemakers' husbands had average earnings that were 20 percent higher than husbands of nonhomemakers, but our confidence in those figures is low.

The response rate to the question about household nonwage income was even lower than to the question concerning husband's earnings, and thus the figures for household nonwage income are not included in table 4.1[18] Figures on the percent of women in each group who came from the upper class are also omitted. Since the divorce rate is so low in Japan, we doubt that Todai women made decisions about full-time homemaking based on whether or not their parents could provide economic insurance for them in case their marriage ended.[19]

A key resource for women who wish to continue their employment after they have children may be a relative who lives nearby and is willing to help with child care in an emergency. We wondered whether employed mothers were more likely than full-time homemakers to have such a resource.

As shown in table 4.1, such was not the case for Stanford women, but it was for Todai women. About half of both groups of Stanford mothers had a relative nearby; if anything, the percentage of full-time homemakers who had such a relative nearby (53 percent) was slightly higher than the percentage of employed mothers (48 percent).[20]

Among Todai women, about 60 percent of employed mothers, compared with only 48 percent of full-time homemakers, had this resource. In some cases, it may be that a female relative lived in the same home as the employed Todai mother, and may have been a critical factor in her ability to combine career and family, especially for those whose jobs required them to work until late in the evening (9, 10 and even 11 P.M.).

Limiting One's Career for One's Husband
Among Stanford women who were mothers, about half of full-time homemakers, compared with about 40 percent of employed mothers, had limited their careers for their husbands. Although limiting a career for a spouse may turn out to have damaging effects on the ability to combine career and family, it may be that it is precisely the willingness to make certain kinds of career compromises that enables women (and men) to remain in committed relationships.

Nonetheless, limiting one's career to "follow" one's husband generally leads to decreased remuneration and career prospects, and diminished ability to negotiate for flexible employment arrangements. Generally, parents of young children are more likely to get approval for flexible employment arrangements when their managers have known them for several years as full-time employees and have come to rely on their talent and contributions. The following are some of the comments that Stanford full-time homemakers made on their surveys about limiting their careers for their husbands.[21]

I was offered an excellent promotion in a small company in Chicago, but turned it down to relocate with my spouse.

I have not pursued a career in order to be able to move frequently and maintain a harmonious home.

If I weren't married, I would live in Los Angeles, where my career interests are. My husband is in the computer field, so Silicon Valley is the right place for us to be.

I was transferred to Boston. I turned it down to remain in Washington, DC, with my husband.

When my husband took a job in Bangkok, I didn't work.

I moved to follow my husband's career and had to find a new job.

We moved to a smaller city with less opportunity for me, for his job opportunity.

I quit a job to move to New York for 2 years so my husband could go to business school. Then I quit another job to move back to California.

I limited my search for grad schools to places where my husband could get a job in EE [electrical engineering].

Lack of support from one's husband was also sometimes mentioned by Stanford women as a barrier to combining career and family:

My goal is to be a teacher.... My spouse has not been enthusiastic about my returning to school for the credential.

Among Todai mothers, there was almost no difference between full-time homemakers and employed mothers who limited their career because of their spouse (44 percent versus 42 percent). As noted earlier, some women who limit their career for their spouse may severely weaken both their economic rewards from staying in the labor market and their ability to negotiate flexible employment arrangements, so that becoming a full-time homemaker is more attractive than remaining employed. However, for other women, limiting their career for their spouse may be a strategy that allows them to combine career and family. Future research needs to look more closely at the details of limiting one's career for one's spouse, so that we may better understand when this strategy assists and when it impairs the combining of employment and motherhood.

Absence of Support from Husband
Having limited their careers to follow their husbands, many Todai women found that their employment choices were now curtailed. In addition, several women reported that they were unable to get their husbands to agree to the furthering of their education or to their pursuing careers in combination with motherhood. Lack of support from husbands was a much more frequent theme among Todai women than among their Stanford sisters.

I had to quit my full-time job in order to be with my husband, who worked far away from my workplace. Then, every time he got transferred, I had to change my part-time job. I really wanted my child, but to say that having a baby was not a disadvantage in my job search would be a lie. But if I have to leave my child and go out and work, the job must be something I feel very strongly about.

My husband is against my taking up a job. I am trying to convince my husband and at the same time asking my professors to help me hunt for work. I felt I could have waited a little longer before I had children, so that I could have had some time to build up my career. My husband strongly feels that babies should be raised by the mother, and he is very uncooperative in my job hunting. Besides, he may be transferred to a different area soon, and that also influences the type of job I can take.

I did not choose to become a full-time housewife. I had to quit due to circumstances. I cannot work for pay in the U.S. without a visa.

I tried to study during my first pregnancy, but my husband was very much against the idea. Because I was a high-risk case and had difficulties during pregnancy, I did not continue to study and did not get the certificate I had wanted.

One woman indicated that her original preference was to have a career instead of children, but that her husband opposed that plan and she acceded to his wishes. It is telling that she felt she could not have both employment and motherhood. She appeared to be content with her decision.

I could not find an answer to the question: Which is more appropriate, to pursue a career or to become a wife and mother? I did not think it is possible to do both.

My husband strongly insisted that I put child rearing before my own career. I did not fully agree, but went along with his opinion. I decided to give up my career completely to concentrate on being a mother and a wife. Now I am thankful that he forced me, because I feel the joy of being a full-time mother.

Failed Efforts to Combine Career and Family

In the Stanford sample, many women were reluctant full-time home-makers; they would have preferred to combine career and motherhood but could not find the type of employment that would enable them to do so.

Some would liked to combine work and family by having part-time employment, but were unable to arrange it.

I tried for a full year to talk my company into creating part-time work. No luck. I finally quit to have the extra time at home I needed. I'd like to have a part-time job with care of children by some other person during hours I am gone (preferably my husband).

I would prefer that both my husband and I work part-time for pay and part-time in the home, but we have not been able to arrange this.

One woman wanted to balance employment and family by working from home, but was unsuccessful in her negotiations with her employer.

I attempted to find work which I could do from home. Although my manager felt the technical end was possible, the company policy rejected it. I contacted consulting companies. Their corporate clients don't usually have an opportunity to work from home either; so I'm concentrating on child rearing.

The type of employment and employers that Todai women had prior to leaving the workforce influenced their decisions to become full-time homemakers. Several full-time homemakers thought it was simply too arduous to combine career and family. The following comments were typical:

The job of a researcher is too time-consuming for a mother.

I decided that it is too difficult to work and raise children at the same time, so I quit my job.

Some full-time homemakers remarked that certain aspects of their former job made it impossible to combine career with motherhood.

Because my job involved dealing with chemicals, I quit after I got pregnant. I had hoped that I could change to a position in the office and continue working. But it did not happen that way.

The following quote is from a woman who saw a conflict between motherhood and the after-hours requirements of her job, and seemed actively relieved to end her employment.

I did two to three times more work than my men colleagues and attended the after-work drinking parties. This type of living became a burden to me. However, if I did not comply, they would not teach me the know-how of the job. I quit my job when I became pregnant with my first child.

Like the previous woman, this full-time homemaker had not been particularly enthralled with her job even before she quit and had a child.

There was a flaw in the character of my boss. He made false promises to female staff, saying that there would be better opportunities for them, and caused chaos in the office. I got very tired and quit the job. I feel very happy about my decision to have children.

Plans for the Future

Most of the Stanford full-time homemakers expected to remain out of the labor market for only a few years. This woman's response was typical.

I have taken a "time out" from my career in order to raise our two sons. When they are at school in about 3 more years, I shall return.

With respect to the potential difficulty of returning to the labor market, there was a wide variation of views, as the following four quotes indicate.

I have a job waiting for me at a great law firm in town any time I want to start again.

I am fearing the return to the workplace.

I expect to earn a teaching credential and work toward becoming a school administrator.

I am hoping to own my own marketing consulting firm.

Ironically, it may be that some Stanford women had an easier time deciding to become full-time homemakers precisely because of their Stanford education, which they felt would stand them in good stead when they decided to return to the workforce. As one woman put it:

My Stanford experience has given me confidence in the decisions I've made concerning motherhood and postponing my career outside the home.... I will be eager to pursue a nursing degree when my child is in school. I am confident my Stanford education will assist me in achieving my goal.

Like their Stanford sisters, most Todai full-time homemakers expected to return to the labor market and seemed to have a mental time limit on their full-time mothering.

I have decided to rest for 5 years to concentrate on child rearing.

I will be a full-time mother at least until my younger children enter kindergarten.

However, unlike the optimism that most Stanford women exhibited, many Todai women expressed concern about their ability to reenter the job market and did not discuss new career possibilities. This did not surprise us, given the differences between the U.S. and Japanese labor markets discussed earlier. Indeed, as we will see in chapter 6, Todai women homemakers were very pessimistic about the earnings they expected in the future.

I wish to go back to my old job in the future, but thinking about my ability, my physical condition, and the time frame, I have no confidence in that happening.

I hope that after the children get a little bigger, I can do something from the house. But in the meantime, I have not found anything yet.

I got pregnant soon after I got my graduate degree, so I missed the chance of getting a full-time job. Now my child is one and I have a blank period in my career, so it will be difficult to find work.

Overall Satisfaction Level

Some Stanford full-time homemakers were happy with the decision they had made.

I worked part-time (32 hours) for 4 years while our daughter was small. I've now opted to "stay home" full time. I am happy with these choices.

But for others, it was bittersweet.

I miss the challenge and adult interaction, but I know it is best for our daughter.

I enjoy my children and I am most happy being at home with them. But still, I feel guilty that I am not applying myself and my education in a profession.

Still others saw the experience as mostly negative.

I am having difficulty finding friends with whom I share common interests. I miss being intellectually challenged.

Finally, some were happy with the role but upset that others denigrated it.

Stay-at-home mothers are still looked down upon when in truth it is a much more difficult and demanding job than most people who do not have children will ever realize.

Now that I've decided to stay home with my kids, the treatment I get from others is unbelievable—like I'm a nonproductive person.

As we have mentioned several times, although many Todai women who wrote comments on their surveys did not seem pleased with the reasons why they had become full-time homemakers, and many were concerned about the future, most appeared to be pleased with their role, as the following two comments indicate.

When I thought about "something that no one else could do except me," I decided that it is not working in society but raising my own children. I am very contented with my decision.

I do not know what it would be like if I had continued to work, but I am happy about raising my own children.

Who Is Responsible for Doing Household Tasks?

We now examine how the graduates divided household tasks in their families. As in the case of the other decisions we have analyzed, bargaining power, labor market structures, individual ideology, and social norms are all important in determining household task division.

In general, theorists assume that most spouses consider household management and tasks as chores (as they are often termed) that each would prefer to have the other partner do. Each partner bargains to do less in the way of household management and tasks, and seeks to get her or his spouse to do more. The more bargaining power a spouse has, the less household work he or she will perform.

Of course, such an assumption is not always correct. Some people like certain tasks, and even if they had enormous bargaining power, they might still prefer to do them (although not necessarily all the time). Indeed, in our own work, Stanford and Todai mothers who are employed full-time are not interested in bargaining away any additional child care tasks. In addition, for some people, issues of identity, self-worth, and the pleasures of caregiving may be tied to successfully performing certain tasks.[22] On the "darker" side, for some women, being the parent in charge of the home may permit greater exercise of power over their children and over their husband's access or relationship to those children. Ironically, the need to rebalance power in a family may sometimes outweigh a wife's bargaining power. For example, it may be that husbands who earn less than their wives seek to rebalance power by doing less (not more) in the way of household tasks. The motivation to rebalance power may also come from wives, who seek to "soften" their greater economic earning power by doing more than their fair share of housework.[23] Nonetheless, the assumption that most people, most of the time, seek to use their bargaining power to do fewer, rather than more, tasks seems reasonable.

Hours of employment play a complex role in determining the household division of labor. On the one hand, from a practical point of view, spouses who spend particularly long hours in employment are not available to do household tasks, and we would expect to see a negative correlation between responsibility for household tasks and hours of employment. On the other hand, the number of hours each spouse is employed is itself affected by the couple's ideology and the distribution of bargaining power in the marriage. In many marriages, hours of employment may be bargained jointly with responsibility for household tasks.

There are at least three different questions that can be asked about household tasks. (1) How many hours of household tasks do you and your spouse perform each day (or week)? (2) What proportion of the total household tasks performed (including those not performed by one of the spouses) does each spouse do?[24] (3) How are household tasks divided between the two spouses? We asked our respondents only the last question.

The survey question about household tasks asked: "How are household tasks divided between you and your partner?" The graduates were asked to circle one of the following five answers: "I do most," "I do more," "About equally," "Partner does more," "Partner does all." The categories in table 4.2 were created by combining responses. Respondents who circled "I do most" or "I do more" were included in the "Self" category; those who circled "About equally" were placed in the "About equal" category; and those who circled "Partner does more" or "Partner does most" were put in the "Spouse" category.

As is clear in table 4.2, Stanford women and men were far more likely than Todai women and men to share household tasks about equally with their spouses. Moreover, whereas the women and men in the Stanford sample were quite similar in the proportions who shared household tasks about equally, Todai men were much less likely to share household tasks about equally than Todai women.

In the Stanford sample, among all married women and men, about half of the respondents had a traditional gender division of household tasks.

Table 4.2
How Household Tasks Are Divided
(percentages)

	Stanford Sample			
	All Married Graduates and Those with Children, by Gender			
	All Men (N = 249)	Men with Children (N = 143)	All Women (N = 200)	Women with Children (N = 115)
I do all or more than half	4.8	4.2	51.5	61.7
Spouse does all or more than half	52.2	64.3	5.0	2.6
About equal division	43.0	31.5	43.5	35.7
Total	100.0	100.0	100.0	100
	All Full-Time-Employed Married Graduates and Those with Children, by Gender			
	All Men (N = 221)	Men with Children (N = 130)	All Women (N = 107)	Women with Children (N = 41)
I do all or more than half	4.1	3.9	34.6	31.7
Spouse does all or more than half	53.9	65.4	7.5	7.3
About equal division	42.1	30.8	57.9	61.0
Total	100.1	100.1	100.0	100.0
	Todai Sample			
	All Married Graduates and Those with Children, by Gender			
	All Men (N = 261)	Men with Children (N = 185)	All Women (N = 128)	Women with Children (N = 101)
I do all or more than half	2.7	2.2	86.7	88.1
Spouse does all or more than half	89.7	91.9	0.0	0
About equal division	7.7	6.0	13.3	11.9
Total	100.1	100.1	100.0	100.0
	All Full-Time-Employed Married Graduates and Those with Children, by Gender			
	All Men (N = 218)	Men with Children (N = 153)	All Women (N = 46)	Women with Children (N = 33)
I do all or more than half	2.3	1.3	76.1	78.8
Spouse does all or more than half	91.7	94.1	0.0	0.0
About equal division	6.0	4.6	23.9	21.2
Total	100.0	100.0	100.0	100.0

Just slightly over 50 percent of the women said they did most or more of the household tasks, and about the same proportion of men said their wives did most or more of the household tasks. However, a significant minority (43 percent) of both the women and the men in the Stanford sample shared household tasks about equally with their spouses. A few of the respondents (5 percent of the men and 5 percent of the women) were in reverse-traditional families, where the husband did most or more of the household tasks.

Stanford men and women were much less likely to share about equally if they had children. Almost 60 percent of Stanford men without children, but only about half that percentage (32 percent) with children, were likely to share household tasks about equally. Among Stanford women, slightly more than half of those without children shared housework equally, compared with only 36 percent of those with children.[25] This is exactly the complaint one often hears from young women: "My husband shared tasks with me until the children came, and then, when the tasks increased, we no longer shared equally."

Stanford women and men were more likely to share housework equally than most Americans. The 1986 Panel of Income Dynamics Study showed that in the United States, married women with and without children spent double the number of hours on housework that married men with and without children spent.[26] In 1992, the Families and Work Institute carried out phone interviews with a randomly selected national sample of 3,381 men and women ages 18 to 64. They found that among women with employed husbands, only 10 percent said they shared cleaning equally, 11 percent said they shared shopping equally, and only 5 percent said they shared cooking equally. Men were more likely to say they shared tasks equally: 12 percent of men said they share cooking equally, 21 percent said they shared cleaning equally, and 30 percent said they shared shopping equally.[27]

In the Todai sample, only a handful of families shared household tasks equally. The vast majority of Todai married women (87 percent) did most or more household tasks, and the vast majority of Todai men (90 percent) had wives who did most or more of the household tasks. Very few couples (8 percent of the men and 13 percent of the women) shared household tasks about equally with their spouses. There was some variation by parental status, with both women and men somewhat less likely to share equally if they had children. Three percent of the Todai men and none of the Todai women reported having reverse-traditional housework arrangements.

These patterns for the Todai sample were similar to those for Japanese families in general at the time. A 1982 survey of women's lives in six countries carried out by the Japanese Prime Minister's Office showed that in 90 percent of Japanese families, it was primarily the wife who performed household tasks.[28] The rate of sharing was lower in Japanese families than for those in the five other countries studied (the Philippines, Sweden, the United Kingdom, the United States, and West Germany). Moreover, while in these other countries sharing rates were higher among young people, in Japan they were lower among young people. The 1987 Sino–Japanese Working Women's Family Life Survey also found very low rates of egalitarian sharing of household tasks. This survey of full-time-employed married mothers whose children were below school age and attending a child care facility, found that equal sharing was reported by only 7 percent of mothers for cleaning the house, 5 percent for washing clothes, and 3 percent for cooking.[29]

Full-Time Workers

Table 4.2 also gives the division of household tasks among full-time workers. Because most married men worked full-time, there were few differences between all married men and married men working full-time. However, married women who worked full-time, whether they had children or not, were much more likely to share household tasks equally than were all married women.[30] This result supports the theory that women with greater economic resources have greater bargaining power and can more easily get their husbands to share household tasks.

In the Stanford sample, 58 percent of all women who were employed full-time shared household tasks about equally with their husbands, almost one-third higher than the percentage of those who were not employed full-time. There was an even larger difference among mothers. Sixty-one percent of mothers who were employed full-time shared household tasks about equally with their husbands, compared with only 36 percent of all mothers.

Like Stanford women, Todai women who were employed full-time were also more likely to share household tasks about equally. About one-fourth of all married Todai women who were employed full-time and 21 percent of mothers employed full-time shared household tasks about equally with their husbands. These percentages were almost double those for all married women and for all mothers.[31] Again, these results are supportive of the bargaining power theory of household task division.

Dual-Earner Couples

Based on bargaining theory, we expected that the graduates in dual-earner couples would be more likely to share household tasks about equally than other graduates. Our expectations were correct, especially for Todai men. There were 328 respondents in dual-earner couples in the Stanford sample (176 men and 152 women) and 113 in the Todai sample (56 men and 57 women). Dual-earner couples in all four samples had sharing rates that were higher than those for all respondents.[32]

Todai men in dual-earner couples were *much* more egalitarian than those in other couples. They had an equal sharing rate of 22 percent, about 3 times higher than the equal sharing rate for all Todai men. In fact, their rate of sharing equally was the same as for Todai women in dual-earner couples.

Full-Time Homemakers

As expected, full-time homemakers were much more likely to do half or more of household tasks than employed mothers. In the Stanford sample, 82 percent of full-time homemakers, compared with 53 percent of employed mothers, did half or more of household tasks. In the Todai sample, 96 percent of full-time homemakers, compared with 83 percent of employed mothers, reported doing half or more of household tasks. It is a measure of the difference between the Todai and Stanford samples that the percentage who did more than half of household tasks was the same for Stanford full-time homemakers and Todai employed mothers.

Satisfaction with Household Task Arrangements

To what extent were Stanford and Todai graduates satisfied with the division of labor in their families? To find out, after we asked about how household tasks were divided, we asked: "Would you prefer to have a different arrangement?" Tables 4.3 and 4.4 look at the graduates' satisfaction with their family household task arrangement.

Table 4.3
Percentages Who Prefer Different Arrangement for Dividing Household Tasks: Married Graduates with Children and Without Children, by Household Task Division, by Gender

| | Prefer Different Arrangement (Stanford) | | | |
| | With Children | | Without Children | |
	Men	Women	Men	Women
I do all or more than half	—	52.2	—	54.8
Spouse does all or more than half	15.2	—	16.2	—
About equal division	17.7	2.5	9.7	8.7
Total	17.1	33.9	14.3	29.8

| | Prefer Different Arrangement (Todai) | | | |
| | With Children | | Without Children | |
	Men	Women	Men	Women
I do all or more than half	—	40.2	—	40.9
Spouse does all or more than half	6.1	0.0	3.3	—
About equal division	10.0	25.0	—	—
Total	6.4	37.5	4.1	33.3

Table 4.4
Percentages Who Prefer a Different Arrangement for Dividing Household Tasks, by Household Task Division: Married Women with Children

| | Prefer Different Arrangement (Stanford) | | |
	Full-Time Homemakers	Part-Time Employed	Full-Time Employed
I do all or more than half	40.0	53.9	76.9
Spouse does all or more than half	—	—	—
About equal division	—	—	0.0
Total	32.4	42.9	27.5

| | Prefer Different Arrangement (Todai) | | |
	Full-Time Homemakers	Part-Time Employed	Full-Time Employed
I do all or more than half	22.2	34.2	61.5
Spouse does all or more than half	—	—	—
About equal division	—	—	—
Total	21.2	33.3	54.5

Stanford Graduates

Regardless of their task arrangement, the vast majority of Stanford men (84 percent) were satisfied with the way they and their wives divided household tasks. Among those who shared household tasks about equally with their wives, the satisfaction rate was 87 percent, and among those whose wives did all or more than half of the tasks, the satisfaction rate was about the same, 84 percent.

On the other hand, Stanford women had a much lower overall satisfaction rate, 68 percent, and it varied considerably for those with egalitarian versus traditional arrangements. Wives who shared tasks about equally with their husbands had a satisfaction rate of 94 percent, double the satisfaction rate of 47 percent for wives with a traditional arrangement. In other words, almost all of the Stanford women in an egalitarian arrangement wanted to keep it; but of those in a traditional arrangement, about half were satisfied and half were not.

How did having children affect satisfaction rates with household task arrangements? Among Stanford men who shared household tasks about equally with their wives, those without children had a slightly higher rate of satisfaction than those with children (90 percent versus 82 percent). The flip side of this finding is that among Stanford women who shared tasks about equally with their husbands, there was a slightly higher rate of satisfaction for mothers (98 percent) than for those without children (91 percent). These findings make sense, since household tasks require more time and effort when there are children in the family; thus fathers might be less pleased, and mothers more pleased, with an egalitarian division (compared with men and women without children).

Table 4.4 compares the rates of satisfaction with household arrangements for mothers who were full-time homemakers, part-time employed, and full-time employed. In the Stanford sample, among mothers with an egalitarian task arrangement, there were no differences in satisfaction among the three groups. All but one of these 40 mothers was satisfied with it. However, there were substantial differences in satisfaction among the three groups for those who had a traditional task arrangement. Satisfaction with the traditional arrangement decreased with increased employment. Sixty percent of full-time homemakers, slightly less than half of part-time-employed mothers, and less than one quarter of full-time-employed mothers were satisfied with their traditional task arrangement.[33]

Stanford women who were dissatisfied were quite specific about the kinds of alternative arrangements they would prefer.

A woman who worked full-time as an artist and had no children:

I would prefer more help with not only household chores, meals, and management, but also maintenance and improvement—i.e., a more 50/50 arrangement re day-to-day living.

A woman physician who was employed 65 hours a week and earned $70,000 was married to a man who was a student and earned no income. The couple had no children. The wife did all of the tasks (as well as all of the household management). Bargaining power theory certainly did not explain the distribution of household tasks in this family. The wife was, perhaps not surprisingly, dissatisfied with the task arrangement and commented specifically:

I'd like him to do more of the shopping, cooking, vacuuming, and laundry.

A woman with two children who worked part-time was less specific about particulars, just generally dissatisfied with the household task arrangement.

I generally enjoy housework, but the load is sometimes overwhelming and isolating.

A Stanford man whose partner did most of the tasks said he would have preferred a more equal division. Although his wife may have seen him as recalcitrant in meeting her standards, he saw the problem, as many men do, as her being more "fastidious" than he thought she needed to be.

My wife is in medical school. I would prefer a more balanced division [of household tasks], but my wife is usually more anxious to complete certain tasks.

Some of the Stanford graduates who were dissatisfied with their household task arrangement would have preferred more hired help.

From a woman still in graduate school:

I used to do more housework, but when I was studying for my qualifying exams, I realized I couldn't keep that up. So now our house is simply not as clean as I'd like it to be. I wish we could afford someone to come and clean from time to time.

And from a male software engineer whose wife was also employed:

We share the housework equally. I would prefer to have an army of French maids take care of the household and an accountant to do the bills (as would my wife).

Todai Graduates

Like Stanford men, Todai men were largely satisfied with the arrangements they had. Of the 90 percent of Todai men who lived in families where housework was done largely or entirely by wives, 95 percent were satisfied with the arrangement. And 95 percent of the Todai men who had an egalitarian division of household labor were also satisfied.

Todai women, like Stanford women, had a much lower rate of satisfaction with household task division than their male classmates. Overall, 63 percent of Todai women were satisfied with their family's arrangement, very similar to the Stanford women's satisfaction rate of 68 percent. Of those in an egalitarian arrangement, 14 percent of the total, the satisfaction rate was very high, 82 percent. But of those in a traditional arrangement, 60 percent were satisfied and 40 percent were not.[34] This satisfaction/dissatisfaction split of 60:40 is similar to the 50:50 satisfaction/dissatisfaction split among Stanford women with traditional household arrangements.

Because of the small number of Todai women without children, we do not compare their satisfaction rates with those of Todai mothers. Among Todai men, the satisfaction rates were above 90 percent for those with children and without, for both traditional and egalitarian arrangements.

As shown in table 4.4, among Todai mothers with a traditional household task arrangement (87 percent of all mothers), about three-quarters of homemakers, two-thirds of part-time employed mothers, and about 40 percent of full-time-employed mothers were satisfied with their household task arrangement.

The following are some of the comments by Todai women who explained why they were dissatisfied with the division of household tasks in their families. Their comments are quite similar to those of their Stanford sisters.

From a woman who has an M.A. degree, works at home, has two children, and whose annual salary is ¥2.4 million:

I want a different arrangement. At least for part of the housework, I want to hire help. Specifically, I want help with cleaning and washing. I can do the cooking.

From a woman with a Ph.D. in science, who has two children and does most of the housework herself:

I am going to take up more work from now on, so I hope my husband will help out more.

The following is an interesting comment from a woman who is dissatisfied although she and her husband share housework equally. She has a master's degree, is a lecturer at the university, has one child, and earns ¥6 million. (Her husband earns ¥7 million.)

My husband and I differ in the amount of housework we each think is indispensable. In my view we need to do more. However, he will not share 50% of the housework that I think is necessary and I do not want to do 100%. So we leave it as is for now, although I really want to raise the total amount.

One unusual man who said he wanted a different arrangement earned ¥11 million per year as a manager in a small company and had two very young children; his wife did all of the housework and child care, and did not work outside of the home:

I want a different arrangement. I hope my wife can take up part of the financial responsibility (like bringing home pay), so I can help with housework, especially the education of my children.

Another unusual man, who had taken his law degree in the United States, had no children and shared housework equally with his wife, who earned almost as much as he (¥19 million a year; he earned ¥21 million a year):

Housework should be fairly shared.

Bargaining Power, Hours of Paid Work, and Household Task Arrangements in Two-Earner Couples

How was bargaining power in two-earner families related to their division of household tasks? Table 4.5 provides the results of probit regressions to examine the relationship between the probability of sharing household tasks about equally and several measures of bargaining power.[35]

Our measures of bargaining power are wife's earnings, husband's earnings, and the ratio of wife's/husband's earnings. We expected that the higher the wife's earnings and the higher the ratio of wife's/husband's earnings, the greater would be the wife's bargaining power and, therefore, the higher would be the probability of sharing. Similarly, we expected that the higher the husband's earnings and the lower the ratio of wife's/husband's earnings, the greater would be the husband's bargaining power and, therefore, the lower would be the probability of sharing.

We also looked at the relationship between the number of hours of the graduate's paid work and sharing. Number of hours is mainly a measure

Table 4.5
Relationships Between Earnings and Hours Employed and the Probability of Sharing Household Tasks in Dual-Earner Couples

	Stanford Men (N = 160)	Stanford Women (N = 139)	Todai Men (N = 56)	Todai Women (N = 56)
Percent sharing	52.5	52.5	23.1	23.2
Regression 1				
effect of wife's earnings	+0.00444**	+0.00014	+0.00072**	+0.00034^
Regression 2				
effect of husband's earnings	−0.00187^	−0.00185*	−0.00050	+0.00004
Regression 3				
effect of ratio of wife's earnings/husband's earnings	+0.3106**	+0.09695^	+0.54357**	+0.13325
Regression 4				
effect of number of hours respondent was employed	−0.00191	+0.01195**	−0.00837*	+0.00316

Probability derivatives are calculated from probit regressions where sharing tasks = 1, not sharing = 0. Regressions have a constant and only one independent variable.
**Significant at 1% level.
*Significant at 5% level.
^ Significant at 10% level.

of availability for household work, but it may also measure bargaining power. We hypothesized that having long hours of employment probably increased one's bargaining power at home (or perhaps provided one with greater more moral suasion), so that we expected hours of paid work to be negatively related to sharing of household management for men and positively related to sharing for women.[36]

For U.S. couples, other researchers have found support, but modest effects, for a bargaining theory of household task division. Goldscheider and Waite found small effects of husband's and wife's earnings on sharing of household work. They also found that wife's hours of employment were more important in determining household task sharing than husband's hours.[37] Ross found that the difference between husband's and wife's earnings (similar to the ratio of husbands' earnings to wife's earnings, the inverse of our measure of bargaining power) had a significant negative effect on husband's participation in housework.[38] Maret and Finlay, looking at women in the National Longitudinal Surveys of Work Experience, found that wives' earnings were positively associated with sharing household tasks while husbands' earnings were negatively associated with sharing household tasks.[39]

As shown in table 4.5, our results also provide modest support for the bargaining power theory in dual-earner couples. The probability of sharing household tasks equally was most sensitive to the ratio of wife's earnings to husband's earnings. For both groups of men, an increase in the ratio of wife's earnings to husband's earnings had a sizable (and statistically significant) relationship to the probability of sharing household tasks. For Stanford women, the relationship was smaller but still significant.

For Stanford men, and Todai men and women, the wife's earnings had a significant, but small, positive relationship to the probability of sharing household tasks. Husband's earnings had a significant, but small, negative relationship to the probability of sharing for Stanford women and men. Number of hours of employment had a small, significant positive relationship to sharing household tasks for Stanford women and a small, significant negative relationship for Todai men.

The Relationship Between Household Task Arrangements, Number of Hours of Paid Work, and Earnings

We turn now from looking at the relationships between number of hours spent in paid work and earnings to household task arrangement for dual-earner couples, to analyzing the relationships between household task arrangement and hours of paid work and earnings for all married graduates. It is important to recognize, however, that the relationships between earnings and hours worked, on the one hand, and division of household tasks, on the other hand, are probably reciprocal. Given the cross-section data we have, we really cannot determine which variables caused the others.

Most economists expect that women who do a substantial amount of housework will both reduce their hours of paid work and earn less per hour. Becker, who seems to think that all married women are responsible for housework, puts forth a kind of conservation-of-energy theory: that married women have less energy to devote to their jobs. Not only are they employed for fewer hours, he contends, but they expend less energy during the hours they are employed (which reduces their productivity), leading to lower earnings per hour. Moreover, he argues, they reduce their investment in their own market human capital, which further lessens their productivity and earnings.[40]

Feminist sociologists and economists dispute the assumption that all married women are responsible for housework tasks. Moreover, the empirical work of Bielby and Bielby contests Becker's suggestion that married women work less hard at their jobs than do others. Feminist social scientists think, rather, that discrimination may cause a relationship between a woman's responsibility for household tasks and lower earnings. This may be particularly true for certain professional and managerial jobs where there is a need to put in "face time," in order to be successful.[41]

Three studies have looked specifically at the effect of household task responsibility on earnings. Their results are conflicting. Using data on married middle managers in a large Canadian corporation, Cannings found that having more responsibility for household tasks did *not* have a significant effect on earnings for women, but decreased earnings for men.[42] Hersch has looked at this matter in two studies. In a study using data from the national 1987 Panel Study of Income Dynamics, she found that additional time spent on household work reduced women's wages but increased men's wages.[43] In a another study, using original data collected in Eugene, Oregon, in 1986, she found that for women, additional housework was negatively related to earnings, but for men, there was no significant relationship. However, when job conditions variables were added to the earnings regression, time spent on housework was no longer significant for women. Moreover, neither housework nor working conditions were important in a decomposition to explain the difference in earnings between women and men.[44]

Hours of Paid Work

Table 4.6 gives the means and standard deviations of the variables in a regression to examine the effect of household task arrangement on number of hours employed for all earners and for full-time earners. All of those in the regression samples are married. About 70 percent of the Todai graduates are parents (74 percent of women in the all-earner sample). Almost 60 percent of the Stanford men are parents. Among the Stanford women, 48 percent are parents in the all-earner sample, but only 38 percent in the full-time-earner sample.

For women, the 0–1 (dummy) variable measuring household task arrangement takes on the value of 1 if she does *more than half* of household tasks and is 0 otherwise. For the men, the variable takes on the value of 1 if he does *at least half* of the household tasks. We expected that both of these variables would be negatively associated with hours of employment, either because those with more household tasks have less time for employment or because those who have taken on fewer hours of employment take on more household tasks because their bargaining power is reduced.

Table 4.6
Means and Standard Deviations of Variables in OLS Regressions to Examine How Household Task Responsibility Affects Hours Employed for All Earners and Full-Time Earners, by Gender

| | All Earners | | | | Full-Time Earners | | | |
| | Stanford | | Todai | | Stanford | | Todai | |
Variables	Men (N = 227)	Women (N = 146)	Men (N = 234)	Women (N = 66)	Men (N = 221)	Women (N = 110)	Men (N = 218)	Women (N = 47)
Number of hours employed/week	55.4 (14.8)	43.55 (17.43)	50.14 (12.81)	38.17 (15.47)	56.4 (13.7)	51.1 (12.4)	52.5 (9.4)	46.3 (7.8)
Number of years employed full-time	6.6 (2.7)	6.3 (2.6)	9.43 (2.53)	7.94 (3.86)	6.72 (2.7)	6.70 (2.7)	9.68 (2.2)	9.53 (2.8)
Number of years employed part-time	0.51 (1.09)	1.04 (1.74)	0.73 (2.12)	1.45 (2.61)	0.48 (1.03)	0.69 (1.67)	0.49 (1.56)	0.43 (1.14)
Percent financial manager	0.09 (0.28)	0.05 (0.21)	—	—	0.09 (0.29)	0.06 (0.25)	—	—
Percent lawyer	0.15 (0.36)	0.08 (0.26)	—	—	0.15 (0.36)	0.08 (0.28)	—	—
Percent marketing manager	0.08 (0.27)	0.12 (0.32)	—	—	0.08 (0.27)	0.15 (0.35)	—	—
Percent medical doctor	0.18 (0.38)	0.08 (0.35)	—	—	0.17 (0.38)	0.15 (0.36)	—	—
Percent misc. manager	0.08 (0.28)	0.10 (0.30)	—	—	0.09 (0.28)	0.09 (0.11)	—	—
Percent technical manager	0.12 (0.30)	0.03 (0.30)	—	—	0.10 (0.30)	0.04 (0.19)	—	—
Percent technical professional	0.12 (0.32)	0.08 (0.26)	0.05 (0.22)	0.05 (0.21)	0.12 (0.32)	0.08 (0.28)	0.05 (0.22)	0.06 (0.25)

	Col 1	Col 2	Col 3	Col 4	Col 5	Col 6	Col 7	Col 8
Percent manager	—	—	0.15 (0.36)	0.03 (0.17)	—	—	0.16 (0.36)	0.04 (0.20)
Percent professor	—	—	0.09 (0.29)	0.15 (0.36)	—	—	0.07 (0.26)	0.09 (0.28)
Percent researcher	—	—	0.14 (0.35)	0.15 (0.36)	—	—	0.15 (0.35)	0.21 (0.41)
Percent teacher	—	—	0.04 (0.19)	0.06 (0.24)	—	—	0.03 (0.16)	0.04 (0.20)
Percent in company ≥ 1000 employees	—	—	0.62 (0.49)	0.21 (0.41)	—	—	0.65 (0.48)	0.28 (0.45)
Percent government employees	—	—	0.18 (0.39)	0.23 (0.42)	—	—	0.20 (0.40)	0.30 (0.46)
Percent parent	0.58 (0.49)	0.48 (0.50)	0.70 (0.46)	0.74 (0.44)	0.59 (0.49)	0.38 (0.49)	0.70 (0.46)	0.70 (0.46)
Percent does *more than half* of household tasks	—	0.42 (0.50)	—	0.79 (0.41)	—	0.34 (0.47)	—	0.74 (0.44)
Percent does *at least half* of household tasks	0.47 (0.50)	—	0.10 (0.30)	—	0.46 (0.50)	—	0.08 (0.28)	—

Among all earners, 42 percent of Stanford women and 79 percent of Todai women did more than half of the household tasks. Among full-time earners, 34 percent of Stanford women and 74 percent of Todai women did more than half of the household tasks. Among men, 46 to 47 percent of Stanford men and 8 to 10 percent of Todai men did at least half of household tasks.

Table 4.7 gives the regression results. For Stanford men and Todai women, holding constant all of the variables listed in the table, number of hours of employment was not significantly related to household task arrangement. However, for Stanford women and Todai men, there was a significant relationship between these two variables. Stanford full-time-earner women who were responsible for doing more than half of household tasks were employed seven hours per week less than other full-time-earner women. Among all-earner Stanford women, those responsible for more than half of household tasks were employed about 9.5 hours per week less than other all-earner women. Todai men who were responsible for at least half of household tasks were employed about 4.5 hours less per week if they were full-time earners and 7.75 hours less per week in the all-earner sample.

Holding all else constant, being a mother had a strong negative effect on hours of employment for Stanford women in the all-earner sample (a reduction of about 6.25 hours per week) and for Todai women in the full-time-earner sample (a reduction of about 7.5 hours per week). In the comments section of the survey, many Todai fathers said they found it difficult to parent their children because of their long working hours. It is interesting that our results show that on average Todai men who were fathers and employed full-time worked about 3.6 hours less per week than nonfathers.

Earnings

Primary responsibility for household tasks had less of an effect on earnings than it had on hours of employment. Although having primary responsibility for household tasks affected earnings by lowering the number of hours of employment per week for Stanford women and Todai men, once hours of employment were accounted for, there was no further effect on earnings.

Table 4.8 shows the means and standard deviations of the variables in a regression to examine the effect of household task arrangement on earnings for all earners and full-time earners. The regressions have the same variables as those discussed in chapter 3, except that the samples are restricted to those who are married and variables measuring participation in household tasks have been added. These household task variables are defined exactly as they were for the regression examining the effect of household task arrangement on hours of employment.[45]

Table 4.9 tells us that except for Stanford men, the effect of household task arrangement on earnings was small and insignificant. Stanford men in the all-earner sample earned about 12 percent less, all other variables held constant, if they did at least half of the household tasks. In the full-time-earner regression, they earned 11 percent less.[46]

It is also interesting that in these regressions for married respondents, there were no significant negative effects on earnings for being a mother, but a significant positive effect for being a father in the Stanford regression for all-earners, and significant positive effects for being a father in both Todai regressions.

The assertion that women pay an earnings penalty if they are married, or if they are mothers, because household and child care tasks make them less productive (either because they are more "tired" or because they are saving their energy for their household responsibilities) does not receive empirical support from these data. On average, the women in these samples have fewer hours per week of employment if they have children, but once hours of work are accounted for, neither Stanford nor Todai women pay an earnings penalty for motherhood, or for doing the lion's share of household tasks.

Rather, it is the men in the sample whose earnings are impacted by family variables: Todai men earn more for being a father (because that is the way Japanese pay is structured), and the few Todai men who share household tasks have significantly lower hours of employment. Finally, those Stanford men who do substantial amounts of housework earn less.

Egalitarian, Traditional, and "Hybrid" Families

In studying the graduates, we were interested not only in their division of household tasks but also in their division of household management and in their division of responsibility for their family's financial well-being. On the questionnaire, we asked separate questions about division of household tasks, division of household management, and responsibility for financial well-being. About division of household management we asked: "Who is mainly responsible for managing the household?" About

Table 4.7
How Do Gender, Parental Status, and Responsibility for Doing Household Tasks Affect Hours Employed?: Parameter Estimates from OLS Regression Analysis Predicting Number of Hours Worked per Week

| | All Earners | | | | Full-Time Earners | | | |
| | Stanford | | Todai | | Stanford | | Todai | |
Variable	Men (N = 227)	Women (N = 146)	Men (N = 234)	Women (N = 66)	Men (N = 221)	Women (N = 110)	Men (N = 218)	Women (N = 47)
Intercept	61.89**	48.15**	43.92**	34.37**	66.17**	61.79**	49.55**	48.06**
Number of years employed full-time	−0.99*	0.01	0.65	−1.29*	−1.32*	−1.05**	0.54	0.63
Number of years employed part-time	−2.15**	−1.85*	−0.61	−1.77**	−1.48^	−0.94	0.52	−0.08
Financial manager	4.44	9.75	—	—	2.76	1.38	—	—
Lawyer	0.32	5.51	—	—	−2.43	1.35	—	—
Marketing manager	−1.22	5.79	—	—	−2.72	−1.81	—	—
Medical Doctor	12.06**	15.99**	—	—	11.66**	7.52*	—	—
Misc. Manager	3.01	4.34	—	—	1.67	−1.92	—	—
Technical manager	−0.60	11.18	—	—	−2.08	3.10	—	—
Technical professional	−7.48*	−1.24	−0.52	−6.99	−8.52**	−9.80*	0.64	13.36**
Manager	—	—	−3.00	−5.60	—	—	−2.98	−0.45
Professor	—	—	−1.42	−1.64	—	—	0.60	−1.36
Researcher	—	—	0.57	−5.13	—	—	−1.02	5.64

Teacher	—	—	-10.11**	-5.06	—	—	-9.81**	-1.90
Company ≥ 1000 employees	—	—	3.71	0.25	—	—	0.65	-0.39
Government employee	—	—	10.30**	1.46	—	—	4.36*	-4.51
Parent	-0.17	-6.26*	-2.83^	-5.73	-0.73	2.15	-3.61*	-7.47**
Does *more than half* of household tasks	—	-9.48**	—	-0.11	—	-7.10**	—	0.20
Does *at least half* of household tasks	-1.00	—	-7.77*	—	-0.67	—	-4.46^	—
Adjusted R^2	0.21	0.26	0.18	0.37	0.30	0.15	0.06	0.16
F	6.59**	5.55**	5.65**	4.45**	9.72**	2.80**	1.97**	1.81^

** Significant at 1% level.
* Significant at 5% level.
^ Significant at 10% level.

Table 4.8
Means and Standard Deviations of Variables in OLS Regressions to Examine How Household Task Responsibility Affects Earnings for All Earners and Full-Time Earners, by Gender

	All Earners				Full-Time Earners			
	Stanford		Todai		Stanford		Todai	
Variable	Men (N = 227)	Women (N = 146)	Men (N = 234)	Women (N = 66)	Men (N = 221)	Women (N = 111)	Men (N = 218)	Women (N = 47)
Ln earnings	4.0720752 (0.5851082)	3.5795464 (0.7958070)	6.5374972 (0.3509090)	6.0373152 (0.7510804)	4.0862447 (0.5717930)	3.8034900 (0.4788985)	6.5455783 (0.3232781)	6.2631805 (0.4291116)
Number of years employed full-time	6.64 (2.69)	6.30 (2.65)	9.43 (2.53)	7.94 (3.86)	6.73 (2.65)	6.68 (2.70)	9.68 (2.15)	9.53 (2.82)
Number of years employed part-time	0.51 (1.09)	1.04 (1.74)	0.73 (2.12)	1.45 (2.61)	0.48 (1.03)	0.69 (1.67)	0.49 (1.56)	0.43 (1.14)
Hours employed/week	54.9 (16.3)	38.5 (24.6)	48.9 (16.1)	33.0 (22.1)	56.4 (13.7)	51.4 (12.6)	52.5 (9.4)	46.3 (7.8)
Percent employed part-time	0.03 (0.16)	0.25 (0.43)	0.07 (0.25)	0.29 (0.46)	—	—	—	—
Number of hours empl/wk times part-time	0.52 (3.28)	5.05 (9.61)	1.22 (5.00)	5.20 (9.91)	—	—	—	—
Number of hours empl/wk times full-time	54.9 (16.3)	38.5 (24.6)	48.9 (16.1)	33.0 (22.1)	—	—	—	—
Percent financial manager	0.09 (0.28)	0.05 (0.21)	—	—	0.09 (0.29)	0.06 (0.24)	—	—
Percent lawyer	0.15 (0.36)	0.08 (0.26)	—	—	0.15 (0.36)	0.08 (0.27)	—	—
Percent marketing manager	0.08 (0.27)	0.12 (0.32)	—	—	0.08 (0.27)	0.14 (0.35)	—	—

Percent medical doctor	0.18 (0.38)	0.14 (0.35)	—	—	0.17 (0.38)	0.08 (0.27)	—	—
Percent misc. manager	0.08 (0.28)	0.12 (0.30)	—	—	0.09 (0.28)	0.11 (0.31)	—	—
Percent technical manager	0.10 (0.30)	0.03 (0.16)	—	—	0.10 (0.30)	0.04 (0.19)	—	—
Percent technical professional	0.12 (0.32)	0.08 (0.26)	0.05 (0.22)	0.05 (0.21)	0.12 (0.32)	0.08 (0.27)	0.05 (0.22)	0.06 (0.25)
Percent manager	—	—	0.15 (0.36)	0.03 (0.17)	—	—	0.16 (0.36)	0.04 (0.20)
Percent professor	—	—	0.09 (0.29)	0.15 (0.36)	—	—	0.07 (0.26)	0.09 (0.28)
Percent researcher	—	—	0.14 (0.35)	0.15 (0.36)	—	—	0.15 (0.35)	0.21 (0.41)
Percent teacher	—	—	0.04 (0.19)	0.06 (0.24)	—	—	0.03 (0.16)	0.04 (0.20)
Percent co. $\geq$ 1000 employees	—	—	0.62 (0.49)	0.21 (0.41)	—	—	0.65 (0.48)	0.28 (0.45)
Percent government employees	—	—	0.18 (0.39)	0.23 (0.42)	—	—	0.20 (0.40)	0.30 (0.46)
Percent parent	0.58 (0.49)	0.48 (0.50)	0.70 (0.46)	0.74 (0.44)	0.59 (0.49)	0.38 (0.49)	0.70 (0.45)	0.70 (0.46)
Percent does *more than half* of household tasks	—	0.42 (0.50)	—	0.79 (0.41)	—	0.33 (0.47)	—	0.74 (0.44)
Percent does *at least half* of household tasks	0.47 (0.50)	—	0.10 (0.30)	—	0.46 (0.50)	—	0.08 (0.28)	—

Table 4.9
How Do Gender, Parental Status, and Household Task Responsibility Affect Earnings for All Earners and Full-Time Earners?: Parameter Estimates from OLS Regression Analysis Predicting the Natural Log of Earnings

| | All Earners | | | | Full-Time Earners | | | |
| | Stanford | | Todai | | Stanford | | Todai | |
Variable	Men (N = 227)	Women (N = 146)	Men (N = 234)	Women (N = 66)	Men (N = 221)	Women (N = 111)	Men (N = 218)	Women (N = 47)
Intercept	3.700**	3.489**	5.893**	5.126**	3.787**	3.218**	6.040**	5.446**
Number of years full-time employment	0.038*	0.019	0.027*	0.057*	0.034*	0.040*	0.016	0.032
Number of years part-time employment	−0.027	−0.018	0.000	−0.045	−0.051	−0.016	0.019	−0.113*
Hours employed/week	—	—	—	—	−0.005^	0.001	0.005**	0.018
Percent employed part-time	−0.877	−1.897**	0.417^	0.123	—	—	—	—
Number of hours employed/wk times part-time	0.025	0.056**	−0.006	0.025^	—	—	—	—
Number of hours employed/wk times full-time	−0.005^	−0.002	0.005*	0.021^	—	—	—	—
Parent	0.048**	−0.071	0.111*	−0.070	0.046	−0.071	0.083^	−0.097
Financial manager	0.810**	0.462^	—	—	0.789**	0.377*	—	—
Lawyer	0.728**	0.717**	—	—	0.707**	0.696**	—	—
Marketing manager	0.519**	0.350^	—	—	0.491**	0.327*	—	—
Medical doctor	0.449**	0.535**	—	—	0.407**	0.358**	—	—
Misc. manager	0.737**	0.254	—	—	0.709**	0.178	—	—
Technical manager	0.459**	0.489	—	—	0.436**	0.426^	—	—
Technical professional	0.306**	0.296	−0.283**	−0.225	0.245*	0.273*	−0.296**	−0.264
Manager	—	—	−0.100	0.074	—	—	−0.082	0.119

Professor	—	—	-0.027	0.340^	—	—	-0.096	0.147*
Researcher	—	—	-0.154*	-0.208	—	—	-0.175**	-0.252^
Teacher	—	—	-0.093	-1.114**	—	—	-0.196	-0.440^
Employed in co. ≥ 1000	—	—	0.178**	0.026	—	—	0.144*	-0.003
Employed in government	—	—	-0.145*	-0.236	—	—	-0.185**	-0.256^
Does *more than half* of household tasks	—	0.047	—	-0.204	—	0.104	—	-0.02
Does *at least half* of household tasks	-0.117^	—	0.002	—	-0.107	—	0.062	—
Adjusted R²	0.318	0.359	0.231	0.531	0.303	0.155	0.223	0.445
F	8.508**	6.787**	5.987**	6.262**	8.984**	2.684**	6.179**	4.072**

** Significant at 1% level.
* Significant at 5% level.
^ Significant at 10% level.

Table 4.10
Percentages of Married Graduates Across Three Types of Families, by Gender

| | Stanford Sample | | Todai Sample | |
	Men (N = 255)	Women (N = 205)	Men (N = 267)	Women (N = 130)
Egalitarian	34.9	37.6	6.4	11.5
Traditional	24.3	36.6	30.3	40.0
Hybrid	40.8[a]	25.9	63.3[b]	48.5
Total	100.0	100.1	100.0	100.0

[a] Includes three reverse-traditional.
[b] Includes 2 reverse-traditional.

financial responsibility we asked: "Who is responsible for your family's financial well-being?" Information about responses to these questions is in the appendix to this chapter.

To obtain a single measure for each married graduate of how traditional or egalitarian his or her family was with respect to division of labor, we aggregated the data on household tasks, household management, and responsibility for family financial well-being, then put each graduate into one of three categories: egalitarian, hybrid, or traditional. We called graduates traditional if their division of family labor was the one traditionally followed by breadwinner/homemaker families: husband in charge of financial responsibility and wife in charge of household management and household tasks. We called them egalitarian if they shared all three household responsibilities. All others we designated as hybrid. The results of this categorization are in table 4.10.

In the Stanford sample, about 38 percent of the women and 35 percent of the men were in egalitarian families. It is interesting that the percentages are approximately the same for the two genders. In the Todai sample, a much smaller proportion of graduates were egalitarian, about 12 percent of the women and only about 6 percent of the men.

On the other hand, 24 percent of Stanford men and 37 percent of the women had traditional household arrangements. A higher percentage of Stanford women than Stanford men were in traditional families. Almost the same percentage of Stanford women were in traditional families as were in egalitarian families, but Stanford men were much more likely to be in egalitarian families than in traditional families.

Among the Todai graduates, the women's families were also more traditional than the men's. About 30 percent of the men's families and 40 percent of the women's families handled household responsibilities traditionally. These percentages were only slightly higher than the percentages for Stanford men and women. The Todai and Stanford samples were much closer to one another on the percentages who were traditional than on the percentages who were egalitarian.

Differences Among Graduates in the Three Types of Families

Graduates in egalitarian families were different from those in other families on a number of dimensions. Stanford and Todai women were less likely, and Stanford men more likely, to turn down career opportunities for family reasons. With regard to occupations, Stanford and Todai women in egalitarian families were more likely to be in occupations that were nontraditional for women, and Todai men in egalitarian families were very likely to be professors. It may be that professors had more flexible time schedules and/or that they had more contact with a Western ideology of sharing than most of their male classmates.

With regard to earnings, in the Stanford sample, where families divided responsibilities in traditional fashion, husbands (both Stanford men and the husbands of Stanford women) had higher earnings than husbands in hybrid or egalitarian families. Moreover (with one exception, Stanford men's families with children), in the Stanford sample, traditional families' total earnings (husband's earnings plus wife's earnings) were higher than total family earnings in either of the other two types of families.

Turning Down Career Opportunities for Family Reasons

How might limiting one's career for one's spouse be related to family type? There are two possible stories. Some couples may have known early on in their relationship that they wanted to be more or less traditional or more or less egalitarian. Those who sought a traditional relationship would then have favored the husband's career from the outset, while those who sought an egalitarian relationship would less frequently have favored the husband's career and sometimes would have favored the wife's career.

But for other couples, the causality might have run the other way. That is, rather than having their ideology determine their career decisions, they may have found that their career decisions ultimately defined their ideology. For example, after several years of unthinkingly advantaging the husband's career, they may have found that, given those earlier decisions, the husband's earnings and career potential were so much greater than the

Table 4.11
Percentages of Women and Men Who limited or Turned Down Career Opportunities Because of Spouse, by Type of Family

	Stanford Sample		Todai Sample	
	Men (N = 76)	Women (N = 85)	Men (N = 20)	Women (N = 48)
Egalitarian	36.0	39.0	11.8	21.4
Traditional	21.0	49.3	7.6	45.1
Hybrid	30.4[a]	38.0	7.3[a]	36.7
Total	30.0	42.5	7.7	38.4

[a] Includes 1 reverse-traditional.

wife's that being traditional in their division of family labor made the most sense in terms of family well-being.

Whichever story applied, we expected that in egalitarian families, men would have a relatively higher rate of limiting their careers and women a relatively lower rate, compared with their same-sex classmates in traditional or hybrid families. We also expected that in traditional families, women would have a relatively higher rate, and men a relatively lower rate, of limiting their careers, compared with their same-sex classmates in other types of families.

As table 4.11 indicates, our expectations were largely borne out: except for Todai men, family type was clearly related to turning down career opportunities for one's spouse. Compared with their male classmates, Stanford men in egalitarian families were more likely (36 percent), and Stanford men in traditional families less likely (21 percent), to have turned down job opportunities because of their spouses.

Among Stanford women, those in traditional families were the most likely to have turned down job opportunities (49 percent), while those in egalitarian and hybrid families were less likely to have turned down job opportunities (39 and 38 percent, respectively). It may be that for Stanford women, agreeing to restrict career geographically is what made an egalitarian relationship possible.

Among the Todai men, those in traditional families had the same (low) rate of turning down career opportunities as those in hybrid families, about 7 percent. The rate of turndown in egalitarian families was only slightly higher, about 12 percent.

For Todai women, those in traditional families had the highest rate of job limitation (45 percent). It is interesting that Stanford and Todai women in traditional families had similar rates of job limitation. In egalitarian families, only 21 percent of Todai women limited their career, a rate less than half of that for Todai women in traditional families.

Occupational Differences

As shown in table 4.12, among Stanford women, those in occupations that are nontraditional for women were more likely to be in egalitarian families. While for all women 38 percent were in egalitarian families, 58 percent of scientist/engineers, 49 percent of managers, 50 percent of medical doctors, and 46 percent of lawyers were in egalitarian families. Women in these nontraditional occupations were also less likely to be in traditional families than other women.

Among Todai women, the occupation that stood out as being different was salaryman, a very nontraditional occupation for women (witness the title). Although the numbers that the percentages are based on are small, 22 percent of Todai women salarymen were in egalitarian families (compared with only 12 percent for all women) and 28 percent were in traditional families (compared with 40 percent for all women).

In other words, Stanford and Todai women who were nontraditional in their occupation were more likely to be nontraditional in their home. Yet, it is still the case that at least half of the women in both samples who were in nontraditional occupations were *not* in egalitarian families.

Among Todai men, two occupations were of interest: technical professional and professor. For all Todai men, 30 percent were in traditional families. But only 23 percent of Todai men who were technical professionals were in traditional families. And professors differed even more from the average. Only 13 percent of professors were in traditional families. Moreover, although only 6 percent of all Todai men were in egalitarian families, 33 percent of Todai men professors were in such families. Of the 17 Todai men who were in egalitarian families, 8 of them were professors. This may be because professors have more flexible work schedules than others and/or because they are more ideologically inclined toward egalitarian relationships at home.

Other Differences

Table 4.13 points out some additional differences among graduates in the three types of families. The data for Todai graduates are not as good here as those for Stanford graduates because the sample sizes in several of the categories are small and because many Todai graduates did not provide information on a number of questions.

Table 4.12
Selected Occupations of Married Graduates by Type of Family, by Gender
(percentages)

Stanford Sample

Men	Egalitarian (N = 89)	Traditional (N = 62)	Hybrid (N = 104)	Women	Egalitarian (N = 77)	Traditional (N = 75)	Hybrid (N = 53)
Engineer, scientist	37.5	34.4	28.1	Engineer, scientist	58.3	25.0	16.7
Finance	22.7	40.9	36.4	Finance	40.0	40.0	20.0
Lawyer	38.9	19.4	41.7	Lawyer	45.5	27.3	27.3
Manager	27.9	23.3	48.8	Manager	48.7	21.6	29.7
Medical doctor	41.2	27.5	31.4	Medical doctor	50.0	19.2	30.8
Technical manager	34.8	26.1	39.1	Nontechnical consultant	30.0	60.0	10.0
Total	34.9	24.3	40.8	Total	37.6	36.6	25.9

Todai Sample

Men	Egalitarian (N = 17)	Traditional (N = 81)	Hybrid (N = 169)	Women	Egalitarian (N = 15)	Traditional (N = 52)	Hybrid (N = 63)
Manager	3.7	33.3	63.0	Homemaker	3.3	46.7	50.0
Professor (lecturer)	33.3	12.5	54.2	Professor (lecturer)	0.0	40.0	60.0
Researcher	5.9	35.3	58.8	Researcher	7.7	38.5	53.9
Salaryman	1.1	32.6	66.3	Salaryman	22.2	27.8	50.0
Technical professional	0.0	23.1	76.9				
Total	6.4	30.3	63.3	Total	11.5	40.0	48.5

Stanford men in traditional families earned, on average, considerably more than Stanford men in other families, and the husbands of Stanford women in traditional families earned more than the husbands of Stanford women in other types of families. Also, the ratio of wife's/husband's earnings was lower in traditional families than in other types of families.[47] These findings are consistent with a bargaining theory of the division of household labor.[48]

Stanford men in traditional families also had higher nonwage income than Stanford men in other types of families. Combined with their higher earned income, these results begin to create a pattern. It is likely that their higher earnings and higher nonwage income gave these men the power to bargain for a traditional division of labor.[49]

If we add the earnings of husbands and wives (including those who reported spouses with zero earnings), we find that with the exception of Stanford men with children, the highest totals of husbands' plus wives' earnings are in traditional families. This may help to explain why so many Stanford women who had a traditional division of household tasks (almost half) said they were satisfied with their task arrangement. Perhaps some of them felt that their relatively high family income "compensated" them for their task responsibilities.

One difference between Stanford women with children in traditional families and those in other types of families was that their average number of hours per week in paid employment (29) was much lower than that of Stanford women with children in egalitarian and hybrid families (46 and 47 hours, respectively.) Clearly, one way that these mothers coped with their double burden of employment plus primary or sole responsibility for household tasks and management was to cut back their number of hours of employment and to give up (or eschew) joint financial responsibility, even though their average earnings were no lower than those of women in other types of families. This finding corroborates our finding for Stanford women in the regressions reported in table 4.8.

Overall, there were bigger differences between traditional families and other families than between egalitarian families and other families.[50] One difference between egalitarian families and other families was that Stanford men in egalitarian families with children were more likely to employ household help than Stanford men in other families with children. Stanford women with children had the same rate of employing household help (56 to 57 percent), regardless of family type. Stanford men with children who were in egalitarian families had this same rate (57 percent). However, Stanford men with children in other family types had much

Table 4.13
Comparisons of Graduates by Type of Family, by Gender and Parental Status

| | Stanford Egalitarian | | | | Stanford Traditional | | | | Stanford Hybrid | | | |
| | With Children | | Without Children | | With Children | | Without Children | | With Children | | Without Children | |
	Men	Women	Men	Women	Men	Women	Men	Women	Men	Women	Men	Women
Earnings of husband	$62,647	$59,548[a]	$56,667	$56,395[a]	$91,000	$79,593[a]	$81,929	$69,062[a]	$70,733	$46,333[a]	$56,000	$51,321[a]
(Standard deviation)	($31,761)	($31,337)	($29,910)	($49,208)	($112,340)	($65,288)	($46,706)	($57,335)	($47,907)	($23,427)	($29,369)	($29,403)
N	34	31	51	38	44	54	14	16	60	21	40	28
Earnings of wife	$45,800[a]	$43,893	$38,680[a]	$46,359	$25,565[a]	$40,912	$38,100[a]	$56,222	$26,114[a]	$45,500	$36,432[a]	$47,913
(Standard deviation)	($31,758)	($27,970)	($20,091)	($20,352)	($27,899)	($52,650)	($27,501)	($37,727)	($16,397)	($26,445)	($19,318)	($25,000)
N	25	28	50	39	23	34	10	16	35	14	37	23
Ratio w/h earnings[b]	0.73	0.92	0.79	1.16	0.46	0.62	0.59	0.93	0.51	1.22	1.04	1.26
(Standard deviation)	(0.39)	(0.70)	(0.49)	(0.94)	(0.49)	(0.79)	(0.45)	(0.57)	(0.45)	(1.07)	(1.14)	(0.97)
N	25	27	48	38	23	34	10	16	34	14	36	23
Household non-wage income[a]	$40,630	$22,714	$26,341	$39,303	$63,659	$26,266	$130,333	$48,750	$30,577	$21,389	$29,895	$49,800
(Standard deviation)	($77,007)	($31,586)	($48,973)	($98,889)	($111,440)	($45,179)	($234,068)	($86,736)	($59,193)	($29,310)	($41,368)	($72,354)
N	27	28	44	33	41	49	12	16	52	18	38	25

Total hours employed	55.67	45.60	55.98	47.38	56.00	29.18	55.93	46.33	54.37	47.26	54.39	47.00
(Standard deviation)	(15.02)	(16.30)	(14.81)	(18.21)	(12.90)	(18.68)	(8.02)	(10.03)	(13.88)	(19.89)	(19.72)	(16.77)
N	33	30	49	39	46	33	14	18	59	15	38	23
Percent who employ Household help	57.1	55.6	37.0	39.0	47.9	57.1	42.9	38.9	36.1	56.5	36.8	26.9
N	35	36	54	41	48	56	14	18	61	23	38	26
H + w earnings[a]	$108,111	$100,037	$97,417	$103,895	$88,379	$118,231	$108,909	$116,375	$90,359	$86,375	$90,579	$93,600
(Standard deviation)	($31,761)	($31,337)	($40,704)	($49,208)	($112,340)	($65,287)	($46,706)	($57,335)	($47,907)	($23,427)	($29,369)	($29,408)
N	27	27	48	38	29	39	11	16	39	16	38	25

Table 4.13 (continued)

	Todai Egalitarian				Todai Traditional				Todai Hybrid			
	With Children		Without Children		With Children		Without Children		With Children		Without Children	
	Men	Women	Men	Women	Men	Women	Men	Women	Men	Women	Men	Women
Earnings of husband	¥8,350,000	—	—	—	¥7,795,439	¥7,525,357[a]	¥6,761,579	—	¥7,330,857	¥7,335,758[a]	¥7,328,542	¥6,574,000[a]
(Standard deviation)	(¥9,452,131)	—	—	—	(¥2,699,581)	(¥2,337,270)	(¥1,710,407)	—	(¥2,737,329)	(¥2,540,405)	(¥2,835,672)	(¥2,133,043)
N	10	9	6	2	57	28	19	6	105	33	48	10
Earnings of wife	—	¥6,146,000	—	—	¥663,704	¥4,571,333	¥1,376,364	—	¥3,470,667	¥3,849,615	¥3,329,000	¥6,777,000
(Standard deviation)	—	(¥2,948,341)	—	—	(¥1,790,125)	(¥1,786,788)	(¥1,764,014)	—	(¥1,884,158)	(¥2,074,927)	(¥2,356,458)	(¥3,652,716)
N	6	10[a]	5	2	27	15[a]	11	5	15	26[a]	209	9
Ratio w/h earnings[b]	—	—	—	—	—	0.66	—	—	0.54	0.72	6	—
(Standard deviation)	—	—	—	—	—	(0.43)	—	—	(0.28)	(0.38)	(0.36)	—
N	6	9	5	2	5	12	6	4	14	21	20	9
Household nonwage income[a]	—	—	—	—	—	—	—	—	—	—	—	—
(Standard deviation)	—	—	—	—	—	—	—	—	—	—	—	—
N	3	4	3	2	9	8	4	2	18	10	8	1

Total hours employed	38.50	39.30	—	—	52.30	31.08	52.79	—	48.42	34.61	51.57	45.09
(Standard deviation)	(15.74)	(14.32)	—	—	(11.38)	(18.57)	(10.62)	—	(11.59)	(17.08)	(2.83)	(17.80)
N	10	10	6	2	60	26	19	8	106	31	49	11
Percent who employ household help	10.0	16.7	—	—	3.2	12.2	5.9	0.0	2.6	18.8	0.0	0.0
N	10	12	7	3	62	41	17	10	116	48	50	14
H + w earnings[a]	—	—	—	—	¥8,700,769	¥11,961,700	¥8,446,364	—	¥8,795,000	¥11,112,900	¥9,100,000	—
(Standard deviation)					(¥2,699,581)	(¥2,485,342)	(¥1,710,407)		(¥4,226,776)	(¥3,534,536)	(¥2,835,672)	
N	6	9	6	2	26	12	11	10	42	21	29	9

[a] Includes spouses whose reported income was zero.
[b] Based only on those whose incomes were > 0.

lower rates (48 percent in traditional families and 36 percent in hybrid families). In the same way that Stanford women in traditional families decreased their average hours of employment to take on sole or primary responsibility for household management and household tasks, Stanford men with children in egalitarian families increased their rate of using household help to reduce the total amount of household work that they had to share.[51]

For the Todai sample, one difference between egalitarian families and other families was that the average number of hours per week that men with children in egalitarian families were employed (39) was considerably lower than the number of hours per week for men with children in traditional families (52) or men in hybrid families (48). This result echoes the one we saw in table 4.8, where in the regression to explain hours worked, there was a significant negative coefficient of about eight hours per week for Todai men who did at least half of household tasks. Moreover, as we noted earlier, half the men in egalitarian families were professors, who had more than average control over their hours of employment.

Homemakers

Stanford mothers who specialized in homemaking and child rearing were much less likely to be in egalitarian families and much more likely to be in traditional families than were employed mothers. Only 13 percent of full-time homemakers were in egalitarian families, compared with 40 percent of employed mothers. At the opposite pole, 60 percent of full-time homemakers were in traditional families, compared with 44 percent of employed mothers. However, although mothers had a much higher chance of being in an egalitarian family if they were employed full-time than if they were full-time homemakers, mothers employed full-time nevertheless had a better than 50–50 chance of being responsible for more than half of household tasks and an almost 50 percent chance of being in a traditional family.

Only a single full-time Todai homemaker (less than 4 percent), compared with 11 Todai employed mothers (15 percent), was in an egalitarian family. The opposite was true for being in a traditional family; 46 percent of full-time Todai homemakers, compared with 38 percent of Todai employed mothers, were in traditional families.

Summary of Major Findings

Bargaining power theory helps us to understand how the interaction between the labor market and family decision-making can perpetuate the breadwinner/homemaker model and create a situation where the difficulty of achieving an egalitarian marriage may become a self-fulfilling prophecy. To the extent that a wife's earnings are lower than her husband's (or the couple anticipates that her earnings will be lower than his), the wife will have less bargaining power in the marriage; her career will be less frequently favored than her husband's, and she will do the lion's share of household tasks. As a result, she will have a lower hourly rate for her work than her husband has for his, and she may work fewer hours than he does, either in order to accommodate her additional tasks at home or because the moves she has made to further her husband's career have left her without the ability to hold a full-time job in her field.

Women in egalitarian families were much less likely to have limited or turned down career opportunities for their spouse's sake. On the other hand, Stanford men in egalitarian families were much more likely to have done so. Todai men, regardless of family type, were unlikely to have limited their career for their spouse's sake.

Women who chose to be homemakers did so for a combination of ideological and economic reasons. Many were reluctant homemakers, having taken on that role because they were unable to find flexible employment. Most expected to return to the labor market, but while Stanford women were optimistic about their return, Todai women, probably with good reason, were not.

Whether or not a mother had a graduate degree was one of the best predictors of whether or not she would be a homemaker. On the other hand, having limited one's career for one's husband did not differentiate homemakers from employed mothers. While limiting one's career for one's husband probably made it more difficult to obtain flexible employment, thereby making a stint as a full-time homemaker more likely, limiting one's career may also have been what made it possible for mothers to remain in a dual-earner marriage.

In the Stanford sample, husband's earnings and family nonwage income were *not* very much higher in homemaker families. Rather, having only one adult in the labor market probably meant that many homemaker families had less in the way of material goods and services than families with two earners. However, it is important to remember that two-earner families had not only additional income but also additional expenses: taxes, child care, commuting, additional clothing, and so on.

Stanford homemakers were much more likely to come from upper-class backgrounds than were Stanford employed women. Having wealth in the extended family may have given some women with upper-class origins the financial "insurance" they needed to take the financial "risk" of giving up continuity of work experience and becoming a full-time home-maker.

Having a relative nearby who can provide child care in an emergency is a valuable resource for parents with jobs. In the Todai sample, it may be that this resource was important in allowing mothers to be employed. However, in the Stanford sample, employed mothers and full-time home-makers were equally likely to have this resource.

While Stanford women and men were more likely to share housework equally with their spouse than most Americans, still less than half of Stanford women and men (about 43 percent) shared household tasks about equally. Moreover, the proportion who shared equally was much lower for those with children than for those without. Among dual-earner couples, the sharing rate for household tasks was about 50 percent for both the Stanford women and the Stanford men.

The difference in the proportion of Stanford and Todai graduates who shared household tasks about equally with their spouse was the single largest difference in our study; only 8 percent of Todai men and only 13 percent of Todai women shared household tasks about equally with their spouse. However, among dual-earner couples, the rate of sharing was much greater; slightly more than 20 percent of Todai women and men in dual-earner couples shared household tasks.

According to bargaining power theory, the greater the wife's bargain-ing power relative to her husband (where each spouse's bargaining power is measured by his or her earnings), the more likely the couple is to share household responsibilities. Our analyses provided modest support for the theory. Among Todai men, professors were particularly likely to share household tasks.

It is highly likely that differences in ideology in the United States and Japan played an important role in the differences in the percentages of couples who shared household work equally in the two samples. One of the reasons why Stanford couples had a higher rate of sharing house-hold tasks about equally is probably that the American women's move-ment has fostered a stronger and more thoroughly discussed ideology of sharing housework than has been true in the Japanese women's movement.

Interestingly, men in both samples were highly satisfied with their family's division of household tasks, and in both samples men with an egalitarian division of household tasks had about the same rate of satisfaction as men with a traditional division of household tasks. Among women, however, there was a large difference in satisfaction rates between those who shared household tasks about equally and those who did not. Those who shared household tasks about equally had high rates of satisfaction, but among women with a traditional arrangement for household tasks, 53 percent of Stanford women and 40 percent of Todai women were dissatisfied. This is a very high degree of dissatisfaction, and provides some insight into the friction that many women experience as society moves away from the traditional breadwinner/homemaker system.

While it is too strong to argue that dissatisfaction with the division of labor in a family leads to divorce, there is empirical evidence in the United States that such dissatisfaction is associated with having thoughts about divorce.[52] The high rate of dissatisfaction with the division of household tasks among women with a traditional division of such tasks is cause for concern.

Our analyses uncovered two strategies that some graduates used for combining career and marriage.[53] Stanford women who had primary responsibility for household tasks and Todai men who shared household tasks equally with their spouses both spent fewer hours in paid work than other women and men. And Stanford men with children who were in egalitarian families were much more likely to employ household help than men with children in less egalitarian family arrangements.

While many employed Todai and Stanford women may have been burdened by a double day (heavy responsibility for household tasks in addition to a paid job), we did not find that doing more than half of household tasks had a significant negative effect on women's earnings. The notion that women who have primary responsibility for household tasks have lower productivity, and therefore lower earnings, was not supported by our findings.

However, we did find a significant relationship between having household task responsibility and Stanford men's earnings. Holding constant work experience, hours of employment, occupation, and parental status, Stanford men who did at least half of household tasks earned about 10 percent less than other married men. It is important to remember, however, that although our analyses suggest that it is increased participation in housework that leads to lower earnings, in fact the direction of causality between these two variables is not established.

Appendix: Responsibility for Family Financial Well-Being and for Household Management

Responsibility for Family Financial Well-Being

In traditional breadwinner/homemaker families, men are responsible for their family's financial well-being.[1] How traditional were the Stanford and Todai graduates on the division of financial responsibility?

Our questionnaire asked the graduates: "Who is responsible for your family's financial well-being?" We coded responses into three categories: self, if the respondent was either entirely or mostly responsible; joint, if responsibility was shared with the spouse; and spouse, if the spouse was either entirely or mostly responsible.

The majority of Stanford men (54 percent) and Stanford women (59 percent) said they and their spouse were jointly responsible for their family's financial well-being. On the other hand, 44 percent of Stanford men and 29 percent of Stanford women had a traditional arrangement for financial responsibility. About 2 percent of the men and 13 percent of the women reported being in reverse-traditional families, where the woman was entirely or mostly responsible for financial well-being.[2]

It is interesting that women report a lower incidence of men having sole responsibility than men report. We know from time-use studies that relative to their spouses' reports, both husbands and wives tend to underestimate the amount of housework their spouse does and to overestimate the amount they do. It may be that Stanford women are simply less likely than Stanford men to be in families where husbands have the sole financial responsibility. But it may also be that Stanford women underreport the degree of financial responsibility their husbands feel.

Todai men and women were much more traditional in dividing family financial responsibility than were Stanford graduates, and Todai men were even more traditional than Todai women. Fully two-thirds of the Todai men said they were entirely or mostly responsible for their family's financial well-being, and only 27 percent of Todai men shared this responsibility with their wives. Todai women, on the other hand, were divided almost equally (47 percent to 45 percent) between a traditional and an egalitarian division of financial responsibility. (Again, it may be that some Todai women underestimated the amount of financial responsibility their husbands felt.) About 7 percent of Todai men and 8 percent of Todai women had a reverse-traditional arrangement for financial responsibility.

In the Stanford sample, those who had children had a more traditional arrangement for sharing financial responsibility. Among men, about 75 percent of those without children shared financial responsibility, but only about half of that percentage with children (38 percent) shared financial responsibility. Among women, the difference between those with and without children was not as great as for the men. Still, while 73 percent of women without children shared financial responsibility, only about half (48 percent) of women with children did so.

In the Todai sample, however, among men there was almost no difference in financial responsibility between those who had children and those who did not; and among the women, there was only a small difference (11 percentage points).

The percentage of Stanford women who shared financial responsibility was much higher (more than double) among women who were employed full-time (77 percent) than among those not employed full-time (35 percent). Interestingly, among Stanford women who were employed full-time, the percentage with joint financial responsibility did not vary much by whether or not they had children. Seventy-four percent of Stanford women who were full-time-employed with children shared financial responsibility, and 79 percent of those employed full-time without children shared jointly.

Among Todai women who were employed full-time, 69 percent shared financial responsibility jointly with their husband. Like Stanford women, Todai women who were employed full-time had a rate of joint financial responsibility that did not vary greatly by whether or not they were mothers. Sixty-eight percent of mothers and 73 percent of women without children shared financial responsibility with their husbands.

Across the two samples, the rates of sharing among respondents in dual-earner couples were much more similar by gender than the rates for all couples. Seventy-nine percent of Stanford men and 64 percent of Todai men in dual-earner couples shared financial responsibility with their wives. This rate for Todai men was more than double the rate for Todai men in most of the other family situations. Among the women, 78 percent of Stanford women and 81 percent of Todai women in dual-earner couples shared financial responsibility with their husbands.

For graduates in dual-earner couples, we ran probit regressions, specified in the same way as those reported in table 4.5, to look at the relationships between earnings and hours worked and the sharing of responsibility for the family's financial well-being. In all four samples, wife's earnings and the ratio of wife's/husband's earnings were significantly positively related to sharing financial responsibility; the higher the wife's earnings and the higher the ratio of wife's/husband's earnings, the greater the probability of sharing financial responsibility. For Stanford men, husband's earnings were negatively associated with sharing financial responsibility; that is, the higher the husband's earnings, the less likely the couple was to share financial responsibility. For the other three groups, however, husband's earnings were not significantly associated with the sharing of financial responsibility.

With regard to hours, wives who were employed more hours were more likely to share financial responsibility with their husbands. However, there was no significant relationship between men's hours of employment and the sharing of financial responsibility in their families.[3]

Responsibility for Managing the Household

The question concerning household management asked: "Who is mainly responsible for managing the household?" Respondents were asked to circle one of four answers: self, partner, both, or other.

The majority of respondents in both samples (between 56 and 64 percent) were in families with joint responsibility for household management.[4] At the other end of the spectrum, in both the Stanford and Todai samples, about 30 percent of the men and about 40 percent of the women were traditional in dividing household management responsibilities.[5] These gender differences may be real, but as was the case with financial responsibility, they may be the result of different perceptions on the part of women and men. It may be that both Stanford and Todai men underestimated the amount of household management their wives did and overestimated their own time spent on management. Or Stanford and Todai women may have overestimated their own contributions to management and underestimated those of their husbands.

For both Stanford women and men, an egalitarian division of labor for household management was less common among those with children. Only 57 percent of men with children shared household management, compared with 75 percent of men without children. Among women, only 45 percent of those with children shared household management, compared with 73 percent of those without children.

For Stanford women, those with children had a markedly higher rate of sharing household management if they were full-time-employed, compared with all respondents with children (73 percent versus 45 percent). But full-time employment had little effect on the rate of sharing for those without children (68 percent versus 73 percent). This is the same pattern we found for the sharing of financial responsibility and household tasks.

Todai men were also more likely to share household management if they did not have children; 55 percent of Todai fathers shared household management, compared with 64 percent of Todai men without children. But this pattern did not hold for Todai women. Todai women were the only group whose rate of sharing was not lower for those with children than for those without children. (This is an anomalous finding; with regard to sharing financial responsibility and household tasks, all groups, including Todai women, were more likely to share if they did not have children.)

Three-fourths of Todai men in dual-earner couples shared household management, a higher percentage than for any other group of Todai men and higher than the rate for the other three groups of dual-earner couples.

Probit regressions specified in the same way as those reported in table 4.5 showed that for Stanford women, the probability of sharing household management was negatively related to their husband's earnings, but positively related to the ratio of wife's/husband's earnings and to wife's hours of employment. For the other three samples, none of the bargaining power variables were significantly related to the probability of sharing household management.

5   How Did the Graduates Care for Their Children?

Stanford married woman, living separately:

Exhaustion, sleep deprivation, social and emotional isolation, sexism, I haven't had energy to deal with them.... I would prefer to live with my spouse rather than duplicating efforts and expenses.... I have postponed having children and regret that I didn't go to Med School earlier.

Stanford man, associate attorney at a law firm:

The largest problems have been balancing professional and personal life and positioning myself to end up where I wish to be in 10 years.... We have delayed having children for a few years.... I expect to be a father of two or three.

Todai father, works for a large company:

Since we are a full-time working couple, my wife is bearing a bigger burden at home. There seems to be no compassion in my company or in society. I wish for a better child-rearing environment. My first child will be born in December.

Todai father:

The problem is I can see my children only on weekends. The only thing I can do is not to go to golf on weekends to stay home with them.

Todai father:

I wish my wife would quit work and send the children to private kindergarten.

Todai mother with Ph.D.:

When I accompanied my husband for his overseas transfer, I gave birth to my child. When we came back to Japan, I was officially accepted as a lecturer at (a Japanese university), but when they found out that I had a baby, they canceled the acceptance.

More than half of the Todai graduates and slightly over a third of Stanford graduates in our samples were parents. This chapter examines their employment patterns, child care arrangements, and satisfaction with those

Table 5.1
Employment Status of Graduates Who Were Parents, by Gender
(percentages)

	Stanford Sample		Todai Sample	
	Men (N = 150)	Women (N = 124)	Men (N = 192)	Women (N = 107)
Employed	97.4	66.1	96.8	68.3
Full-time	92.0	40.3	87.5	39.3
Part-time	2.7	25.8	5.7	26.2
Unclear	2.7	—	3.6	2.8
Unemployed	0.0	0.0	0.0	0.9
Not Employed	2.0	33.1	1.0	27.1
Students	1.3	0.8	1.0	0.9
Full-time homemakers	0.7	32.3	0.0	26.2
Missing	0.7	0.8	2.1	3.7
Total	100.1	100.0	99.9	100.0

arrangements. As we shall see, the ability to combine employment with an active role in child rearing remained elusive for many of these parents. We look particularly at the very few Stanford and Todai fathers who were active in their children's care and compare the characteristics of active and inactive fathers.

Employment Status of Graduates Who Were Parents

Table 5.1 presents the employment status of graduates who were parents. Among both Stanford and Todai fathers, about 97 percent were employed, the vast majority full-time. Among mothers, Stanford and Todai women were remarkably similar. About two-thirds of both groups were employed, and their division into full and part-time employment was virtually identical. About 40 percent who were employed worked full-time, and about 26 percent part-time.[1]

The percentage of Stanford mothers who were employed (about 66 percent) was only slightly higher than the 62 percent of all U.S. mothers who were living with their husbands and were employed in 1990; the Todai women who were mothers had much higher rates of employment (about 68 percent) than all Japanese mothers (54 percent) in 1988.[2]

Compared with all U.S. mothers living with their husbands, Stanford mothers had about the same rate of working full-time, but a higher rate of working part-time. In the United States, among mothers living with their husbands, 43 percent were employed full-time, (three percentage points higher than the rate for the Stanford mothers) and 19 percent were employed part-time (seven percentage points lower than the rate for Stanford mothers).[3]

Mothers who were employed were frequently conscious of the ongoing and tremendously difficult task of balancing work and family. One mother of two preschoolers, in answer to our question about the problems faced in pursuing a career, said that combining marriage, career, and child rearing had been her toughest problem. In response to our question about how she had dealt with this problem, she responded:

Like every other working mom, I haven't. We just make it through day after day.

A woman medical resident, whose child spent three days a week in a child care center and two days a week with her mother-in-law, lamented:

I have changed the type of job I am training for since my child was born. I often feel I'm doing neither job well.

Flexibility in the job was often very important for Stanford mothers who were employed. One mother of one child who worked full-time (45 hours a week) said:

It's frustrating knowing I could do more professionally, but that family must come first in my life. I've taken a job which provides flexibility in hours and is less demanding and has less responsibility than I'm otherwise capable of handling.

Being employed part-time was clearly a strategy that Stanford women pursued as a means of balancing career and family. Many intended to return to full-time work in the future. As in the case of this next comment, sometimes the wife's choice to work part-time was colored by earlier decisions she and her husband had made to favor his career.

Relocations for spouse's upward mobility left long gaps while job hunting and caused discontinuity. Family is my chosen priority. My turn to delve into full-time career will come. In the meantime, I pursue part-time endeavors that I can build on in the future and have started my own business. (woman who works 25 hours a week and earns $24,000 a year; husband earns $50,000 a year)

Unfortunately, sometimes reducing hours of employment and taking a part-time job did not always leave the woman more time for her children, as in the case of this mother.

When we had no children and I was working full-time, we split tasks 50/50. Now that I am working 3 days/week so that I can spend some time with our son, I am responsible for 100% of the household duties *and* repairs. Needless to say, I don't have that much free time to spend with my son.

In contrast to Stanford mothers, whose rate of full-time employment was similar to that of all U.S. mothers and who were more likely to work part-time than all U.S. mothers, Todai mothers were much more likely to work full-time than all Japanese mothers and slightly less likely to work part-time. About 23 percent of all Japanese mothers had full-time jobs (17 percentage points lower than Todai mothers) and 31 percent held part-time jobs (about five percentage points higher than Todai mothers).[4]

Todai mothers probably were less likely to work part-time than either Stanford mothers or other Japanese mothers at least in part because in the kinds of work they sought, part-time jobs were unavailable. For example, one Todai mother with a Ph.D. in science opined:

In Japan there are no part-time researchers, so in order to have both a family life and work, I chose the present situation, where I work as a researcher but I do not get paid.

One mother of two young children, now working only a few hours a week as an English teacher in her own home, had been employed in a large company for three years before her marriage, but then was forced to quit. She would have preferred to combine career and motherhood:

Looking back, I should have gone into a career that would have allowed me to work after marriage and childbirth.

The Decision to Have a Child

To learn about the graduates' decision-making process regarding having a child, the survey asked: "Has your working affected your decision to have children?"[5] A follow-up question asked: "If yes, how?"

As shown in table 5.2, the majority of *parents* in both samples said that their decision to have children was not affected by work. Only 10 percent of Todai men answered "yes" to the question. Among Stanford men and Todai women, about 30 percent said that work affected their decision to have children. The group with the highest "yes" response to the question was Stanford women (41 percent).

Stanford graduates who responded to the follow-up question said that two considerations caused them to answer positively: concern about their financial capacity to support a child and concern about balancing work and family. And for those couples who thought that having children would move them from a dual-earner to a single-earner situation, the concern about balancing led to a concern about financial capability.

Some typical responses from Stanford women were as follows:

Table 5.2
Has Working Affected Decision to Have Children?: Proportion of Graduates with Children Whose Decision to Have Children Was Affected by Work, by Gender (percentages)

	Stanford Sample		Todai Sample	
	Men (N = 139)	Women (N = 111)	Men (N = 186)	Women (N = 104)
Yes	31.7	41.4	9.7	30.8
No	68.4	58.6	90.3	69.2
Total	100.1	100.0	100.0	100.0

Among those with children, 11 Stanford men, 13 Stanford women, 6 Todai men, and 3 Todai women did not answer this question.

Working made me hesitant to have kids. Very difficult to do both. I'll probably wait until I am more established. I have mixed feelings about this decision. Ticking biological clock, etc. Also bitter that companies aren't more supportive of women (i.e., giving time off or granting part-time status while rearing kids).

From an assistant professor who shared household tasks and household management equally with her husband and who earned about 20 percent more than her husband:

I have put off having children until I achieve tenure.

A woman financial analyst also was putting off having children:

I want to time the births of any children so that they occur when I am secure in my position and can afford to take 3 months off.

A woman who was pregnant with her first child noted that career plans can sometimes result in moving up the time to have a child:

I've decided to have children now—earlier than I want—so it will fit into my future plans to return to school.

A Stanford man, still in a residency program and working 100 hours a week, noted:

I postponed having children because I don't have enough time to properly raise them.

A man with an MBA, who worked as a management consultant:

I hope to be able to fully enjoy raising a family, ... but the decision to attend graduate school brought along with it financial burden in the form of student loans, which will be haunting me for a few more years.

The fact that such a small proportion of Todai men said that work affected their decision to have children is perhaps not surprising, given their relative job security and relative nonparticipation in household tasks and household management (and, as we shall see, in child care). With regard to Todai women, there are two ways to look at the low proportion of women who said that work affected their decision to have children. The first is to be surprised that the percentage was so low. Given the investment that Todai women made in their education and the knowledge that they would face difficulties in combining career and family, one might have expected more of them to have thought long and hard about the decision to have children.

But a second possible reaction is to be surprised that the percentage was as high as it was. Given the cultural "mandate" in Japan to be married and have a child by one's late twenties or early thirties, one might have expected that, as some wrote on their questionnaire, they did not see having children as a choice. The 30 percent figure is probably the net result of these two conflicting factors.

Two Todai men wrote about the effect of their jobs on their decision not to have children. First,

The pay I get from my company is not enough for us to buy a house. So I started some side business, but no income from that yet. We have decided not to have children yet, because I might be moved to another province at any time, and we don't want to have children while moving around.

And

The problem with my career is the imbalance between pay and the amount of work, such that I find it difficult to maintain a household. My wife also works, so we are not planning to have children. I cannot join in child rearing and the education of children because I return home so late. So, although it is very sad, because of hardship, financially and physically, we cannot have children.

This last quote is particularly interesting because the man earned a fairly high income relative to his classmates and his hours of work were by no means among the highest. Moreover, from other comments on his survey, his wife appeared to work part-time.

Women's comments on this matter follow. From a woman who has a master's degree, is a lecturer in a university, and had one child at the beginning of her career:

It was really hectic. My working situation made it nearly impossible to have a child. But I decided to have the child. Now I feel happy about the decision, but there are things that I have lost.

A woman physician:

As a doctor I have always wanted children, but we can have only one, because we both work. Because of having a child both timewise and moneywise, we had to sacrifice (like hiring paid help at home), but I am very satisfied about the decision.

A woman government employee who, in order to keep her job, lived separately from her husband when he was transferred to another city:

I was moved around from department to department, and each time I thought it was not realistic to ask for child leave at a new position, so I kept refraining from getting pregnant. I still have not made up my mind about having children. Now I think I should not have worried that much and should have had children at a younger age.

Several of the graduates commented on the importance of children in their lives, and some alluded to a somewhat humanizing effect that their children had on their work lives. The following two comments are from men whose wives provided full-time care for their children. The first comes from a Todai man.

Having children adds a personal perspective to my speeches.

A Stanford man:

Kids make it all worth it. All the long hours go easier.

How the Graduates Cared for Their Children

We divide our discussion of child care into three sections. We look first at how children were cared for during usual working hours; we then turn to arrangements for care during after-work hours. Finally, we examine care patterns for children when they were sick.

During Usual Working Hours

The terms used to describe Japanese child care facilities are often confusing to Americans and vice versa. Nursery schools in Japan are what are called child care centers in the United States. Both provide care all day and all year. Public Japanese nursery schools are under the aegis of the Ministry of Health, and there are also private nursery schools. American child care centers may be run by the state, by community organizations, by private companies, or by private individuals. Japanese children go to nursery schools from infancy to age five. Children whose parents are both employed may start nursery school as early as six weeks of age. In the United States, children also may go to child care centers from infancy to age five.

Kindergartens for three- and four-year-olds in Japan are equivalent to what are termed nursery schools in the United States. They provide only part-day care (and often only part-year care). In Japan, kindergartens are run by municipalities or prefectures, under the supervision of the Ministry of Education. In the United States, nursery schools are run by private individuals. Because Japanese kindergartens and American nursery schools provide only part-day care, working parents who use them must have additional care arrangements.

Japanese kindergartens for five-year-olds are equivalent to U.S. kindergartens for five-year-olds. Both provide only part-day, part-year care, and both are publicly owned and operated—in Japan under the aegis of the Ministry of Education and in the United States by the public school districts. Again, for working parents, kindergartens do not provide a sufficient number of hours of care, and parents who use public kindergartens must supplement their care arrangements.

In the United States, there are also family day care homes that care for children from infancy to age five, and also after kindergarten and school. Family day care homes are run by private individuals in their own homes, and parents pay the providers directly for the care services. Family day care providers often have young children of their own, and care for them while they care for other children. In Japan, family day care homes are rare.

Table 5.3 looks at how full-time-employed parents cared for their children during usual working hours. The question we asked was "Who cares for your children during usual working hours? Circle as many as applicable." The survey then listed all of the possibilities given in table 5.3.[6]

The most common response for the men, not unexpectedly, was that their wife provided child care during usual working hours. About three-fourths of Todai fathers and 70 percent of Stanford fathers circled this arrangement. Only 9 percent of Stanford mothers and 15 percent of Todai mothers said their husbands provided child care during usual working hours. In one family, where the husband was a Stanford graduate and he and his wife both cared for their child, the arrangement worked as follows:

We have an ideal arrangement wherein I stay for about $2\frac{1}{2}$ hours in the morning until my wife returns from part-time teaching, and then I work from about 11 A.M. to 7 P.M., using [my company's] "flextime."

Table 5.3
How Full-Time Earners Cared for Their Children During Hours of Employment, by Gender
(multiple responses permitted)
(percentages)

	Stanford Sample	
	Men (N = 133)	Women (N = 47)
I do it	8.3	8.5
Spouse does it	69.9	8.5
Relative in my home	0.0	4.3
Relative in their home	3.8	4.3
Baby-sitting coop	2.3	2.1
Paid employee	21.1	25.5
Family day care	13.5	19.1
Child care center	12.0	23.4
Nursery school	8.3	8.5
School	4.5	6.4
	Todai Sample	
	Men (N = 144)	Women (N = 34)
I do it	11.1	8.8
Spouse does it	74.3	14.7
Relative in my home	6.9	20.6
Relative in their home	6.9	17.6
Baby-sitting coop	—	—
Paid employee	2.8	26.5
Family day care	—	—
Child care center	—	—
Nursery school[a]	18.8	70.6
School[b]	8.3	11.8
Other	3.5	11.8

[a] Nursery schools in Japan are equivalent to child care centers in the United States. Of the 27 men, 19 used a public nursery and 8 used a private one; of the 24 women, 17 used a public nursery and 7 used a private one.
[b] Kindergartens take children age 3 to 5 for half a day. They are thus the U.S. equivalent of nursery schools for 3- and 4-year-olds and of kindergartens for 5-year-olds.

The most common arrangement for Stanford women (and the second most common for Stanford men) was that a paid employee cared for their children during usual working hours. About 26 percent of Stanford women and about 21 percent of Stanford men cited this arrangement.

About one-fourth of Stanford women used child care centers and 19 percent used family day care. Among Stanford men, only 12 percent used child care centers and only 14 percent used family day care.

Only three Stanford graduates said a relative cared for their children in the child's/children's home. Here is a description of one of these arrangements, from a woman who worked 80 hours a week and for whom being a mother was extremely satisfying.

As a resident, I have no control over my schedule, which makes it tough to have a family. My husband is much more flexible and my mother lives with us to take care of the children. Having children has has been the most rewarding thing I have done.

Compared with all employed (part-time as well as full-time) women with children under the age of five in the United States in 1990, Stanford parents employed full-time were much more likely to use a paid employee in the child's home and much less likely to use care by a relative (either in the relative's home or in the child's home). Among those employed full-time, 21 percent of Stanford men and 26 percent of Stanford women reported using a paid employee in their home, compared with less than 3 percent of all U.S. employed mothers with children under five. And only 4 percent of Stanford full-time-employed men and 4 percent of Stanford full-time-employed women used a relative to care for their child, whereas, nationally, among all employed women with a child less than five years of age, 20 percent used a relative. Stanford graduates employed full-time were also somewhat less likely to use group care (child care centers or family day care homes) than all employed mothers in the national survey.[7]

Among Todai mothers, the most common child care arrangement (70 percent) was nursery school (equivalent to a child care center in the United States). This was a much higher percentage than the 42.5 percent of Stanford women who used either form of full-time, formal day care (child care centers plus family day care homes).[8] Two other common arrangements for Todai mothers were a paid employee (27 percent) and a relative in the child's home (21 percent). (Recall that the questionnaire permitted multiple responses to this question.) It is interesting that about the same percentage of Stanford and Todai mothers used a paid employee

Table 5.4
Percentage of Stanford Full-Time Earners Who Preferred a Different Arrangement for Child Care During Hours of Employment, by Gender

	Men (N = 121)	Women (N = 31)
Preferred different arrangement	22.3	22.6

Twelve men and 16 women full-time earners who provided information about how their children were cared for during hours of employment did not respond to the question about whether they preferred a different child care arrangement.

to care for their children. Among Todai fathers, only 19 percent used nursery schools. One of the reasons why school may have been a more popular arrangement for Todai parents than for Stanford parents is that Todai parents tended to have older children. (See table 2.1.)

Like their Stanford sisters, a few Todai women with successful careers had a relative to look after their children. These are the comments of a government employee with two children who had spent a year in the United States studying and had been promoted twice.

Without my mother looking after my children, I would never have been able to have 2 children and work at the same time. Other than when they attend nursery school and school, all other times my mother takes care of the children.

In general, Stanford parents who were employed full-time were satisfied with their child care arrangements, but a significant minority, 22 percent of the fathers and 23 percent of the mothers, would have preferred a different arrangement. (See table 5.4.) In the United States as a whole, questions about satisfaction with child care arrangements elicit similar responses.[9] Many people who are not satisfied with their child care switch to other arrangements, so that at any point in time, most people say they are satisfied. It is interesting that the same proportions of Stanford men and women who were full-time earners were satisfied (and dissatisfied) with their arrangements.

In looking at the surveys of full-time employees who said they wanted a different child care arrangement, we were struck by the absence of a pattern; every type of dissatisfaction seemed represented. Fathers who wished their wives would quit their jobs to provide full-time child care were about equally balanced by fathers who wished their full-time homemaker wives would return to employment. Some fathers whose children were currently cared for in child care or family day care homes, or by a relative wanted care by a nanny. Others with care by a nanny wanted care by a relative. And several whose children were in child care centers wished both they and their wives could provide more care for their children.

The mothers' reasons for dissatisfaction tended to be more specific, and most said they could not have what they wanted because they felt they could not afford it. One woman would have liked a family day care home with fewer children; a second, a single-parent, would have liked her nanny to live in; a third would have preferred a higher-quality child care center; and a fourth would have liked to share a nanny with another family who had a child. Finally, several women would have preferred to provide child care themselves, either by reducing the number of hours they worked or by quitting their jobs altogether, but implied that they could not afford to do so.

The following are comments from two fathers at quite different ends of the spectrum on satisfaction with child care. The first is from a software engineer who was quite satisfied with his son's child care center.

Our child care center is wonderful, and our son would not have as much opportunity to play if he were home all the time. (There are no kids in the neighborhoods of the 1990s—they are all at day care.)

The second is from a lawyer, who was not in favor of child care at all.

We tried day care; but in the end our generation will regret what it does to our family nucleus. My wife takes care of our kids now.

Although the question about satisfaction with child care was inadvertently omitted from the Todai survey, a number of Todai parents commented on their difficulties with child care. In response to the survey question about problems faced in pursuing a career, one Todai mother responded as follows:

Child care problems. No matter what you do, if you are raising a child, there is no flexibility for you in Japanese society. If the society does not give you a chance, you can do nothing.

Another Todai woman, a postdoctoral student at the university with a one-year-old and a four-year-old, also lamented about the difficulty of finding suitable child care that was conveniently located.

I quit my first job in a big company because I could not find a solution to the care of my first child. Now I have put my children in a nursery. I know this is about the best situation I can hope for now, but I spend so much time commuting to work and picking up my children. My son says: "It would be so nice if we lived on the second floor of the nursery and your university were next door." I agree with him.

Table 5.5
How Stanford Graduates and Their Spouses Shared Child Care During Hours Not in Employment, by Gender
(percentages)

	Men (N = 134)	Women (N = 104)
I do all or more than half	11.2	68.3
Spouse does all or more than half	33.6	1.9
Equal	55.2	29.8
Total	100.0	100.0

Two men answered "other" to this question. Their responses are not included in the analysis.

A father, a high school teacher who wanted to spend more time with his child, also found the location of the nursery too far from his workplace.

I find the place of my work and the nursery of my child too far from each other. In order to remedy this situation I am studying on my own and am planning to move.

One mother had problems with child care because her children were not eligible for a public nursery.

Public nurseries are for full-time working mothers. I wish for institutions that would accept self-employed mothers' children. Now I can work only when my children are sleeping. I wish, say every other day, just in the morning, I could send them to public nurseries.

During After-Work Hours

Sharing Patterns for Stanford Graduates
To what extent did parents share in the care of children outside of usual working hours? To answer this question, Stanford respondents were asked: "During other than usual working hours, what share of the child care do you do?" and were given the following choices to circle: All, More than half, About half, Less than half, Almost none, Other (please specify). We collapsed these responses into three categories: I do all or more than half, Spouse does all or more than half, About equal. Table 5.5 shows the Stanford parents' responses to this question. Note that while tables 5.3 and 5.4 include only parents who were employed full-time, table 5.5 includes all parents.

About half of Stanford fathers (55 percent) said they shared equally (did about half) of the child care during hours that they were not employed.

Table 5.6
How Stanford Graduates and Their Spouses Shared Child Care During Hours Not in Employment, Full-Time Earners Only, by Gender

	Men (N = 121)	Women (N = 33)
I do all or more than half	11.6	78.8
Spouse does all or more than half	32.2	0.0
Equal	56.2	21.2
Total	100.0	100.0

Two men answered "other" to this question. Their responses are not include in the analysis.

This was a much higher percentage than among Stanford mothers, where only 30 percent reported equal sharing. Such a large disparity between the women and men in reports of equal sharing raises red flags. Recall that Stanford women's and men's reports of sharing household tasks (and also household management) were quite similar.

It is also interesting that about 11 percent of Stanford fathers reported doing more than half of the child care in hours of nonemployment. This, too, was a much higher rate than what Stanford mothers reported for their own husbands (2 percent).[10]

It may be that, in fact, Stanford fathers shared child care to a greater extent than did the husbands of Stanford mothers. Or it may be that when women and men think about child care, they have different tasks in mind. In any event, given the differences in men's and women's responses, the data on the sharing of child care tasks should be interpreted cautiously.

The pattern of child care sharing for full-time-employed graduates only was quite enlightening in terms of understanding the work–family balancing that full-time-employed mothers do. (See table 5.6.) For the fathers, there was virtually no difference in the results for all fathers versus those who were employed full-time. However, Stanford mothers who were employed full-time, and therefore not with their children during usual working hours, seem to have spent *more* nonemployment hours (evenings, weekends, etc.) with their children, compared with other mothers. The percentage of full-time-employed mothers who did more than half of child care during nonemployment hours was 79 percent, 11 percentage points higher than the percentage for all mothers. And the percentage of full-time-employed mothers who shared about equally was 21 percent, nine percentage points lower than that for all mothers.

Table 5.7
Percentages of Stanford Graduates Who Preferred a Different Arrangement for Sharing Child Care During Nonemployed Hours, by Type of Child Care Arrangement, by Gender

	Men (N = 134)	Women (N = 101)
I do all or more than half	13.3	42.6
Equal	5.4	3.2
Spouse does all or more than half	27.2	—
Total	13.4	29.7

One man answered "other" to this question. His response is not included in the analysis.

Satisfaction with Sharing Patterns for Stanford Graduates
Table 5.7 analyzes Stanford parents' satisfaction with their arrangement for sharing child care during other than usual working hours. We found that those with equal sharing arrangements had very high rates of satisfaction, 95 percent for fathers and 97 percent for mothers. Among fathers, the lowest rate of satisfaction was for those who participated least in caring for the children: 27 percent of fathers who did none or less than half of the child care would have preferred a different arrangement. Among mothers, the same pattern held: those whose husbands participated least in child care had the lowest rate of satisfaction. Among mothers who did all or more than half of child care in nonemployed hours, about 43 percent were dissatisfied and would have preferred a different arrangement. In the words of one such mother:

I wish my husband would take more interest and time with the children—for his sake and theirs.

And from another mother:

I would prefer that my husband was more aware of the need to participate in child care—ongoing discussion.

The fact that 27 percent of Stanford fathers who did less than half of child care would have preferred a different child care arrangement is interesting. This is a larger degree of dissatisfaction than we saw in table 4.3 among Stanford fathers who did less than half of household tasks (16 percent). We see the mirror image of this pattern among Stanford women, where dissatisfaction was greater among those who did all or half of the household tasks (53 percent) than among mothers who did all or more than half of child care (43 percent).

These findings may result from the fact that child care is simply more intrinsically rewarding than household tasks. It would appear that unless bargaining power changes between women and men or an egalitarian ideology becomes more popular in general, there will be an increase in the frequency of shared child care before there is an increase in the frequency of shared household tasks.

Fathers who said they were dissatisfied with the amount of child care they did wrote as follows.

From a father who worked 50 hour a week as a technical manager:

I wish I had the energy to do more [child care]. I don't like being a weekend father.

From a father who was a surgical resident and worked 115 hours a week:

I would like to be home more to help out and watch my child grow.

From a father who was a lawyer working 115 hours a week:

I would like to be with my children more, but at this stage of developing my business it is next to impossible to get out of my office.

Full-time-employed Stanford mothers were much more likely to be satisfied with doing all or more than half of after-work child care than were Stanford mothers who were full-time homemakers. Table 5.8 compares satisfaction rates for these two groups. While almost two thirds of the full-time homemakers who did all or more than half of the after-work child care would have preferred a different arrangement, only about one-third of the full-time employed mothers with this arrangement were dissatisfied with it.

This difference in dissatisfaction rates between full-time homemakers and full-time-employed mothers with respect to child care was the reverse

Table 5.8
Percentages of Stanford Women Graduates Who Preferred a Different Arrangement for Sharing Child Care During Nonemployed Hours: Homemakers and Full-Time-Employed

	Homemakers (N = 36)	Full-Time Employed (N = 32)
I do all or more than half	65.0	32.0
Equal	0.0	14.3
Spouse does all or more than half	—	—
Total	36.1	28.1

Three homemakers and 15 full-time-employed did not answer this question.

of the pattern of dissatisfaction rates with respect to household tasks. Table 4.4, which compared the satisfaction and dissatisfaction rates of full-time homemakers with all full-time-employed women (both mothers and women who were not mothers) with respect to household tasks showed that full-time-employed women who did more than half of household tasks had a dissatisfaction rate of 77 percent, almost double the dissatisfaction rate of (40 percent) for their full-time homemaker sisters. Full-time homemakers had a much higher rate of dissatisfaction when they did all or most of the child care in after-work hours (65 percent) than when they did all or most of the household tasks (40 percent). It appears that there are substantial numbers of Stanford full-time-employed mothers who, while they find doing the lion's share of household tasks onerous, are content to do the lion's share of child care during the hours when they are not in the labor market. On the other hand, while most full-time homemakers seem to see full responsibility for household tasks as part of their job description, they would prefer to share responsibility for child care in nonwork hours.

Sharing Patterns for Todai Graduates

Due to an error in translating the survey into Japanese, Todai and Stanford graduates were asked slightly different questions about their child care responsibilities during hours not in employment. The question about child care during hours of nonemployment that was asked of the Todai graduates was "What percentage of your own time after work do you spend on child care?" Respondents were given five possible answers and asked to circle one: All, More than half, About half, Less than half, Almost none. The Todai parents' answers to the question are provided in table 5.9.

Table 5.9
Percentage of Their Own Time After Work That Todai Graduates Spent on Child Care, by Gender

	Men (N = 181)	Women (N = 88)
All	1.1	38.6
More than half	18.2	37.5
About half	21.5	20.5
Less than half	40.3	1.1
Almost none	18.8	2.3
Total	99.9	100.0

One man answered "other" to this question. His response is not included in the analysis.

Table 5.10
Percentage of Their Own After Work That Todai Graduates Spent on Child Care: Full-Time-Employed Only, by Gender

	Men (N = 150)	Women (N = 32)
All	0.6	25.0
More than half	20.7	43.8
About half	20.7	31.3
Less than half	41.3	0.0
Almost none	16.7	0.0
Total	100.0	100.1

One man answered "other" to this question. His response is not included in the analysis.

Perhaps the most striking finding was that almost 20 percent of the Todai fathers did almost no child care after work. Another 40 percent of fathers reported that they spent less than half of their after-work hours on child care. Thus, 60 percent of the Todai fathers in our sample spent almost none or less than half of their after-work time with their children. One is reminded of the frequent lament about absentee fathers in Japan.

The responses for Todai mothers were the mirror image of those for Todai fathers. Unlike the Stanford case, where fathers and mothers had quite different reports about sharing arrangements, the Todai women and men provided essentially the same reports. About 40 percent of mothers spent all of their after-work time caring for their children and another almost 40 percent spent more than half of their after-work time caring for their children. Among mothers who worked full-time (table 5.10), about 70 percent spent more than half of their after-work time caring for their children.

Satisfaction with Sharing Patterns for Todai Graduates
A few fathers wrote in their surveys that they wished they had more time to spend with their children. One father who spent less than half of his nonwork time with his children was not happy about the situation and hoped to remedy it by being more efficient.

I have too many responsibilities at work. I need to divide my time in a better way. If I could have more time of my own, I would like to help out with the housework and I want more time with the children, too.

One father, a research department head who had spent a year in the United States as a postdoctoral fellow and who spent more than half of

Table 5.11
Percentages of Todai Graduates Who Would Have Preferred a Different Proportion of Their After-Work Time Doing Child Care, by Proportion of Time Spent, by Gender

Proportion of Time Spent	Men	Women
All or more than half	20.0	31.3
About half	18.4	23.5
Less than half or none	13.3	0.0
Total	15.7	28.6

One man answered "other" to this question; his response is not included in the analysis. Fourteen men and 23 women did not answer this question.

his time at home caring for his infant child, was looking forward to less child rearing.

I am trying to concentrate on my research. My child is small, and because my wife is tired, I have to help her with the baby. I hope the baby will grow up fast so I can have more time of my own.

But by and large, Todai parents were satisfied with the proportion of their after-work time they spent on child care. (See table 5.11.) Among fathers, 84 percent were satisfied; and the satisfaction rates were about the same for those who spent little time with their children as for those who spent all or more than half of their after-work time with their children. Only 13 percent of Todai fathers who did less than half or none of the child care after work said they would have preferred a different arrangement.

Among mothers, the overall satisfaction rate was about 70 percent, and there were also relatively few differences among the various categories. Most Todai parents seemed to have found an after-work child care pattern that pleased them.

In table 5.12 we look at the satisfaction rates of Todai mothers who were homemakers, compared with the satisfaction rates of Todai mothers who were employed full-time. About one-third of homemakers did not answer this question. Among those who did, almost all spent all or more than half of their time in so-called nonwork hours doing child care, and almost all were satisfied with the arrangement. Among mothers who were employed full-time, the overall rate of satisfaction was 70 percent, and the rate of satisfaction for those who spent all or more than half of their after-work time in child care was two-thirds.

In summary, assuming that the husbands of Todai mothers have the same attitudes about child care as Todai fathers, we see the difficulty here

Table 5.12
Percentages of Todai Women Graduates Who Would Have Preferred a Different Proportion
of Their "After-Work" Time Doing Child Care, by Proportion of Time Spent: Homemakers
and Full-Time-Employed

Proportion of Time Spent	Homemakers	Full-Time-Employed
All or more than half	18.8	33.3
About half	0.0	—
Less than half or none	0.0	0.0
Total	16.7	30.0

Ten homemakers and 5 full-time-employed did not answer this question.

for Todai mothers. The vast majority of Todai mothers (70 percent) spent
all or more than half of their time doing child care in nonwork hours,
and of those, about a third were dissatisfied. On the other hand, the
majority of Todai fathers spent less than half or none of their after-
work time doing child care, and only 13 percent of these men said they
would like a different arrangement. On the face of it, the situation looks
deadlocked.

Comparison of Satisfaction Among Todai and Stanford Mothers
Although the questions posed to Todai and Stanford graduates were different, it is interesting that Todai homemakers were much more satisfied
than Stanford homemakers (81 percent versus 35 percent) but that Todai
full-time-employed mothers had the same rate of satisfaction as Stanford
full-time employed-mothers (67–68 percent). The difference in satisfaction
among homemakers across the two samples may be due in part to the low
response rate among Todai homemakers on this question, but it may also
be due to a belief among many Japanese women that homemaking is a
prestigious career, a belief that Stanford homemakers were less likely to
hold.

Caring for a Sick Child

We asked the graduates: "If your child is sick on a workday and needs
adult care, who provides it?" We then gave them the following choices
and asked them to circle one: I stay home, Spouse or partner stays home, I
take turns with spouse or partner, Other. In table 5.13, we provide the
responses of graduates who were employed full-time.
    The litmus test for egalitarian arrangements often occurs when a child
is sick, as indicated in the following comment from a Stanford father:

Table 5.13
How Full-Time Earners Cared for a Sick Child on a Workday, by Gender
(percentages)

	Stanford Sample	
	Men (N = 120)	Women (N = 36)
I stay at home	4.2	13.9
Spouse stays at home	63.3	2.8
Spouse and I take turns	20.8	52.8
Other	11.7	30.6
Total	100.0	100.1
	Todai Sample	
	Men (N = 151)	Women (N = 33)
I stay at home	0.7	33.3
Spouse stays at home	73.5	0.0
Spouse and I take turns	22.5	48.5
Other	3.3	18.2
Total	100.0	100.0

Eighteen Stanford men, 14 Stanford women, 12 Todai men, and 9 Todai women did not answer this question.

We have 1 child. My wife is also a physician. When our child is sick, our lives
become very stressful. We love our day care situation except when our kid is sick.
Illness is the only reason that we would consider a nanny.

If it is assumed that the mother will always be the one to change her
usual employment schedule to care for a sick child, it becomes very difficult for the mother to pursue a career. Not all fathers were as pragmatic as
the Stanford father who said:

If our son gets sick, I take care of him. I have more vacation and sick leave benefits
than my wife.

About half of Stanford and Todai mothers who were employed full-
time said they took turns with their husbands in providing sick child care.
And although the vast majority of Stanford and Todai fathers relied on
their wives for such care, about 20 percent of the men in both samples
reported taking turns with their wives to care for a sick child. This result
was unexpected, particularly given the stereotypes about Japanese fathers.
Fathers who take turns providing sick child care are at the cutting edge of
social change, and we will look further at them in the next section of the
chapter.

Table 5.14
Proportions of Graduates with Children Who Had a Relative Nearby Available to Help with Child Care in an Emergency, by Gender

	Stanford Sample		Todai Sample	
	Men (N = 143)	Women (N = 115)	Men (N = 183)	Women (N = 98)
Yes	58.0	48.7	59.6	58.2
No	42.0	51.3	40.4	41.8
Total	100.0	100.0	100.0	100.0

Seven Stanford men, 9 Stanford women, 9 Todai men, and 9 Todai women did not answer this question.

Still, about one-third of Todai mothers and about 14 percent of Stanford mothers who were employed full-time had sole responsibility for sick child care. Once again we see the greater difficulty Todai mothers faced in combining a full-time career with motherhood. The reason so many more Todai mothers were solely responsible for sick child care than their Stanford sisters was that a much lower percentage of Todai mothers than Stanford mothers had other arrangements, including paid help at home (18 percent versus 31 percent).

Sometimes grandparents or siblings who live nearby are willing to help with sick child care in an emergency. We asked the graduates "Do you have any relatives nearby who are available to help with child care in an emergency?" The answers to this question are presented in table 5.14.

Interestingly, although the United States is considered to have much more geographic mobility than Japan, the percentages of graduates with children who had a relative nearby to help with child care in an emergency were not that different in the two samples. Among Todai women and men, about 60 percent had a relative nearby; among Stanford men, the percentage was the same. Stanford women had a somewhat lower percentage, about 50 percent.

Fathers Who Actively Participated in Child Care

Twenty-three Stanford fathers and exactly the same number of Todai fathers actively participated in the care of their children in after-work hours and when their children were sick. What distinguished these few active fathers from the majority of their male classmates who were less active in child rearing?

Table 5.15
Comparison of Stanford Men Graduates Who Were "Active" Fathers and "Inactive" Fathers

	"Active" Fathers	"Inactive" Fathers
	Mean	Mean
Hours employed per week	48.8	55.5
(Standard deviation)	(14.2)	(12.9)
N	23	102
Graduate's annual earnings	$67,783	$76,284
(Standard deviation)	($33,536)	($80,966)
N	23	102
Wife's annual earnings[a]	$37,818	$23,934
(Standard deviation)	($33,316)	($26,185)
N	22	61
Ratio wife's earnings/graduate's earnings[b]	0.63	0.55
(Standard deviation)	(0.43)	(0.50)
N	21	49
Household nonwage income[a]	$20,750	$47,943
(Standard Deviation)	($29,863)	($89,310)
N	20	88
Percent in traditional family[c]	17.4	39.3
N	4	42
Percent in egalitarian family[c]	43.5	18.7
N	10	20
Percent in "hybrid" family[c]	39.1	42.1
N	9	45

"Active" fathers did all or most sick child care or shared sick child care *and* did at least half of the child care during nonwork hours.
[a] Includes those with zero spouse's income or nonwage income.
[b] Ratio calculated only for those where both husband's income and wife's income >0.
[c] Percentages based on 23 active fathers and 107 inactive fathers.

We called Stanford fathers "active" if they took turns with their wives doing sick child care or did it themselves *and* did at least half of the child care during other than usual work hours. We called Todai fathers active if they took turns with their wives doing sick child care or did it themselves *and* spent at least half of their after-work time doing child care. Only 18 percent of Stanford fathers and 13 percent of Todai fathers were active.

One of the major requisites for being an active father is time at home. Fathers whose jobs keep them away from home for long hours have much more difficulty being active fathers. As shown in tables 5.15 and 5.16, in both the Stanford and the Todai samples, the average number of hours of

Table 5.16
Comparison of Todai Men Graduates Who Were "Active" Fathers and "Inactive" Fathers

	"Active" Fathers	"Inactive" Fathers
	Mean	Mean
Hours employed per week	44.5	49.9
(Standard deviation)	(15.5)	(11.7)
N	23	149
Graduate's annual earnings	¥7,582,273	¥7,550,140
(Standard deviation)	(¥6,347,610)	(¥2,819,360)
N	22	143
Wife's annual earnings[a]	¥346,214	¥767,097
(Standard Deviation)	(¥2,809,610)	(¥1,658,710)
N	14	62
Ratio wife's earnings/graduate's earnings[b]	0.75	0.50
(Standard deviation)	(0.14)	(0.27)
N	11	13
Percent in traditional family[c]	17.4	35.2
N	4	56
Percent in egalitarian family[c]	30.4	1.3
N	7	2
Percent in "hybrid" family[c]	52.2	62.9
N	12	100

"Active" fathers did all or most sick child care or shared sick child care *and* spent at least half of their nonwork hours caring for their child. Note that the definition is different from the definition of "active" father for the Stanford sample.
[a] Includes those with zero spouse's income or nonwage income.
[b] Ratio calculated only for those where both husband's income and wife's income >0.
[c] Percentages based on 23 active fathers and 158 inactive fathers.

employment was considerably lower for active fathers than for inactive fathers. In the Stanford sample, inactive fathers were employed an average of 55.5 hours per week while active fathers were employed an average of 48.8 hours a week, 6.7 hours a week less. Among Todai fathers, those who were inactive were employed 49.9 hours a week, compared with 44.5 hours a week for active fathers, a difference of 5.4 hours a week.[11]

There are at least two reasons why active fathers might have lower earnings than inactive fathers: it could be that active fathers were less focused on earning and more focused on having time to spend with their children; or it could be that their lower earnings gave them less bargaining power vis-à-vis their wives (so that their wives were more successful in getting them to share child care).[12]

One could also hypothesize that active fathers had wives with higher incomes than did other fathers. The wives' higher incomes might have allowed the fathers to put less effort into earning income themselves, thereby leaving them more time available to concentrate on child care. In addition, the wives' higher income might have increased their bargaining power in efforts to get the fathers to do more child care. Finally, a bargaining theory would lead one to expect that the ratio of wife's earnings to husband's earnings would be higher in families with active fathers.

All of these hypotheses found support in the Stanford data, but not in the Todai data. (See tables 5.15 and 5.16.) Active Stanford fathers had earnings that were 13 percent lower than those of inactive Stanford fathers. At the same time, the wives of active Stanford fathers had earnings that were almost 60 percent higher than those of inactive Stanford fathers. And the ratio of wives' earnings to husbands' earnings was about 10 percentage points higher in active fathers' families compared with the families of nonactive fathers (0.63 versus 0.55).[13] Stanford fathers who were active in child rearing had more time available for it and may well have had less bargaining power in their families than fathers who were inactive.

However, to the extent that earnings are a measure of bargaining power, the results for the Todai sample do not support the theory that fathers are likely to be more active in families where their bargaining power is weaker. In the Todai sample, earnings were virtually the same for active and nonactive fathers, and wives' earnings were *lower* in active fathers' families.[14] We know that Todai women with low earnings were employed more hours than other women. It may be that this was true for the wives of Todai men as well, and that Todai men whose wives had low earnings and worked longer hours were more likely to spend a larger proportion of their after-work time doing child care.

For both the Stanford and the Todai fathers, division of household responsibilities was a good predictor of division of child care responsibilities. Active fathers were unlikely to be in traditional families and inactive fathers were unlikely to be in egalitarian families.

In terms of occupations, among Stanford fathers, engineers/scientists and physicians were more likely than others to be active fathers (table 5.17). Among Todai fathers, professors were more likely than others to be active fathers (table 5.18).

Table 5.19 looks at graduates who were parents and had an egalitarian arrangement for sharing household responsibilities and child care. The table's bottom line will be disappointing for those who think that highly

Table 5.17
Major Occupational Categories of Stanford Men Graduates Who Were "Active" Fathers and "Inactive" Fathers

	"Active" Fathers		"Inactive" Fathers		Total	
	#	%	#	%	#	%
Engineer/scientist	5	33.3	10	66.7	15	100.0
Financial manager	0	0.00	10	100.0	10	100.0
Lawyer	3	15.8	16	84.2	19	100.0
Other manager	3	13.0	20	87.0	23	100.0
Physician	6	27.3	16	72.7	22	100.0
Other	3	12.5	21	87.5	24	100.0
Technical manager	3	17.6	14	82.4	17	100.0
Total	23	17.7	107	82.3	130	100.0

"Active" fathers did all or most sick child care or shared sick child care *and* did at least half of the child care during nonwork hours.

Table 5.18
Major Occupational Categories of Todai Men Graduates Who Were "Active" Fathers and "Inactive" Fathers

	"Active" Fathers		"Inactive" Fathers		Total	
	#	%	#	%	#	%
Manager	3	7.5	37	9.3	40	100.0
Professor	6	40	9	60	15	100.0
Other	9	28.1	23	7.2	32	100.0
Researcher	3	11.1	24	88.9	27	100.0
Salaryman, no title	4	7.1	52	92.9	56	100.0
Technical professional	0	0	12	100	12	100.0
Total	25	12.6	157	87.4	182	100.0

"Active" fathers did all or most sick child care or shared sick child care *and* spent at least half of their nonwork hours caring for their child. Note that the definition is different from the definition of "active" father for the Stanford sample.

Table 5.19
Married Graduates Who Were Egalitarian on Household Responsibilities and on Child Care
Responsibilities

	Stanford Sample		Todai Sample	
	#	%	#	%
Total families with children	274	100.0	299	100.0
Egalitarian families with children	71	25.9	22	7.4
Egalitarian families who shared child care in nonworking hours	31	11.3	9	3.0
Egalitarian families who shared child care in nonworking hours and sick child care	10	3.7	7	2.3

Thirteen egalitarian families in the Stanford sample said "other" for sick child care arrangement.

educated women and men are at the vanguard of the movement toward
egalitarian families. Only ten Stanford parents (4 percent of all Stanford
parents) and seven Todai parents (2 percent of all Todai parents) were
egalitarian in dividing both household and childcare responsibilities.

Summary of Major Findings

Perhaps the clearest indicators of the changes that have (and have not)
taken place in the traditional breadwinner/homemaker model are the employment rates for the parents in our samples. As in earlier times, almost
all of the fathers were employed full-time. However, among mothers, in
both samples about two-thirds were employed, clearly not adhering to
the old system. In both samples, 40 percent of mothers were employed
full-time and about 26 percent were employed part-time. It is rather remarkable how similar the employment patterns were for parents in the
two samples.

That women experience more difficulty than men in the new system of
combining career and children was evident from the fact that a larger
proportion of women than men said that working affected their decision
to have children. Still, overall, the majority of those with children said
that working had not affected their decision to become parents.

Among fathers who were employed full-time, the vast majority gave a
traditional response to the question about how their children were cared
for during usual working hours. "My wife" was their answer. However,
among Stanford fathers about 20 percent said a paid employee cared for
their children, and among Todai fathers 25 percent said their children
were cared for in school and about 20 percent said their children were

cared for in nursery school. (Multiple responses were permitted to the question.)

Among women employed full-time, in both samples about one-fourth used a paid employee to care for their children. Stanford women also used child care centers (about one-fourth) and family day care (about 20 percent), while Todai women relied on nursery schools (70 percent), schools (about one-fourth), and relatives, both in the child's home (about 20 percent) and in the relative's home (about 18 percent).

In general, Stanford parents who were employed full-time were satisfied with their child care arrangements, but slightly over 20 percent were not. Mothers generally would have preferred more expensive arrangements than they said they could afford. (Todai parents were not asked about their satisfaction with their child care arrangements during usual working hours.)

Stanford and Todai parents were asked slightly different questions about their sharing of child care during after-work hours. Stanford parents were asked what share of the child care they did, whereas Todai parents were asked what proportion of their own time they spent on child care.

Although Stanford women and men gave consistent reports about their patterns of sharing household tasks, their reports about sharing child care were contradictory, with men much more likely to say that they shared child care with their wives than women were to say they shared child care with their husbands. We are therefore inclined to be cautious in interpreting Stanford parents' responses.

Among Stanford parents who shared child care equally, there were very high rates of satisfaction among both mothers (97 percent) and fathers (95 percent). For those mothers who did more than half of the child care, the dissatisfaction rate was about 40 percent—high, but not as high as the 53 percent dissatisfaction rate among Stanford married women who did more than half of the household tasks.

Mothers who were employed full-time and did more than half of child care after working hours had a much lower rate of dissatisfaction (one-third) than full-time homemakers (two-thirds). Caring for children after a whole day of caring for them is obviously much less enjoyable than caring for children after a day away from them.

The old breadwinner/homemaker dictum that mothers should provide care for children was alive and well in the Todai sample. Sixty percent of Todai fathers spent less than half of their nonwork hours caring for children! On the other hand, 80 percent of mothers spent more than half of their nonwork hours caring for children.

Fathers had a high degree of satisfaction with their child care arrangement (84 percent) regardless of whether they spent a large or a small proportion of time with their children. Mothers had an overall satisfaction rate of 70 percent, which did not vary by the proportion of their after-work hours spent on child care.

Todai mothers were much more likely to have sole responsibility for caring for a sick child than were Stanford mothers, in part because Stanford mothers were more likely to have paid help who provided sick child care. About 20 percent of Stanford and Todai fathers took turns with their wives in providing care for a sick child.

We defined active fathers as those who shared sick child care with their wives and also either did half or more of the after-work child care (Stanford) or spent half or more of their own after-work time on child care (Todai). Only 18 percent of Stanford fathers and 13 percent of Todai fathers were active fathers.

Bargaining theory was successful in predicting the correlates of being an active father in the Stanford sample, but not in the Todai sample. Stanford fathers who were active earned lower incomes than other fathers, had wives who earned higher income than other wives, and had a higher (more equal) wife/husband earnings ratio than other fathers. But Todai fathers' earnings were about the same for active and inactive fathers, and the earnings of wives were actually *lower* in active fathers' families.

In both samples, active fathers were employed fewer hours than inactive fathers, and were unlikely to be in traditional families. Inactive fathers were unlikely to be in egalitarian families.

Truly egalitarian families with children, where parents shared financial responsibility, household management, household tasks, child care in non-work hours, and sick child care, were rarities. Only 4 percent of Stanford parents and 2 percent of Todai parents were in such families.

Is it likely that in the future the graduates in our samples will combine work and family in more egalitarian fashion than they were doing at the time they were surveyed? Once the graduates' children are grown, it may be easier for them to have more egalitarian relationships. Having young children makes egalitarianism more difficult; women with young children are more likely to be out of the labor market than other women; and for those women who are in the labor market, having young children reduces their hours of work, and hence their total earnings. It is also the case that couples with children are less likely to share household tasks.

However, because of the structures of the American and Japanese labor markets, we think it likely that our graduates will have even *less* gender equality in their future than they had approximately a decade after graduation. At work, men will rise in their chosen careers and will benefit from steep age–earnings profiles. Only those women who remained full-time in their careers during their thirties will see substantial increases in their responsibilities and earnings; but unless they are in traditionally male occupations, and unless they are able to break currently existing glass ceilings, even they will not reap the same earnings rewards as their male classmates.

In the home arena, as men move up in their careers and their obligations at work become more demanding, they will have even less time for home tasks, and as their economic bargaining power vis-à-vis their wives increases, it is unlikely that these men will share more equally in household tasks unless their wives become highly career-oriented as their children leave home. However, for those few men who change their career path and take more leisure at a fairly early age, egalitarian relationships at home may become part of a new lifestyle.

This chapter looks to the future by analyzing the responses of the graduates to questions about two points in their future: 10 years post survey (that is, about 20 years after college graduation) and at the peak of their career. While the graduates' hopes and expectations must be viewed with caution, they confirm our predictions. The future gender earnings ratio for these graduates is likely to be even more unequal than the one based on earnings approximately a decade after graduation. And the reasons for the differences in men's and women's earnings expectations provide a sobering window on the difficulties of achieving more egalitarian ways of combining work and family.

How Accurate Are the Graduates' Predictions About Their Own Future Earnings Likely to Be?

The questions we asked the graduates about their own future earnings were as follows: "At the high point of your career, what is the highest annual salary in 1990 dollars (yen) that you *hope* to earn per year?" "At the high point of your career, what is the highest annual salary in 1990 dollars (yen) that you *expect* to earn per year?" Blank spaces were left for filling in the amounts.

How much credence should we put in the answers to these questions as predictors of the future gender earnings ratios for the two sets of graduates? Tests of the extent to which highly educated people are able to successfully predict their own earnings are rare and somewhat contradictory. Clearly, caution is warranted in interpreting our results on predicted earnings.

One study found that recent male MBAs from Stanford University were able to predict their future earnings accurately. Like the Stanford and Todai graduates, the Stanford MBAs were asked to predict their earnings at the peak of their career. The study found that the men's predictions corresponded quite closely to the current earnings of Harvard MBAs who were 25 years into their careers, probably quite close to the peak of their careers.[1]

A second study looked at income expectations 10 years later among college seniors at two state universities. For both women and men seniors, the predictions about what their classmates would earn, by gender, were very close to what college graduates 10 years out were actually earning. However, while women's average prediction of their own earnings was the same as women's average prediction about the earnings of other women in their class, men's average prediction about their own earnings was *greater* than their average prediction about others in their class. That is, the men tended to "self-enhance." This was particularly so for the men from the more prestigious university.[2]

The Graduates' Expectations

Ten Years Hence

In the section of the questionnaire on future plans, we asked: "In general, what do you expect to be doing ten years from now professionally, occupationally and personally?" As in the case of earnings predictions, it is as yet unknown whether in fact the graduates' prediction will become actualized.

Stanford Graduates
A number of Stanford graduates responded to this question by saying, in effect, "In 10 years, I expect to be doing about the same as what I am doing now."
    A male assistant professor:

In ten years I hope to be teaching, writing, researching—living happily, soberly and with peace.

    A businesswoman:

I expect to be running my business, still married and raising my kids.

    However, several Stanford men graduates thought they would be leading a quite different life, some with more service to others and others with more time for themselves and/or their families.
    An investment banker and venture capitalist:

In ten years I will be building start-up companies and doing volunteer work for a homeless shelter.

    An MBA man who works in the field of finance:

In ten years, I hope to put together the financing and management for a home for homeless families/children.

    And three businessmen:

Ten years from now I will be teaching high school and coaching. I will have made enough money in real estate and will then devote my time and energy to positively impacting the youth.

In ten years I expect to be semi-retired, running my own investment firm, raising a family and traveling.

In ten years, I intend to be semi-retired, and spending time with my children, traveling, hunting and enjoying the outdoors.

Other men expected to remain on the path they had already taken, but with some changes in their lives. A physician hoped to do more public service as part of his work:

In ten years—same thing—physician, hopefully more work with the uninsured or underinsured.

A researcher who shared household tasks and child care equally with his wife hoped to be even more family-oriented:

I expect to be the leader of a large research group ... I expect to spend a lot of time with a large family.

Finally, one graduate indicated he would be grateful simply to be around in 10 years.

In ten years, hopefully I'll still be alive. I have a terminal illness.

Among women graduates, several planned to make career shifts. One woman, currently working part-time to achieve the flexibility she felt she needed for her children, hoped to have even more flexibility as a business owner.

I would like to own my own business. Hopefully, I will be able to run it out of my home, so I can still spend time with my children.

Other women, like some of their male classmates, wished to do more service-oriented work. A woman manager, married with no children:

I've found that there's more to life than making $ pushing paper.... I want to make a difference. For me, that's being a teacher. I'm working toward a credential now.

Other women couldn't predict exactly where they would be in 10 years. A woman currently an administrator in a nonprofit organization could see two different possible career paths.

I hope to still be married and hope to have 2–3 children, either working part-time and taking career back seat or promoted and be a senior administrator at a major institution.

Todai Graduates
Among the Todai graduates, several women indicated they expected to continue to be single in 10 years. One was concerned mostly with career and finances.

I envision myself as single in ten years. I want to move away from Tokyo to [smaller city] and work for the local government. It is more stable and less expensive.

Other women expected to continue the difficult task of trying to balance their work ambitions with their family responsibilities. Although U.S. women often see their children's teenage years as a time when they can pursue more of their own career interests, women in Japan often expect that their tasks, particularly as an educator, will continue in those years. Some Todai women certainly thought that their job as a mother would continue to be time-consuming during their children's teenage years.

Ten years from now my older daughter will be 14 and my youngest child will be 12. They will be preparing for their entrance examinations. I would like to be a counselor or translator by then, but since they will be busy, I may have to help them.

One woman thought she might have to leave the country in order to attain her multiple goals.

I want to have my own company. In ten years I probably will be struggling between family and work. In order to make this all possible, I may have to leave Japan.

Another woman, whose mother played a major role in caring for her children, thought she might have to leave her marriage to attain her goals.

I gave birth to children too early and lost a lot of freedom. In ten years I will be divorced and will raise the children on my own. If my salary is not sufficient, I will become a lawyer.

Another woman, for whom extended family was important in planning for the future:

I quit my first job to build a family. I am not carrying a heavy workload now for the sake of my children. But, in ten years I will have a bigger company specialized in doing tax accounting. My children will be in primary school, and in order for them to come home to a place where they can see family faces, I am planning to move close to my mother.

Type of Organization at Peak of Career

We asked Stanford graduates what type of organization they hoped to work for at the high point of their career and gave them four choices: self-employed (e.g., professional or sole proprietorship), your own business

Table 6.1
Types of Organizations That Stanford Graduates Hope to Work for at High Point of Their Career, by Gender

	Men (N = 373)	Women (N = 302)
Self-employed	34.3	33.1
Own business	23.3	17.2
Public	12.1	19.9
Private	30.3	29.8
Total	100.0	100.0

(other than self-employed), public (e.g., government), or private (e.g., business firm). Stanford graduates' responses are presented in table 6.1. (This question was omitted from the Todai survey.)

Overall, Stanford women and men were quite similar in the types of organizations they hoped to work for. About one-third of both groups wanted to be self-employed, and about 30 percent of both groups wanted to work for a private company. A slightly higher proportion of men than women (23 percent versus 17 percent) wanted to own a business, and a somewhat lower proportion of men than women (12 percent versus 20 percent) wanted to be employed by a public institution.

Some graduates hoped that at the peak of their career they would be in a markedly different environment. Several hoped to be giving back to their communities.

A Stanford man, a software engineer with quite high income aspirations and early retirement plans:

At the high point of my career I hope my job title will be philanthropist.

Hoped-for and Expected Earnings at Peak of Career[3]

Although most of the graduates answered our questions about income aspirations in dollars or yen, some resisted. A Stanford single man who had no earned income and $24,000 of unearned income indicated at several points on his questionnaire that he was annoyed with the survey's interest in money. When he finally got to the question about income aspirations, he exploded:

Enough is enough! I don't hope to achieve more than I need.

In a similar vein, another Stanford man wrote:

Position, power, and money are of low value to me. I hope at the height of my career to be serving the greatest and most vital needs of others in a manner that is detached from my own personal material needs.

Despite the similarity in the type of organization that Stanford women and men hoped to work for, neither they nor the Todai women and men were similar in their earnings aspirations and expectations. Mean and median responses, by gender, for both samples, to the questions about hoped-for and expected earnings at peak of career are in table 6.2.

In all cases, but particularly for the Stanford graduates (and certainly for the Stanford men graduates), the mean hoped-for and expected earnings exceeded the median. This is because in each of the samples there were a few people with very high hopes and expectations. Also, in all cases, as might be expected, hopes far exceeded expectations.[4]

In the Stanford sample, among men, the mean hoped-for earnings was $336,611 and the median $200,000; among women the mean was $158,536 and the median $100,000. In each case, the female/male ratio was about 50 percent.

In the Todai sample, among men, the mean hoped-for earnings was ¥27,279,710 and the median ¥20,000,000; among women the mean was ¥11,152,450 and the median ¥10,000,000. The female/male ratio was 41 percent for the means and 50 percent for the medians. In other words, in both the Stanford and Todai samples, the female/male ratios for the medians were about the same. Women hoped to earn about half of what men hoped to earn.[5]

While expected earnings were lower than hoped-for earnings for all groups, the gender differences and the differences across the two samples were about the same. In the Stanford sample, the mean expected earnings for men was $271,693 and the median was $150,000; for women the mean expected earnings was $124,669 and the median was $80,000. For the means, the female/male ratio was 46 percent. For the medians, it was 53 percent. Roughly speaking, then, Sanford women hoped and expected to earn about half of what Stanford men hoped and expected.

In the Todai sample, the female/male expected earnings ratio was a few percentage points higher than in the Stanford sample. For men, the mean expected earnings was ¥17,634,740 and the median was ¥15,000,000. For women, the mean was ¥9,898,864 and the median was ¥8,500,000. The female/male ratio was 56 percent for the means and 57 percent for the medians.[6]

When we looked at the distribution of current earnings in chapter 3, we saw that Todai earnings were more evenly distributed than Stanford

Table 6.2
Salary Aspirations of Graduates: Mean and Median Hoped-for and Expected Earnings at Peak of Career, by Gender

	Stanford Sample			Todai Sample			Todai/Stanford Comparison[a]	
	Men	Women	W/M Ratio	Men	Women	W/M Ratio	Men Todai/ Stanford	Women Todai/ Stanford
Mean hoped-for earnings	$336,611	$158,536	47.1	¥27,279,710	¥11,152,450	40.9	56.0	48.6
(Standard deviation)	($311,058)	($172,800)		(¥21,415,51)	(¥11,690,00)			
				$188,409	$77,025			
Coefficient of variation	92.4	109.0	—	78.5	85.2	—	—	—
Median hoped-for earnings	$200,000	$100,000	50.0	¥20,000,000	¥10,000,000	50.0	69.1	69.1
				$138,131	$69,066			
N	337	263		295	77			
Mean expected earnings	$271,693	$124,669	45.9	¥17,634,740	¥9,898,864	56.1	44.8	54.8
(Standard deviation)	($281,212)	($126,902)		(¥13,933,390)	(¥7,142,724)			
				$121,795	$68,367			
Coefficient of variation	103.5	101.8	—	79.0	72.2	—	—	—
Median expected earnings	$150,000	$80,000	53.3	¥15,000,000	¥8,500,000	56.7	69.1	73.4
				$103,598	$58,705			
N	329	245		290	72			

[a] Based on an exchange rate of 144.79 yen to $1.00.

earnings. That pattern is also manifest in earnings aspirations and expectations. The coefficient of variation (the standard deviation divided by the mean) of hoped-for earnings was 92 percent for Stanford men and 109 percent for Stanford women. But for Todai men it was only 79 percent and for Todai women, 85 percent. Similarly, for expected earnings, the coefficients of variation were 104 percent for Stanford men and 102 percent for Stanford women, compared with 79 percent for Todai men and 72 percent for Todai women.

For Stanford women, the coefficient of variation of expected earnings (102 percent) was just about the same as the coefficient of variation for current earnings (98 percent). However, for men, the dispersion of expected earnings (104 percent) was about 20 percentage points greater than it was for current earnings (81 percent).

Among Todai earners, the coefficients of variation for expected earnings differed even more from the coefficients of variation for current earnings than they did among Stanford earners. The coefficients of variation for expected earnings were 79 percent and 72 percent for Todai men and women, respectively. Each of these was about 30 percentage points higher than the respective coefficient of variation for current earnings. Thus, except for Stanford women, the dispersion in expected earnings was greater than the dispersion in current earnings.

The gender differences in expectations noted in table 6.2 are consonant with those found in other samples of highly educated women and men. The more prestigious the school from which graduates come, the later in their career they are surveyed, and the further out in time the prediction is for, the greater the difference between women's and men's earnings expectations.

Among university seniors at two state universities, the female/male ratio in expected earnings 10 years later was 80 percent for those in the less prestigious state university (exactly the same as the differential for Stanford and Todai graduates 10 years out) and 74 percent for those in the more prestigious state university. Among management interns at the State University of New York at Buffalo, the female/male ratio in expected earnings at career peak was 69 percent.[7] In a study of seniors at the University of California, Berkeley, the female/male differential in expected earnings at the peak of their careers was 47 percent.[8]

Among Stanford MBAs, the gender differential in expected earnings at career peak was about 60 percent at the time of the first survey, during their last year of the MBA program; but when they were resurveyed four years later, men and women had a much greater difference in expectations, with women expecting to earn only 40 percent of what men expected to earn at the peak of their careers.[9]

Earnings Aspirations, Expectations, and Parents' Social Class

In tables 6.3 and 6.4, we look at earnings aspirations and expectations by parents' social class. The remarkable finding, in both tables, is that Stanford men from the upper class had so much higher hoped-for and expected earnings than Stanford men with other social class origins.

For Stanford men, hoped-for earnings (table 6.3) rose linearly with social class origins. But the hoped-for earnings of men from the upper class were $560,000, 1.67 times higher than the mean hoped-for earnings for all Stanford men. For Stanford women and for Todai women and men, the pattern was quite different, with much less variation in earnings aspirations by social class.

If we move to table 6.4 and examine expected earnings, we find that, again, Stanford men from the upper class were "off-scale." Stanford men from the upper class expected $451,250 at the peak of their career, again 1.67 times higher than mean expected earnings for all Stanford men. For Stanford women and Todai women and men, as in the case of hoped-for earnings, there was relatively little variation across social class in mean expected earnings. The high, positive effect of upper social class origins on expected earnings for Stanford men remained even when other variables were held constant, as we shall see when we discuss the regressions reported in table 6.7.

Earnings Aspirations, Earnings Expectations, and Family Type

In table 6.5, we see that in the Stanford sample, men in egalitarian families had the lowest mean earnings aspirations and expectations, while men in traditional families had the highest. In the Todai sample, egalitarian men also had the lowest mean earnings aspirations and expectations. In both samples, egalitarian men's mean expected earnings were about 70 percent of those of traditional men. There is clearly a trade-off between equality in home tasks and husband's earnings expectations.

For women, the results concerning earnings aspirations and expectations and family type were the mirror image of those for men. Stanford and Todai women in traditional families had the lowest mean earnings aspirations and expectations. Stanford women in egalitarian families had mean earnings expectations that were 35 percent higher than those for

Table 6.3
Hoped-for Earnings by Parents' Social Class, by Gender

	Stanford Sample			
	Men		Women	
Social Class	N	Mean Earnings (Standard Deviation)	N	Mean Earnings (Standard Deviation)
Lower or working	8	—	16	$150,313 ($114,127)
Lower middle	16	$235,312 ($247,612)	18	$152,333 ($139,972)
Middle	112	$280,000 ($276,259)	64	$164,453 ($200,491)
Upper middle	174	$348,724 ($312,002)	135	$159,926 ($177,494)
Upper	27	$559,814 ($381,566)	28	$154,929 ($137,650)
	337		261	
	Todai Sample			
	Men		Women	
Social Class	N	Mean Earnings (Standard Deviation)	N	Mean Earnings (Standard Deviation)
Lower or working	44	¥26,999,300 (¥23,508,300)	9	—
Lower middle	75	¥26,087,600 (¥19,588,700)	16	¥10,000,000 (¥4,147,288)
Middle	116	¥27,913,200 (¥22,137,000)	38	¥12,460,500 (¥6,740,741)
Upper middle	65	¥26,261,200 (¥18,274,600)	26	¥17,134,200 (¥18,669,900)
Upper	3	—	1	—
	303		90	

Table 6.4
Expected Earnings by Parents' Social Class, by Gender

	Stanford Sample			
	Men		Women	
Social Class	N	Mean Earnings (Standard Deviation)	N	Mean Earnings (Standard Deviation)
Lower or working	8	—	14	$119,643 ($125,629)
Lower middle	8	—	17	$121,059 ($123,530)
Middle	109	$203,183 ($234,569)	59	$126,322 ($147,018)
Upper middle	166	$289,849 ($281,562)	128	$124,062 ($121,677)
Upper	28	$451,250 ($375,257)	27	$128,815 ($115,174)
	319		245	
	Todai Sample			
	Men		Women	
Social Class	N	Mean Earnings (Standard Deviation)	N	Mean Earnings (Standard Deviation)
Lower or working	44	¥19,181,600 (¥18,397,100)	9	—
Lower middle	74	¥16,832,400 (¥9,319,064)	14	¥8,285,714 (¥3,625,308)
Middle	115	¥17,912,000 (¥15,157,900)	34	¥10,352,900 (¥8,889,498)
Upper middle	62	¥17,282,100 (¥13,524,500)	26	¥10,292,300 (¥6,841,165)
Upper	3	—	1	—
	298		84	

Stanford women in traditional families. (Because of the small number of Todai women in egalitarian families, it was not possible to compare earnings aspirations and expectations for women in egalitarian and traditional families.)

Table 6.5 also provides ratios for the mean earnings aspirations and expectations of egalitarian women compared with egalitarian men and for traditional women compared with traditional men. In the Stanford sample, women from egalitarian families aspired to and expected to earn about half as much as men from egalitarian families. This was about the same ratio as for the sample as a whole. But the aspirations and expectations ratios for Stanford traditional women compared with Stanford traditional men were much lower (less equal), only 32 and 25 percent, respectively.

For the Todai sample, the aspiration and expectation ratios for traditional women compared with traditional men were about the same as for the Todai sample as a whole (in part because such a large proportion of the Todai sample was in the traditional category) and were much higher (more equal) than in the Stanford sample; traditional women hoped to earn about 40 percent of what traditional men hoped to earn and they expected to earn about 50 percent of what traditional men expected to earn.

Determinants of Expected Earnings

In table 6.6 we provide the means and standard deviations of the variables used in OLS regressions to examine the determinants of the natural log of earnings expected at the peak of the respondents' career. The specifications of the regressions for expected earnings are exactly the same as the ones for current earnings (table 3.5), except that current earnings is included as an additional dependent variable in the expected earnings regressions.

Because fewer graduates responded to the question about expected earnings than responded to the question about current earnings, the sample sizes given in table 6.6 for expected earnings are smaller than those given in table 3.5 for current earnings. Moreover, as was the case for current earnings, the regression samples (table 6.6) are smaller than the total samples (table 6.2). And because the regression samples were restricted to those who were employed, the means of expected earnings of the regression samples were lower than the means of expected earnings in the total samples. For Todai women, there was only a very small difference between mean expected earnings for the whole sample and for the

Table 6.5
Salary Aspirations by Family Type: Married Graduates Only, by Gender

	Stanford Sample					
	Men			Women		
	Egalitarian	Traditional	Hybrid[a]	Egalitarian	Traditional	Hybrid
Mean salary hope to achieve	$278,240	$396,731	$309,886	$158,064	$116,754	$151,471
(Standard deviation)	($279,662)	($305,360)	($299,279)	($175,362)	($140,080)	($175,618)
N	75	52	88	62	61	34
Mean salary expect to achieve	$228,176	$330,961	$252,176	$113,625	$83,509	$121,500
(Standard deviation)	($231,260)	($298,583)	($256,063)	($90,238)	($63,849)	($99,396)
N	74	52	85	56	57	30

	Ratios			
	Men Egalitarian/ Traditional	Women Egalitarian/ Traditional	Egalitarian Women/ Egalitarian Men	Traditional Women/ Traditional Men
Salary hope to achieve	0.70	1.35	0.56	0.32
Salary expect to achieve	0.70	1.36	0.50	0.25

Todai Sample

	Men			Women		
	Egalitarian	Traditional	Hybrid[b]	Egalitarian	Traditional	Hybrid
Mean salary hope to achieve	¥19,400,000	¥27,581,900	¥30,199,200		¥11,189,700	¥12,925,900
(Standard deviation)	(¥10,273,400)	(¥18,120,200)	(¥24,008,800)	—	(¥7,238,801)	(¥6,972,065)
N	15	73	140	6	29	27
Mean salary expect to achieve	¥12,300,000	¥18,328,800	¥19,858,500		¥9,114,815	¥9,732,143
(Standard deviation)	(¥7,140,928)	(¥11,413,700)	(¥16,139,200)	—	(¥9,444,889)	(¥5,698,411)
N	15	73	138	6	27	28

Ratios

	Men Egalitarian/ Traditional	Women Egalitarian/ Traditional	Egalitarian Women/ Egalitarian Men	Traditional Women/ Traditional Men
Salary hope to achieve	0.70	—	—	0.41
Salary expect to achieve	0.67	—	—	0.50

a Excludes 3 reverse-traditional.
b Excludes 1 reverse-traditional.

Table 6.6
Means and Standard Deviations for Variables in OLS Regression Analysis Predicting Natural Log of Earnings Expected at Peak of Career, by Gender

	Stanford Men (N = 300) Mean	Stanford Women (N = 204) Mean	Todai Men (N = 269) Mean	Todai Women (N = 53) Mean
	(Standard Deviation)	(Standard Deviation)	(Standard Deviation)	(Standard Deviation)
Expected earnings	$277,357	$129,848	¥18,289,900	¥9,858,491
	($281,927)	($128,477)	(¥13,196,100)	(¥4,426,078)
Log of expected earnings	12.1162564	11.4935508	7.353787	6.8008637
	(0.8923443)	(0.7090941)	(0.5277640)	(0.4508696)
Number of years employed full-time	6.58	6.35	9.14	8.08
	(2.68)	(2.63)	(2.74)	(3.69)
Number of years employed part-time	0.65	1.05	0.80	1.02
	(1.36)	(1.83)	(2.22)	(2.36)
Number of hours employed/wk	53.8	48.8	50.1	42.8
	(15.2)	(17.3)	(12.8)	(14.3)
Percent financial manager	0.09	0.74	—	—
	(0.29)	(0.07)		
Percent lawyer	0.14	0.09	—	—
	(0.35)	(0.30)		
Percent marketing manager	0.06	0.08	—	—
	(0.24)	(0.27)		
Percent medical doctor	0.15	0.15	—	—
	(0.36)	(0.36)		
Percent misc. manager	0.09	0.10	—	—
	(0.29)	(0.30)		

Percent technical manager	0.08 (0.28)	0.02 (0.16)	—	—
Percent technical professional	0.13 (0.34)	0.09 (0.29)	0.07 (0.25)	0.04 (0.19)
Percent manager	—	—	0.15 (0.36)	0.04 (0.19)
Percent professor	—	—	0.10 (0.30)	0.19 (0.39)
Percent researcher	—	—	0.14 (0.35)	0.19 (0.39)
Percent teacher	—	—	0.03 (0.18)	0.02 (0.14)
Percent in company ≥ 1000 employees	—	—	0.63 (0.48)	0.25 (0.43)
Percent government employee	—	—	0.17 (0.37)	0.26 (0.45)
Percent married	0.66 (0.48)	0.54 (0.50)	0.76 (0.43)	0.68 (0.47)
Percent parent	0.40 (0.49)	0.27 (0.45)	0.55 (0.50)	0.49 (0.50)
Current earnings	$67,477 ($56,816)	$51,627 ($51,733)	¥7,195,242 (¥3,059,655)	¥5,349,434 (¥2,116,142)

regression sample. For Stanford men and women and for Todai men, the differences in mean expected earnings between the whole sample and the regression sample were, respectively, about $5,600, $5,200, and ¥655,000 (about $4,500, based on the 1990 exchange rate).

The female/male earnings ratio for the Stanford regression sample was 0.468, one percentage point higher (more equal) than the ratio for the whole Stanford sample (0.459) given in table 6.2. The female/male earnings ratio for the Todai regression sample was 0.539, two percentage points lower (less equal) than the ratio for the entire Todai sample (0.561) given in table 6.2.

As shown in table 6.7, the regressions for the four samples explained between 33 and 36 percent of the variance in expected earnings. In all of the regressions, current earnings was positively and significantly associated with expected earnings.

For Stanford men, work experience, which was significant for explaining current earnings, was not significant for explaining expected earnings, but the reverse was true for hours of employment. Stanford men who expected to earn more worked more hours per week; and an additional hour per week of employment was associated with a 2 percent increase in expected earnings. Neither being married nor being a parent was significantly associated with expected earnings. Being a financial manager was associated with a very large increase in expected earnings (67 percent), and being a miscellaneous manager, a lawyer, or a marketing manager was associated with increases in expected earnings of 52, 35, and 34 percent, respectively.

Interestingly, for both Stanford men and women, although being a medical doctor had a significant positive coefficient in the regressions for current earnings, it was *not* associated with an earnings premium in the expected earnings regressions. Doctors clearly do not expect their earnings to rise over time in the same way that their classmates in business and law do.[10]

The results for Stanford women were similar to those for Stanford men, except that more work experience was associated with significantly *lower* expected earnings. This troubling finding raises the possibility that the more work experience women have, the more discouraged they become about their future earnings capability.

Stanford women who were married expected to earn 15 percent more than their nonmarried classmates. Stanford women who were employed more hours had significantly higher expected earnings. And those who were technical managers expected a 64 percent premium, while financial

Table 6.7
Determinants of Expected Earnings at Peak of Career: Parameter Estimates for Regression Analysis Predicting Natural Log of Earnings Expected at Peak of Career

	Stanford Men (N = 300)	Stanford Women (N = 204)	Todai Men (N = 269)	Todai Women (N = 53)
	Parameter Estimate	Parameter Estimate	Parameter Estimate	Parameter Estimate
Intercept	10.71**	10.97**	7.08**	6.09**
Number of years employed full-time	0.02	−0.04*	−0.01	0.01
Number of years employed part-time	−0.05	−0.002	−0.02	−0.06*
Number of hours employed/week	0.02**	0.008**	−0.009	0.001
Financial manager	0.67**	0.40*	—	—
Lawyer	0.35**	0.25	—	—
Marketing manager	0.34^	0.40*	—	—
Medical doctor	−0.12	0.18	—	—
Misc. manager	0.52**	0.21	—	—
Technical manager	0.19	0.64*	—	—
Technical professional	−0.14	−0.15	−0.18	−0.15
Manager	—	—	0.06	0.51^
Professor	—	—	−0.33**	0.35*
Researcher	—	—	−0.29*	0.08
Teacher	—	—	−0.43**	−0.16
Married	−0.08	0.15^	0.15^	−0.05
Parent	−0.03	−0.01	−0.04	0.14
Current earnings	0.005**	0.0005**	0.001**	0.001**
Employed in company ≥ 1000	—	—	0.19*	0.05
Employed in government	—	—	−0.21*	0.17
Adjusted R^2	0.35	0.34	0.33	0.36
F-Value	13.45**	8.90**	11.30**	3.23*

** Significant at 1% level.
* Significant at 5% level.
^ Significant at 10% level.

managers and marketing managers each expected a 40 percent premium. Having children was not significantly associated with expected earnings.

Among Todai men, being employed in a large company was associated with a 19 percent expected earnings premium, and being employed by the government was associated with about the same size (21 percent) earnings penalty. Teachers, professors, and researchers expected earnings penalties of 43 percent, 33 percent, and 29 percent, respectively. In addition, Todai men who were married expected to have 15 percent higher earnings than unmarried men.

Among Todai women, having had part-time work experience was significantly associated with lower expected earnings. Being a manager was associated with an expected earnings premium of 51 percent, and being a professor with an expected earnings premium of 35 percent.[11] Unlike the situation for Todai men, being employed in a large company or by the government had no significant effect on expected earnings for Todai women. Again, this is a troubling finding, for it suggests that women in large companies are aware of gender barriers to advancement.

We ran several additional regressions to look at possible effects on earnings expectations of coming from an upper-class background and sharing household tasks. For Stanford men, coming from an upper-class background was associated with an increase of earnings expectations of 46 percent (holding constant all of the other variables listed in tables 6.6 and 6.7). In none of the other samples was upper-class background significantly associated with either current earnings or earnings expectations.

Recall that for Stanford men, doing at least half of household tasks had a small, significant, negative effect on current earnings (see table 4.9); however, doing at least half of household tasks had no significant effect on Stanford men's expected earnings. For the other samples, doing household tasks had no significant effect either on current earnings or on expected earnings.

We also wanted to see whether being a full-time homemaker had a negative effect on earnings expectations. To do this, we had to look at earnings expectations for the entire sample of women rather than just for women who were employed. We therefore reran the regressions for women, removing all of the variables related to current employment and including, instead, only the following variables: number of years of full-time and part-time work experience, and dummy variables for being married, being a parent, and being a homemaker. For Stanford women, being a homemaker was not significantly associated with earnings expectations; but Todai women homemakers expected an earnings penalty of

124 percent (significant at the 1 percent level). This finding lends support to our view, discussed in chapter 4, that while Stanford homemakers are optimistic about their future in the labor market, Todai homemakers are not.[12]

Analysis of Gender Differences in Expected Earnings

Table 6.8 provides a decomposition of the female/male expected earnings ratio for the Stanford and Todai samples. Like table 3.7, which provides the same kind of decomposition for current earnings, table 6.8 has two different decompositions for the Todai sample. Version I excludes the two dummy variables that measure type of work organization (employed in a company of at least 1,000 employees and employed by the government), and is therefore comparable with the Stanford decomposition. Version II includes the type of work organization and is based on the Todai regression means and coefficients given in tables 6.6 and 6.7.

In the Stanford sample, the major explanation for the gender difference in expected earnings was that Stanford women expected a lower return to work experience and hours of employment than their male classmates. These gender differences in expected returns to experience and hours of employment dwarfed the contributions to the difference in expected earnings made by the gender difference in current earnings or current hours of employment.

This finding is quite interesting, since in the decomposition of the gender difference in current earnings, the major contributor to the gender earnings difference was also gender differences in returns to work experience and hours of work. Stanford women and men seem to have expected that the kind of gender discrimination that existed in 1990 not only would continue into the future but would in fact worsen.

In the decomposition Todai I, the percentage of the gender difference in expected earnings attributable to gender differences in mean characteristics was 27 percent, almost the same as the 30 percent for the Stanford sample. Turning to the coefficients, we find that both women and men expected that husbands and fathers would continue to receive an earnings premium as compared with wives and mothers. However, we don't learn much else from the coefficients column about what contributed to the other 73 percent of the gender difference in expected earnings. Most of the variables make a negative contribution to the gender difference in expected earnings (that is, Todai women expect to get larger returns to experience, occupation, and current earnings than their male classmates),

Table 6.8
Analysis of Gender Differences in Expected Earnings at Peak of Career (Decomposition of Regressions)

	Stanford			Todai I			Todai II		
	Means	Coefficients	Total	Means	Coefficients	Total	Means	Coefficients	Total
Experience	0.0289	0.3321	0.3610	-0.0022	-0.1601	-0.1592	-0.0083	-0.1607	-0.1690
Hours	0.0819	0.3817	0.4636	-0.0144	0.0962	-0.1106	-0.0062	-0.0244	0.0182
Occupation	0.0144	0.0041	0.0186	0.0534	-0.2110	-0.1576	0.0364	-0.2240	-0.1873
Current earnings	0.0805	-0.0201	0.0604	0.1043	-0.1610	-0.0567	0.0860	-0.2931	-0.2071
Demographics	-0.0138	-0.0030	-0.0169	0.0093	0.0409	0.0503	0.0107	0.0661	0.0774
Type of work organization	—	—	—	—	—	—	0.0913	0.0652	0.0262
Constant	—	-0.2640	-0.2640	—	0.9789	0.9709	—	0.9946	0.9946
Total	0.1919	0.4307	0.6227	0.1534	0.3994	0.5528	0.2106	0.3421	0.5526

and most of the "explanation" for the difference in expected earnings is in the constant term, which means, in effect, that there is not much explanation to be had from the analysis.

The same is true for the decomposition of Todai II. Although type of work organization made a large contribution to the explanation of the gender difference in current earnings, such was not the case for expected earnings.

Summary of Major Findings

We have already seen, in chapter 3, that a decade or so out of their undergraduate programs, Stanford and Todai women who were employed full-time had mean earnings that were about 80 percent of those of their male classmates. When we looked at all earners, including those who worked part-time, we found that the female/male earnings ratio was 76 percent in the Stanford sample and 72 percent in the Todai sample.

The female/male earnings ratios (based on both means and medians) for hoped-for and expected earnings at career peak were even lower (more unequal), ranging between 46 and 53 percent for the Stanford sample and 41 and 57 percent for the Todai sample. These findings bode poorly for the ability of the graduates to develop (or, indeed, continue) egalitarian arrangements for combining work and family.

Both Stanford and Todai men who were in egalitarian families had lower mean earnings expectations than other men, revealing a trade-off between equality in home tasks and husbands' earnings expectations. In the same vein, among both Todai and Stanford women the lowest mean earnings expectations were for those in traditional families.

For Stanford men, as in the case of current earnings, coming from an upper-class background had a large and significant positive effect on earnings expected at peak of career. In the case of Todai women, being a homemaker had a large and significant negative effect on earnings expected at peak of career.

The major source of the female/male differences in expected earnings in the Stanford sample was that women expected a lower return to work experience and hours of employment than men did. In the Todai sample, decomposition of the expected earnings regressions for women and men did not yield much information about the sources of the gender difference in earnings expectations.

7   Major Findings and Policy Reccomendations

Major Findings of the Study

Our summary of the major findings of this study is organized around the book's four themes: that the Todai and Stanford graduates are on the leading edge of social change with respect to more egalitarian work/ family models to replace the old breadwinner/homemaker model; that although much progress has been made in developing these new models, the two groups of graduates still face a long and difficult road; that although the Stanford graduates may be farther along the road than the Todai graduates, the latter are not as far behind as is sometimes stereotypically assumed; and that the labor market affects couples' arrangements for combining career and family both by conferring bargaining power and by constraining their choices.

The Graduates Are the Vanguard of Social Change

As noted in chapter 1, what led us to study the Todai and Stanford graduates was our belief that they, like other college graduates, were pioneers of social change in their respective countries with respect to developing more egalitarian models of combining work and family. We also noted, however, that because many of these graduates are part of the elites in their societies, some aspects of their lives are not likely to generalize to the overall population, or even the overall population of college graduates.[1]

With respect to pursuing nontraditional majors, graduate degrees, nontraditional occupations and increased labor force participation, the Todai and Stanford women are clearly pioneers, and future generations of college graduates are likely to follow in their footsteps. Similarly, we think that the families of the Stanford graduates, and to a lesser extent some of the families of the Todai graduates, may well be leading the way with respect

204 Chapter 7

to the sharing of household tasks and sick child care. However, it is not likely that the graduates' patterns of paying for help in their own homes for household tasks or child care will be emulated to the same extent by others with lower incomes. Nor is it likely that the graduates will be models with respect to their extreme gender differences in income aspirations.

Majors
Compared with all women college graduates in their respective countries, Stanford and Todai women were less likely to major in subjects that are traditional for women (such as humanities) and more likely to major in subjects that are nontraditional for women (such as engineering). Todai women were also less likely than their contemporaries to major in education and somewhat more likely to major in science and math. Being in a nontraditional major often leads to being in a nontraditional career, which we found to be correlated with being in a more egalitarian family.

Graduate Degrees
Egalitarian family arrangements were also more likely for women with an advanced degree. Stanford women were more likely to obtain advanced degrees than Todai graduates (60 percent versus 34 percent). Those with advanced degrees were more likely to be in nontraditional occupations, which, as we have already seen, was associated with being in a more egalitarian family. In addition, full-time homemakers were less likely to have advanced degrees, compared with other mothers in both the Stanford sample (43 percent of full-time homemakers versus 56 percent of other mothers) and the Todai sample (14 percent of full-time homemakers had advanced degrees, compared with 34 percent of other mothers).

Labor Force Participation and Commitment to Paid Work
Stanford and Todai women, like other college graduates, were more likely to be in the labor force than other women in the United States and Japan in the same age range. The difference was more marked in the Japanese case, where the labor force participation rate for Todai women (74.3 percent) was about 20 percentage points higher than for all Japanese women 25–34 (56.6 percent). In the American case, the rate for Stanford women (83.6 percent) was 10 percentage points higher than the rate for all women in the 25–34 age range (73.6 percent).

Among mothers, the percentage of Stanford mothers who were employed (about 66 percent) was only slightly higher than the 62 percent of all U.S. mothers who were living with their husbands and were employed in 1990; the Todai women who were mothers had much higher rates of employment (about 66 percent) than all Japanese mothers (54 percent) in 1988.

Compared with all U.S. mothers living with their husbands, Stanford mothers were more likely to be employed part-time. Forty percent of Stanford mothers were employed full-time (three percentage points lower than the rate for all U.S. mothers living with their husbands) and 26 per-cent were employed part-time (seven percentage points higher than the rate for all U.S. mothers living with their husbands).

Todai mothers, on the other hand, were much more likely to work full-time than all Japanese mothers and slightly *less* likely to work part-time. About 23 percent of all Japanese mothers had full-time jobs (17 percent-age points lower than Todai mothers) and 31 percent held part-time jobs (about five percentage points higher than Todai mothers).

Both Stanford and Todai women had very high rates of commitment to paid work, with 80 percent of both groups saying they would continue to work even if they did not need the income. The women's rates were only slightly below those of the men, which were 85 percent in both samples.

Earnings

The female/male earnings ratio is a measure of social and economic change not only for reasons of equity in the labor market but also because of its effect on the relative bargaining power of spouses in their families. The gender earnings ratio was much higher (more equal) for Stanford and Todai graduates than for the two respective economies as a whole. For full-time earners, it was 80 percent in both samples, compared with only 55 percent for all workers in Japan and 69 percent for all workers in the United States. However, the gender earnings ratio for the Stanford and Todai graduates was about the same as for college graduates 25–34 in the two countries.

Sharing of Household Tasks

Stanford graduates were clearly at the forefront of change with regard to sharing household tasks. Forty-three percent of married Stanford men and 44 percent of married Stanford women reported sharing household tasks about equally with their partner, whereas a 1992 national sample of adults 18 to 64 in the United States found that in families with employed husbands, less than 20 percent said they shared cooking and cleaning equally and less than 30 percent said they shared shopping equally. (In the national study, the men's and women's responses about sharing were quite different, with men reporting equal sharing much more frequently than women.)

On the other hand, Todai graduates were no more likely to share household tasks than other Japanese. Ninety percent of Todai men and 87 percent of Todai women reported that the woman in their family had primary responsibility for household tasks, virtually the same percentage found in a 1982 national survey of all Japanese families, where household tasks were defined as cleaning, laundry, shopping, preparing meals, cleaning up after meals and washing the dishes, and infant care.

To obtain a single measure for each married graduate of how traditional or egalitarian his or her family was with respect to division of labor, we aggregated the data on household tasks, household management, and responsibility for family financial well-being and put each graduate into one of three categories: egalitarian, hybrid, or traditional. We called graduates traditional if their division of family labor was the one followed by breadwinner/homemaker families: husband in charge of financial responsibility and wife in charge of household management and household tasks. We called them egalitarian if they shared all three household responsibilities. All others we designated as hybrid.

Thirty-five percent of Stanford men and 38 percent of Stanford women were in egalitarian families, a ratio likely to be far above that for the general population or even the general college graduate population in the United States. Among the Todai graduates, the percentages in egalitarian families were much lower, 6 percent for Todai men and 12 percent for Todai women.

However, there was an interesting pattern of egalitarianism among Todai men who were professors. Of the 17 Todai men who were in egalitarian families, half were professors. Moreover, only 13 percent of Todai men professors were in traditional families. Todai men professors, whether because of their flexible work schedules or their more frequent exposure to Western ideology (or both), are certainly at the forefront of social change for men in Japan.

Among Todai married graduates, only 3 percent of men and 13 percent of women employed household help. But among Stanford married graduates, 42 percent of men and 48 percent of women employed household help. Among men with children in egalitarian families, 58 percent employed household help, a percentage far greater than for men in any other type of family. This high percentage employing household help is clearly a by-product of the very high incomes earned by Stanford graduates. We do not think that achieving an egalitarian marriage by employing household help is an avenue open to most U.S. families.

In addition to having a wife with an advanced degree or a nontraditional occupation, egalitarian families had several other characteristics. Stanford graduates in egalitarian families were more likely to have favored the wife's career over the husband's; Stanford women in egalitarian families were less likely to have turned down a career opportunity for their husband than were other women; and Stanford men in egalitarian families were more likely than other men to have accommodated their own career to their wife's. Second, Todai men in egalitarian families were employed fewer hours than other men. Third, Stanford men in egalitarian families with children were more likely to employ household help than fathers in other types of families.

Child Care

The child care arrangements during usual working hours made by Todai mothers and Stanford parents were probably more reflective of their elite status than their pioneer status. Twenty-seven percent of Todai mothers, 26 percent of Stanford mothers, and 21 percent of Stanford fathers used a paid employee in their child's home. In a national U.S. sample, employed mothers were much less likely to use a paid employee in the child's home and more likely to use group care than Stanford parents. For reasons of affordability, we think the model for the future is more likely to be the one that already exists in the population at large, not the one exhibited by Stanford parents and Todai mothers.

However, with respect to sick child care, it may that the graduates in both samples are leading the way. About half of Todai and Stanford mothers employed full-time reported that they took turns with their husbands in providing sick child care, and slightly more than one-fifth of fathers said they took turns with their wives in providing such care. While taking turns doesn't necessarily mean equal sharing, and while we don't have national data on the provision of sick child care with which to contrast our findings, we think that these rates of taking turns are high.

The Future

The expectations that Stanford and Todai graduates have about their own future incomes and the gender earnings ratio of about 50 percent that derives from these expectations is likely to be correct. However, neither the graduates' expectations nor the gender earnings ratio that derives from them is likely to be predictive of the experience of other college graduates or of the population as a whole.

Until women and men have more similar labor market experience and more similar probabilities of being promoted, the gender earnings ratio will be lower (less equal) at the peak of people's careers than when they are in their early thirties. But, compared with the Stanford and Todai graduates, other groups are likely to have a much less precipitous change in their gender earnings ratio over time. This is largely because in both the United States and Japan, the kinds of jobs that the men in the Stanford and Todai samples have are the kinds that receive particularly large pay-offs when their incumbents are in their forties and fifties, at the peak of their careers.

To the extent that the degree of gender equality at home is based on the degree of gender equality at the workplace, if the female/male earnings ratio declines (becomes less equal) in this population, sharing household tasks may also decline and Stanford women may wind up doing a higher percent of this work. (Given the low rates of equal sharing to begin with among Todai women, it is hard to predict much of a decline in their sharing.) However, in other families, where male breadwinners are not in the kinds of jobs that are so highly rewarded at the peak of their career, both the female/male earnings ratio and the degree of sharing of household tasks are likely to decline by much less than in the families of our graduates. As a result, while Stanford and Todai graduates in their early thirties may be on the cutting edge of gender equality in the labor market, they may be less likely to remain there when they move toward the peak of their careers.

The Road Winds Uphill All the Way

While the graduates may have been pioneers in the labor market and in their families, they continued to face considerable obstacles on the road to more egalitarian models of combining employment and family. And some of the graduates appeared to be quite content with the old breadwinner/homemaker arrangement.

Employment
Despite the substantial investments they had made in their education, only two-thirds of the Stanford women and only about half of the Todai women were employed full-time, compared with almost 90 percent of the Stanford and Todai men; and almost one-third of Stanford mothers and about one-quarter of Todai mothers were full-time homemakers. For some women in both samples, the greatest return on their educational investment may have been marrying a high-earning husband.

We did not inquire directly about the women graduates' satisfaction with their hours of work or their full-time-homemaker status. However, from comments they made on their surveys we learned a great deal about their preferences. For some, being a full-time homemaker was clearly their first choice. But for others, reducing hours of employment or leaving the labor market entirely was not their preferred strategy; rather, it was the only arrangement they could make to accommodate their lives to those of their husbands and/or cope with the family responsibilities they had assumed.

Earnings
Stanford and Todai women who were employed full-time earned 80 percent of the annual earnings of their full-time-employed male classmates. In the Stanford case, the earnings differential among full-time workers was largely explained by two factors: women were less likely than men to be in the high-paid occupations, and women faced labor market discrimination by earning lower returns on years of work experience and hours of employment than men did. In the Todai sample, three factors were largely responsible for the full-time earnings difference by gender: women were less likely to be employed in large firms, which paid high wages and bonuses, and more likely to be employed by the government, which paid low wages and bonuses; women who were employed in large firms got a smaller payoff than men who were employed in those firms, and women who were employed by the government paid a larger wage penalty than men employed by the government; and women who were wives and mothers were paid less than men who were husbands and fathers.

Turning Down Career Opportunities
Women were more likely than men to have turned down career opportunities for their spouse. About 40 percent of the women in both samples reported doing so, compared with 30 percent of Stanford men and only 8 percent of Todai men.

Responsibility for Household Tasks
Household responsibilities were distributed very unequally between the women and men in our samples. Among those who were married (almost two-thirds of the Stanford sample and three-fourths of the Todai sample), housework generally remained women's work. In the Todai sample, only about 10 percent of the women and men reported that they shared housework "about equally" with their spouse and about 90 percent said

it was done by the woman in the family. And even among Todai dual-earner couples, who were most likely to share household tasks, only about 25 percent did so.

In the Stanford sample, while the sharing rate was much higher than in the Todai sample, it was much lower among those with children than among those without. Slightly more than half of both Stanford women and men without children reported that they shared household tasks with their spouse. But among those with children, only about one-third of the graduates did so. Even among Stanford women who were employed full-time and had children, 40 percent had the lion's share of responsibility for household tasks.

The vast majority of men were satisfied with their household task arrangements. And women in egalitarian arrangements also had a high rate of satisfaction. But among women with traditional arrangements (where the woman does all or most of the household tasks) about half of the Stanford women and about 40 percent of the Todai women were dissatisfied. We find this a worrisome statistic from the point of view of marital satisfaction and the possibility of ongoing marital discord.

Very few graduates had families who were in the egalitarian category: 38 percent of Stanford women, 35 percent of Stanford men, 12 percent of Todai women, and 6 percent of Todai men.

We did not find support for the notion that women who have primary responsibility for household tasks have lower earnings. However, we did find that Stanford women who did more than half of the household tasks in their family were employed fewer hours per week. To the extent that this decrease in work hours meant they were in part-time jobs, they paid a wage penalty over and beyond their loss of income from working fewer hours a week.

Among Stanford men, those who did at least half of household tasks did face a wage penalty; they earned about 10 percent less than other married men, all else held constant.

Child Care

Most fathers were not active in raising their children. Seventy percent of Stanford fathers and 74 percent of Todai fathers were in marriages where their wives cared for their children during usual working hours. Moreover, most fathers were not active in raising their children in after-work hours. In the Todai sample, 60 percent of fathers spent almost none or less than half of their after-work hours on child care, and almost 90 percent of these fathers said they were satisfied with this arrangement. About half of Stanford fathers said they shared equally in child care during the hours they were not employed, but only 30 percent of Stanford mothers said their husbands shared equally during the hours they were not employed. Among fathers who did less than half of child care during the hours when they were not employed, about three-fourths said they were satisfied with that arrangement.

We categorized Stanford fathers as active fathers if they took turns with their wives doing sick child care or did it themselves *and* in addition did at least half of the child care during other than usual work hours. We called Todai fathers active if they took turns with their wives doing sick child care or did it themselves *and* in addition spent at least half of their after-work time doing child care. Only 18 percent of Stanford fathers and 13 percent of Todai fathers were active. Only ten Stanford parents, (4 percent of all Stanford parents) and seven Todai parents (2 percent of all Todai parents) were egalitarian in dividing both household and child care responsibilities.

Aspirations and Expectations

In both the Todai and the Stanford samples, the difference in earnings aspirations and earnings expectations between women and men was even greater than the difference in their current earnings, suggesting that in the future the female/male earnings ratio may well be even lower (more unequal) than it was at the time of our survey. The earnings that Stanford women expected at the peak of their career were only 50 percent of those expected by men. In the Todai sample, this expectations ratio was only slightly higher, about 56 percent.

The United States May Not Be as Far Ahead of Japan with Respect to Gender Equity as Conventional Wisdom Suggests

On balance, Stanford graduates were in situations with greater gender equity than their Todai counterparts. Yet, we were struck that in several respects the Stanford and Todai graduates were pretty much on a par. And with regard to child care, it may be that the Japanese are ahead of Americans; our data suggest that the Japanese group child care system is more acceptable to highly educated parents than the U.S. system.

Labor Force Participation

Although the percentage of Stanford women in the labor force (84 percent) was higher than the percentage of Todai women in the labor force

(77 percent), that was largely because a higher percentage of Todai women were mothers compared with Stanford women. If we look at the labor force behavior of mothers only, in both samples about two-thirds of mothers were in the labor force. Moreover, the percentages of Todai and Stanford mothers who worked full-time (40 percent) and part-time (26 percent) were virtually identical.

The Gender Earnings Ratio and the Ratio of Women's to Men's Hours of Employment

A particularly salient finding is that the earnings ratio for full-time workers was the same in the two samples, 80 percent. In addition, in both samples, among full-time workers the ratio of women's hours of employment to men's hours of employment was the same, 95 percent for the Stanford graduates and 93 percent for the Todai graduates.

Family Matters

Stanford and Todai women were similar with respect to the percentage who limited their careers for their husbands: 43 percent of Stanford women and 38 percent of Todai women. And the percentage of women in the two samples who were in traditional families was also similar: about 37 percent for the Stanford women and 40 percent for the Todai women.

In both samples, only a small percentage of fathers reported staying home with sick children. But in both samples, the percentage was the same, 20 percent. Moreover, although the definition of "active father" was somewhat different for the two samples, neither had very many active fathers: 18 percent in the Stanford case and 13 percent in the Todai case.

With respect to child care arrangements, Stanford and Todai mothers were equally likely to use a paid employee in their home to care for children. Twenty-six percent of mothers in both samples reported doing so. Interestingly, although many Todai parents complained about the availability or convenience of nursery schools (the equivalent of child care centers), a higher percentage of Todai mothers (71 percent) used nursery schools than Stanford women used child care centers (23 percent) or family day care homes (19 percent).

Differences Between the Stanford and Todai Samples

There were, however, several important differences between the two samples. The largest difference in the study concerned the sharing of housework. Here the difference among men was even larger than the already mentioned difference among women. Forty-three percent of Stanford men shared housework about equally with their wives, but only 8 percent of Todai men did so.

Turning to the labor market, we find additional important differences between the two samples. The percentage of men who limited their careers for their wives was *much* higher among Stanford men (30 percent) than among Todai men (8 percent). Also, the index of occupational segregation was lower for the Stanford graduates than for the Todai graduates, and Stanford women were more likely than their Todai sisters to be in nontraditional occupations. Thirteen percent of Stanford women were physicians, 8 percent were lawyers, and 8 percent were scientists and engineers. In the Todai sample, about 14 percent of the women were "salarymen" and about 12 percent were researchers. With respect to managers, in the Stanford sample, 17 to 18 percent of both women and men were managers; in the Todai sample, while 15 percent of the men were managers, only 2 percent of the women were in that occupation.

Finally, the Stanford women faced a more flexible and "forgiving" labor market than did the Todai women. As reflected in their respective comments, Stanford women who had left the labor market to raise children full-time (sometimes because the American labor market was insufficiently flexible for them) were on the whole optimistic about returning to work in the future. Given the difficulties that Japanese women face in trying to return to the labor market after time out for child rearing, Todai women were (appropriately) not optimistic. These qualitative differences in optimism were corroborated in the regressions on expected earnings. Todai women who were full-time homemakers expected earnings at the peak of their career that were 124 percent lower than those of other Todai women, all else held constant. In the Stanford sample, full-time homemaking did not lead to any significant penalty in expected earnings.

Earning Power in the Workplace Affects What Happens at Home

Relative bargaining power of the two spouses was a factor in determining their division of household tasks and household management responsibilities, although the effects were small. That economic bargaining power affects the division of labor at home is an important finding; it means that labor market policies against discrimination in hiring, promotion, and earnings bear fruit not only in the market sector of the economy but also in families. Moreover, since in democratic societies there are no public policies that can easily impact the division of household labor directly, it is of interest to know that antidiscrimination policies, by increasing women's bargaining power, can have some modest indirect influence.

Women who were employed full-time were much more likely to be in families where household tasks are shared equally. Forty-four percent of all Stanford women, but 58 percent of women employed full-time, shared tasks about equally with their husbands. Among Stanford mothers, 60 percent of those who were employed full-time, but only 22 percent of those employed part-time and only 19 percent of homemakers, had an egalitarian arrangement for sharing household tasks.

In the Todai sample, 13 percent of all women, but 24 percent of those employed full-time shared household tasks about equally in their families. Among Todai mothers, the difference in sharing rates between full-time and part-time employed mothers was much smaller than for Stanford mothers; 21 percent of Todai mothers who were employed full-time, compared with 10 percent of Todai mothers who were employed part-time (and one full-time homemaker), shared household tasks.

For the men, the percentages who shared tasks about equally with their wives were much higher if they were in a dual-earner family. This was especially true for Todai men; among all Todai men, only 8 percent shared household tasks about equally with their wives, but among those in dual-earner couples, 23 percent shared about equally.

For dual-earner couples in all four samples, at least one measure of bargaining power (wife's earnings, or husband's earnings, or the ratio of wife's earnings to husband's earnings) was significantly related to the couple's division of household tasks.

In the Stanford sample, egalitarian families tended to have husbands (both Stanford men and the husbands of Stanford women) who earned less than other husbands. Moreover, by and large, total earnings (husband's earnings plus wife's earnings) in traditional families were higher than total family earnings in either egalitarian or hybrid families. In other words, on average, Stanford families paid an economic price for egalitarian arrangements. Or, viewed alternatively, women in traditional families paid for their higher family income by doing a greater share of household tasks.

Moreover, in both the Stanford and Todai samples, men in egalitarian families had mean expected earnings that were about 70 percent of those of traditional men. There was clearly a trade-off between equality in home tasks and husband's earnings expectations.

On the other hand, Stanford women in egalitarian families had mean earnings expectations that were 35 percent higher than those for Stanford women in traditional families. (Because of the small number of Todai women in egalitarian families, it was not possible to compare earnings aspirations and expectations for women in egalitarian and traditional families.)

Although bargaining theory was successful in predicting the correlates of being an active father in the Stanford sample, it was not in the Todai sample. Stanford fathers who were active earned lower incomes than other fathers, had wives who earned higher income than other wives, and had a higher (more equal) wife/husband earnings ratio than other fathers. But Todai fathers' earnings were about the same for active and inactive fathers, and the earnings of wives were actually *lower* in active fathers' families.

Two Additional Findings of Interest

Although they did not relate to the main themes of the book, two additional findings about the graduates are of interest.

Inequality in Earnings Was Much Greater Among Stanford Graduates Than Among Todai Graduates
It is well known that the distribution of earnings in Japan is considerably more egalitarian than in the United States. We found the same pattern in comparing the earnings of the two sets of graduates. Among full-time earners, the measure of income inequality we used (the coefficient of variation, the standard deviation of the income distribution divided by the mean of the distribution) was 0.79 for the Stanford men, about double that of 0.41 for the Todai men. Among the women, the difference in inequality was even greater; the coefficient of variation for the Stanford women was 0.90, more than double that of 0.41 for the Todai women.

If expected earnings are predictive of future earnings, at the peak of their careers the disparity in earnings among Stanford graduates will continue to be greater than the disparity among their Todai counterparts, although the difference in disparity will be less, because the Todai graduates expected a great deal more disparity in future earnings than they had in current earnings. For the Stanford graduates, the coefficient of variation of expected earnings was 104 percent for men and 102 percent for women. Among Todai respondents, the coefficients were 79 percent and 72 percent for Todai men and women, respectively.

The Importance of Social Class in the Stanford Sample

While many Americans argue that social class does not matter (or no longer matters, as some put it), we found that having social origins in the upper class (as self-identified by the respondents) mattered quite a bit. Among women, those who came from upper-class families were more likely to be full-time homemakers than Stanford women with other social class origins. At the same time, men who came from the upper class had greater nonwage income, higher earnings, and higher earnings aspirations than their male classmates. Men from the upper class had nonwage income that was two-thirds higher than that of their male classmates. Controlling for other factors that determine earnings and earnings expectations, Stanford men from upper-class backgrounds had earnings that were 19 to 24 percent higher than those of their male classmates and earnings expectations that were 46 percent higher. As a result of these patterns, women and men with upper-class origins were more unequal in terms of earnings and earnings expectations than women and men from other social classes.

Policy Recommendations

What policies could be adopted in the United States and Japan to facilitate the combining of work and family in nontraditional ways? The answer to this question is of interest not only to the women and men in the trenches (so to speak), but also to those in government and business wishing to ensure that human resources are used effectively.

In the Japanese case, there is particular interest in these matters. Because of the low birthrate in Japan (in 1989 Japan's birthrate fell to an all-time low of 1.57, below replacement rate),[2] there is pressure on Japanese women to have children. Although some Japanese in leadership positions might prefer that women choose children instead of a career, in fact many women have been choosing a career instead of children. Some of these leaders are now beginning to understand that if they want more women, particularly highly educated women, to have children, they will need to make it possible for women to combine career and family.[3]

We suggest that a three-pronged approach is necessary. First, three sets of changes are needed in the labor market. Second, changes are required in the societal ideology about gender roles and particularly in the ways these roles are portrayed in the legal system, the schools, the media, and the culture at large. Third, we make some suggestions for individuals interested in developing egalitarian work/family patterns in their own lives.

Labor Market Policies

A new career–family system must ensure that highly educated women are able to get an equitable return on their educational investment. This will require three kinds of policies: (1) eliminating gender segregation by occupation and industry (ensuring that similarly qualified women and men have the same opportunities to enter particular occupations, industries, and firms); (2) eliminating earnings discrimination (ensuring that women and men who are equally productive receive the same pay); and (3) providing flexible employment options for both women and men during the years they are raising young children.

Eliminating Gender Segregation by Occupation, Industry, and Firm
In the Todai sample, one of the major causes of the gender difference in earnings was women's exclusion from large firms that paid high salaries and their more frequent employment by government agencies that paid relatively low salaries. The Equal Employment Opportunity (EEO) Law, which was passed in 1985 and was described in chapter 1, was designed to deal with this problem. But it has been unsuccessful, in part because many large companies have circumvented the law by creating a new secondary track, *ippanshoku*, and employing women there instead of on the primary track, *sogoshoku*, where most men are employed. The newly amended 1998 version of the EEO prohibits such discrimination. However, no affirmative action is included in the new law. Affirmative action is needed in recruitment and promotion to ensure that highly educated women get their fair share of the most highly paid jobs.[4]

In the Stanford sample, one of the major contributors to the gender earnings differential was occupational segregation: women were less frequently employed in the high-paying occupations than men were. It is difficult to determine how much of women's exclusion from high-paying occupations is due to their "true" preferences and how much is due to discrimination or to the dampening effects of expected discrimination on women's occupational preferences.

To the extent that women exclude themselves from high-paying jobs because of their true preferences (preferences untainted by expected discrimination), there is no labor market problem to be remedied. However, most labor market analysts think that many more women would like to be in high-paying jobs than are currently found there. The policy strategy in the United States to accomplish this has been affirmative action, where employers who are either government contractors or under court order to remedy prior discrimination are required to take affirmative steps (including wider recruiting) to hire women into occupations from which they have been excluded or in which they have been underrepresented.[5] Despite the fact that affirmative action is under attack in the United States, many employers have found that widening the pool during the recruitment process and using the advantages that a diverse workforce brings is simply good business. We continue to recommend affirmative action to bring more women into high-paying jobs.

Another way to get women into high-paying jobs is to increase the pay in the jobs that they already have, to provide "comparable worth" pay adjustments where employers agree to adjust the pay of women in certain low-paid occupations who are deemed to be as productive as men in higher-paid occupations.[6] In this situation, the earnings gap is reduced not because more women move into higher-paid occupations, as is the case with affirmative action, but because more women's occupations become more highly paid.[7]

In recommending a continuation of affirmative action in the United States and further amendments to the EEO Law in Japan to include affirmative action, we are not recommending that women who move into formerly all-male jobs should necessarily be expected to behave like men in those jobs. Henry Higgins, frustrated with Eliza Doolittle, asked: "Why can't a woman be more like a man?" Unlike Prof. Higgins, and some high-level managers and administrators, we do *not* think the goal of occupational, industrial, or firm integration is to make women more like men.

Women who have recently been promoted to management positions often plaintively ask us: "Do we have to become like men to succeed as managers in this company?" They tell us, for example, sometimes with great consternation, that their company has set up a mentoring system for women who have recently moved into management positions formerly reserved for men. The mentoring system is supposed to be teaching them to be managers, but it is actually teaching them to be male managers.

Some women, as they move into what used to be all-male careers, may want to be just "one of the boys."[8] But most women do not. Nor is it necessary for them to do so. Managers can be successful with a wide variety of styles; companies who force all managers into a single style are often failing to harness a great deal of potential creativity and innovation.[9]

Eliminating Earnings Discrimination
As we have seen, in the Stanford sample, a major cause of the earnings difference between women and men was that women faced earnings dis-

crimination; the returns they received for a year of work experience or an hour of employment were lower than the returns that men received. In the Todai sample, discrimination took a slightly different form; husbands and fathers were paid more than wives and mothers because they received family premiums. The 1998 amendments prohibit gender discrimination in premiums, indicating that premiums should be paid to the head of the family. But since in most marriages the husband is considered the head of the family, there will continue to be differences in the benefits paid to married women and men.

In the United States, the remedy for earnings discrimination is stricter enforcement of existing state and federal laws prohibiting such discrimination and better funding of agencies whose job it is to enforce these statutes.[10] In the Japanese case, wage practices must be changed so that a greater proportion of compensation is derived from basic salary instead of on premiums connected to family conditions.[11]

Providing for Flexible Employment and High-Quality, Affordable Child Care
Highly educated women and men who wish to combine career and family in nontraditional ways often would like more flexibility in their paid work than they are generally able to obtain. Because many of their careers are intense, requiring long hours, frequent and often unpredictable travel, and willingness to transfer to distant geographic locations, they often find it more difficult to combine work and family than women and men with other kinds of jobs.

Paradoxically, because their jobs are so difficult to combine with raising children, and because they are often in dual-earner families where both spouses earn enough for the family to manage with less than two full incomes, many highly educated women (and a few highly educated men) seek more flexibility in employment arrangements than women and men with other kinds of jobs. Also, because they have made large investments in their education, they are often more concerned than other workers about the impact that flexible work arrangements may have on their long-term career progress.

Highly educated women and men trying to combine career and family may desire one or more of three types of flexibility: (1) the opportunity to work fewer hours a week or fewer hours a year during times when family responsibilities are heavy, without incurring a wage rate penalty for being a part-time employee;[12] (2) the opportunity to leave the labor force for several years without sacrificing the ability to return to the workforce and resume one's career; and (3) the opportunity to stay on the job, either full-

or part-time, by moving to a position with less career intensity (less direct line responsibility, less travel, etc.) but still being able to move back to a position with more career intensity at a later date.

Many highly educated women and men would like to "have it all" (a demanding career, marriage, and young children), but not necessarily all at once. For several years, at the beginning of their career, they would like to concentrate their full efforts on their jobs and get their career off to a running start. Then, when they have young children, they would like to step off the fast track and work part-time, leave the labor force altogether for a few years while their children are young, or stay on the job (full- or part-time) but move onto a slower track for a few years. When their major child-rearing duties lessen, many of these women and men are ready to turn their full energies once again to paid work.

The problem is that in both the United States and Japan, women and men who have stepped off the fast track are not able to get back on, and those who have left the labor force entirely may not be able to resume their career. In Japan, because the fast track is so often tied to the lifetime employment system, continuity of full-time employment is an administrative prerequisite for having a career that leads to high-level promotions. A man who wants such a career cannot in the present situation also be an active father. A woman who wants such a career generally does not have the option of having her husband raise her children. Instead, she must either forgo a family or try to have career and family at the same time.

As we noted in chapter 1, as a result of the Equal Employment Opportunity Law, many Japanese firms developed a two-track system of employment similar to the "mommy track" in the United States. The fast track (or main track), *sogoshoku*, has the more challenging jobs, requires those on it to be available for transfer to locations a long distance away, and offers the possibility of promotion to the most senior positions. A woman who wants to have it all, but not all at once, is forced onto the secondary, *ippanshoku* track, where jobs are less challenging, job transfer is required only in the local geographic area, and promotion opportunities are highly constrained. In other words, if she does not have career and family all at once, she must give up having a career that leads to a major position. Once she steps off the main track and onto the secondary track, she can never return to the main track. Indeed, unless she promises never to get off the main track, she can never get onto it in the first place.

In the United States, while "tracking" is less formalized than in large Japanese companies, it nonetheless exists. Some law firms and accounting firms have in fact set up "mommy tracks." Like those in Japan, these tracks offer less demanding work and do not permit switches back to the main or fast track. Those who ask to be on the mommy track are doomed to perpetual secondary citizenship in these firms; they are never eligible to become partners.

Similarly, in academe in the United States, unless a college or university has a provision that "stops the tenure clock" for a few years while a mother or father cares full-time for a child, parents who are actively raising their child are expected to do the research and writing necessary for a favorable promotion and tenure review within the same six-year period that others are given to prove themselves. If they have not produced enough high-quality publications within that time period, they often are not promoted and are then obliged to take positions as lecturers or research associates, which do not carry professorial titles or lifetime employment guarantees.

These traditional administrative rules and arrangements for moving to partnership in a firm or becoming a professor in a university were clearly designed with the breadwinner/homemaker system in mind. No system designed for women and men who wish to have fulfilling careers and also be active in rearing their children would arrange to have the major career testing period come at the same time of life when a woman's biological clock begins to whisper "now or never."

In the Japanese case, to permit crossover from the secondary to the primary track is to change fundamentally the entire lifelong employment and *nenko* wage system. The system was possible so long as only a minority of the workforce (only certain men) were guaranteed lifetime employment. Having the vast majority of women leave the workforce at the time of marriage, before they were eligible for higher pay based on their seniority, allowed the system to remain financially viable.

It has been argued that it is only coincidental that the development of the two-track system in large firms came about at the same time the EEO Law took effect, that the need to further differentiate the track leading to management was independent of the need to comply with the new legislation. What Japanese management has been doing, the argument goes, is to use the lifetime employment system to recruit only the most able workers, and thus be able to compete effectively in international markets while simultaneously maintaining the maximum amount of employment flexibility possible in order to control labor costs.[13] The revised EEO prohibits such policies. Also, the prolonged economic recession of the nineties forced firms to lay off workers and to review the viability of lifetime employment. Companies need new ways to cope.

One way is to allow people to switch back and forth between primary and secondary tracks. This is not necessarily incompatible with the management goals of hiring the best and reducing costs. Companies who now compete for the best and the brightest recruits with promises of lifetime employment can be equally successful by promising a combination of flexibility in work intensity over the life cycle and the opportunity to go for the gold ring at multiple points in a career. Also, the total number of people on the fast track at any point can be fixed, thus keeping a lid on the costs of paying certain people particularly high wages.

Another important element in providing flexibility of employment for parents is providing paid child care leave and sufficient, affordable, high-quality child care services. Unlike many countries in Western Europe, neither Japan nor the United States provides for paid child care leave, although both require an employer to rehire a an employee who has taken an unpaid child care leave.[14]

Improvements in the child care system are necessary in both countries to further nontraditional forms of combining work and family. In the United States this would mainly take the form of improving the quality of child care;[15] in Japan it would take the form of increasing the availability of child care services.[16]

Changing Societal Ideology About Gender Roles

Changes in ideology are connected in complex ways to economic, demographic, educational, and cultural changes. The next stages in the transition to nontraditional ways of combining work and family will require additional changes in ideology about gender roles.

A combination of sweeping economic and demographic change and a resurgence of feminist ideology and political power, has produced major changes in the U.S. legal system, education system, and media, as well as movement away from the breadwinner/homemaker model and toward a more egalitarian model of combining work and family. Japan has had some of the same underlying economic and demographic forces as the United States, particularly an increase in the demand for women workers and a marked fall in the birthrate. But Japan has not had the kind of vocal feminist movement that exists in the United States. Instead, Japan's contact with a new ideology about gender roles has come from abroad. Through the media, travel, and trade, the Japanese have been exposed to new ideas about what are and are not "appropriate" roles for women and men in the workplace and in the family.

In part because the feminist movement has not been as strong in Japan as in the United States, and because the Japanese began their ideological shifts later than the Americans, there have been fewer changes in Japanese institutions and smaller shifts in gender ideology. However, Japan is rapidly catching up to the United States. Some examples follow.

In December 1991, the Japanese newspaper *Asahi Shimbun* asked 2,400 registered voters "Do you find men who place primary importance on their work attractive?" Among those between 20 and 40 years of age, more than 70 percent answered "no." In the same survey, while 55 percent of respondents of all ages said they agreed with the breadwinner/ homemaker ideology that "men should go out and work and women should stay home and care for the children," the percentage of agreement was much lower than the 72 percent that agreed with a similar statement in a 1980 poll.[17]

Beginning in April 1994, after many years of pressure by Japanese feminists, by national law it became mandatory for boys as well as girls to take home economics courses in middle school and in high school. Also, the media and government agencies have begun, since the early 1990s, to take sexual harassment seriously, and for the first time women have begun to take positions of leadership in government.[18]

Japanese women have also become less willing to get into or put up with unsatisfactory marriages. One Japanese man characterized the following changes in the marriage market: " 'Why,' more women are asking themselves, 'should I marry a man who not only doesn't help with housework and child care but can't even care for his own day-to-day needs?' ... this growing disillusionment with marriage on the part of women is beginning to drive home to younger men the message that they cannot expect to act the way their fathers have until now if they hope to be accepted by today's young women."[19]

The divorce rate in Japan, still far below the rate in the United States, is nonetheless rising, particularly among couples who have been married more than 20 years and the husband is about to retire. The majority of divorces among these older couples are initiated by the wife.[20]

It also seems to be the case that a few men are becoming weary of the lack of leisure time associated with guarantees of lifetime employment in large companies and are beginning to quit their jobs, something that was unheard-of in earlier times. A name for these men has even been coined: *datsusara*, meaning escaped or runaway salarymen.[21]

For further changes to take place in the old breadwinner/homemaker system, there will need to be a further diffusion of the new ideology and additional changes in the ways in which women and men are portrayed in the media and in the culture. It is unlikely that the policy changes we have suggested will take place without further changes in ideology in the two countries.

Actions That Individuals Can Take

Armed with an understanding of the difficulties of achieving egalitarian work/family arrangements, those who wish to have egalitarian arrangements in their own lives need to be sure to talk with their potential spouses about this subject in advance of marriage. If egalitarian arrangements are not specifically sought, planned for, and often fought over, couples tend to fall back on arrangements that are more traditional in the society, arrangements that they probably saw in their own homes when they were growing up.

Women and men seeking egalitarian arrangements need to be particularly careful that in the early stages of their relationship, they value both careers and take care that sacrifices in careers are shared, that one career does not suffer too much for the sake of the other. Both partners need to remember that when they seek flexibility at the time they have young children, they will need to have established good track records with their employers in order to negotiate successfully for such flexibility. Inequalities in labor markets will often lead to situations where the man will be choosing among jobs that have higher earnings and more attractive career prospects than the woman. In such situations, the couple must take care that it is not the woman's career that is consistently compromised.

Individuals who find themselves in pioneer positions with regard to new work/family roles need support groups and networks. It is very difficult, and often impossible, to pioneer alone. In Myra's work as a consultant to businesses, she has seen several instances where networks have served to support women and men seeking more flexibility in employment in order to spend more time with their families, and where these same networks have become powerful enough to negotiate successfully with management to bring in consultants and eventually to bring about the desired changes.

Parents seeking new ways to combine work and family also find it useful to form groups that work for change at the community level, so that community institutions—child care centers, nursery schools, schools, religious organizations—support egalitarian families.

If the road to egalitarian work/family arrangements winds uphill all the way, it is those who wish to forge new arrangements who must do the climbing, who must work to create the new ideological, cultural, legal, economic, family, and community structures that will make the new arrangements possible. People who climb major mountains never go unprepared and never go alone. Those who consciously plan egalitarian work/family arrangements and who form networks and support groups are far more likely to reach their goals.

Individuals who seek egalitarian arrangements must also recognize that they must be engaged in changing the system as well as their own decision-making behavior. Egalitarian arrangements are far more likely in a system that accommodates or fosters them than in a system that makes them almost impossible. It is crucial that those working for change in this arena seek to affect public policy, organizing politically to achieve the policies suggested here and advocating for politicians and interest groups who support these policies.

Getting businesses and governments to adopt the policy changes suggested in this chapter may well require international cooperation. Just as governments within countries level the playing field among businesses by legislating certain labor benefits so that companies who offer them are not undercut by companies who don't, so international agreements on benefits providing more flexibility for working parents can prevent international businesses from competing at the expense of families. International advocacy may be as crucial as national and local advocacy.

Conclusion

There is no going back to the old breadwinner/homemaker system. There are now too many women and men with a vested interest in moving to a new, more egalitarian, and more fulfilling system.

But the transition from the old to the new remains painful, and it would be a mistake to underestimate the enormity of the changes we are discussing here or the powerful societal resistances to these changes. The breadwinner/homemaker system has been forcefully entrenched in both the United States and Japan. Its underlying assumption, that men should provide for their families and should be given the better jobs in order to do so, will not die quickly. Also slow to expire will be many men's sense of rightful privilege in the workplace and their disdain of household and child-rearing tasks. For those interested in moving to more egalitarian models of combining work and family, the road winds uphill all the way. But, as we have seen from the Stanford and Todai graduates, change is indeed in the works. May their stories and our analyses provide optimism as well as realism for the road ahead.

Appendix: List of Tables

Notes

Chapter 1

1. In keeping with current practice, we call the breadwinner/homemaker system "traditional". However, we recognize that the terms "traditional" and "nontraditional" are somewhat problematic in the context of work–family arrangements. The breadwinner/homemaker arrangement, whereby women are full-time homemakers and are not employed for pay, while men are the sole family breadwinners and participate little, if at all, in household tasks and child care, has not been, and is not today, traditional for all families. Today in families that own small farms or small businesses, the traditional arrangement is for women to work without pay not only in the home but also in the family business. Moreover, in many working-class families, and in most African–American families in the United States since the end of slavery, wives and mothers traditionally worked in the home and also were often employed. For these families, the breadwinner/homemaker model, far from being the traditional model, in fact represented a modern model to which many aspired. For discussion of the origins and decline of the breadwinner/homemaker system, see Kingsley Davis, "Wives and Work: A Theory of the Sex-Role Revolution and Its Consequences," in Sanford M. Dornbusch and Myra H. Strober (eds.), *Feminism, Children, and the New Families* (New York: Guilford Press, 1988), pp. 67–86.

2. We define the term "ideology" in accordance with *Webster's Unabridged New Twentieth Century Dictionary* (1979), p. 902: "the doctrines, opinions or way of thinking of an individual, class, etc." Using the same source (p. 444), we define culture as "the concepts, habits, skills, art, instruments, institutions, etc. of a given people in a given period." Thus, culture includes ideology.

3. In 1950, only 50 percent of Japanese girls entered high school, and only 15 percent of male high school graduates and 5 percent of female high school graduates entered university-level education. Sorifu, *Fujin no Genjo to Shisaku* (Tokyo: Office of the Prime Minister, 1989).

4. "The most highly educated husbands take almost a third more responsibility for household tasks compared with those with little education (30 percent compared to 23 percent)." Frances K. Goldscheider and Linda J. Waite, *New Families, No Families?* (Berkeley: University of California Press, 1991), p. 129. Also see Catherine E. Ross, "The Division of Labor at Home," *Social Forces*, 65 (3) (March 1987): 827. The role of wife's education is less clear-cut. Ross found that wife's education did not significantly affect the division of household tasks. Goldscheider and Waite found that wife's higher education influenced husbands to share more only when there were children in the family. Blair and Lichter found that that both

wife's education and husband's education were positively correlated with greater sharing of household tasks, but even those women and men with sixteen or more years of education still had a highly segregated task division at home. See Sampson Lee Blair and Daniel T. Lichter, "Measuring the Division of Household Labor: Gender Segregation of Housework Among American Couples," *Journal of Family Issues*, 12 (1) (March 1991): 91–113.

5. Bina Agarwal, *A Field of One's Own: Gender and Land Rights in South Asia* (Cambridge: Cambridge University Press, 1994), and "Bargaining and Gender Relations: Within and Beyond the Household," *Feminist Economics*, 3 (1) (1997): 1–51.

6. Claudia Goldin, "Career and Family: College Women Look to the Past," in Francine D. Blau and Ronald Ehrenberg (eds.), *Gender and Family Issues in the Workplace* (New York: Russell Sage, 1997) pp. 20–58. Goldin defines career more narrowly than others might. She excludes those with part-time careers and those with careers whose earnings are low (less than the median of women college graduates' earnings). See also Myra H. Strober, "Commentary on Chapter 2," in the same volume.

7. We are *not* arguing that all women who are trying to combine career and family *should* have full-time employment, but pointing out that most don't.

8. Hannah Papanek, "Men, Women and Work: Reflections on the Two-Person Career," *American Journal of Sociology*, 78 (1973): 852–72, calls this situation a "two-person career." For a discussion of the lives of American corporate wives whose husbands have demanding two-person careers, see Myra H. Strober, "Valuing the Invisible Work of Women." (Cambridge, MA: Radcliffe Public Policy Institute, 1998).

9. Todai is said to have the most difficult entrance exam of any Japanese university. See Yoshio Higuchi, "Higher Education and Income Distribution in Japan." Discussion Paper, Keio University, 1994, p. 8.

10. Japan Statistics Bureau, Prime Minister's Office. *Japan Statistical Yearbook, 1982* (Tokyo: JSB, 1982), table 418. Japanese statistics are often given in terms of enrollment, since the drop-out rate is very low.

11. U.S. Department of Education, *Digest of Educational Statistics* (Washington, DC: U.S. Government Printing Office, 1983). In 1980–81, women received 49.8 percent of the bachelor's degrees awarded.

12. Todai women in the classes we are observing were also much more egalitarian-minded than women students in other educational situations at that time. In the early 1980s, women students at two-year colleges, four-year universities, and Todai University were asked, What do you think is the ideal marriage? Their answers fell into three categories: (1) a breadwinner/ homemaker model; (2) both work outside the home, but the woman's job is secondary; (3) both work outside the home and share household tasks. Sixty-two percent of Todai women said their ideal marriage was one where both spouses were employed and shared household tasks, but only 38 percent of women in four-year universities and only 16 percent of women in two-year colleges chose that response. See Aya Yoshida, "The Social Life and Consciousness of Female Students of Tokyo University," *Higher Education in the Present*, no. 259 (1985): 52–57 (in Japanese).

13. See Higuchi, "New Graduates Must Sell Themselves Harder: Young Entries Finding It Tough to Crack Job Market." *The Nikkei Weekly*, March 20, 1995, cited in James R. Lincoln and Yoshifumi Nakata, "The Transformation of the Japanese Employment System: Nature, Depth and Origins," *Work and Occupations*, 24 (1) (February 1997): 40.

14. See Ronald Dore, Jean Bounine-Cabale, and Kari Tapiola, *Japan at Work: Markets, Management and Flexibility* (Paris: OECD, 1989).

15. See Yoko Kawashima, "Wage Differentials Between Women and Men in Japan" (Ph.D. dissertation, Stanford University, 1983), and "The Place and Role of Female Workers in the Japanese Labor Market," *Women's Studies International Forum* 10 (6) 1987: 599–611; Mary Saso, *Women in the Japanese Workplace* (London: Hilary Shipman, 1990); Alice C. L. Lam, *Women and Japanese Management* (London: Routledge, 1992); and Mary C. Brinton, *Women and the Economic Miracle: Gender and Work in Postwar Japan* (Berkeley: University of California Press, 1993).

16. Japan Statistics Bureau, *Report on the Special Survey of the Labor Force* (Tokyo: JSB, 1981 and 1990), cited in Lam, *Women and Japanese Management*, p. 225. By exempting the first ¥1 million of spousal earnings from income tax, the Japanese tax system encourages women (who are generally the lower-earning spouse) to work part-time (up to a maximum of the exemption). See Brinton, *Women and the Economic Miracle*, p. 89.

17. Lam, *Women and Japanese Management*, p. 62, cites evidence that in some companies, if a woman is still employed full-time at age thirty, the company will begin to invest in her through on-the-job training and job rotation.

18. See Brinton, *Women and the Economic Miracle*, p. 187.

19. See Lam, *Women and Japanese Management*, p. 53.

20. Ibid., pp. 60–62.

21. For a summary of theories of occupational segregation, see Barbara F. Reskin and Heidi I. Hartmann (eds.), *Women's Work, Men's Work: Sex Segregation on the Job* (Washington, DC: National Academy Press, 1986).

22. The more disaggregated the occupations, the more occupational segregation we find and the higher the index. That is because when occupations are more aggregated, much of the segregation within those larger aggregations is not considered. The following discussion is based on the most detailed occupational breakdowns available. For the period 1900 to 1960, the U.S. segregation index remained stable at about 67 percent. See Edward Gross, "Plus Ça Change ...? The Sexual Structure of Occupations over Time," *Social Problems*, 16 (1) (Fall 1968): 198–208. However, during the 1970s and 1980s, it fell about ten or eleven percentage points. See Francine D. Blau and Marianne A. Ferber, *The Economics of Women, Men and Work* (Englewood Cliffs, NJ: Prentice-Hall, 1992), p. 127. For a fuller discussion of occupational segregation, see Myra H. Strober, "Gender and Occupational Segregation," in *The International Encyclopedia of Education* (Oxford: Pergamon Press, 1994), pp. 248–52.

23. See Brinton, *Women and the Economic Miracle*, p. 61.

24. See ibid. It is not easy to measure the index of occupational segregation in Japan, partly because "job" is not clearly defined, especially among white-collar workers. Segregation is often more discernible in terms of rank and work content within the same job category. We are grateful to Yoko Kawashima for this point.

25. For a discussion of the earnings penalty, see Joyce P. Jacobsen and Laurence M. Levin, "Effects of Intermittent Labor Force Attachment on Women's Earnings," *Monthly Labor Review*, 118 (9) (September 1995): 14–19. Myra H. Strober, in a study of MBA graduates from Stanford University, found that in the late 1970s women who had taken even a short leave from the labor force faced a large penalty in earnings. See Strober, "The MBA Degree: Same Passport to Success for Women and Men?" in Phyllis Wallace (ed.), *Women in the Workplace* (Boston: Auburn House, 1982), pp. 25–44.

26. See Blau and Ferber, *The Economics of Women, Men and Work*, p. 193. Also note their discussion of the possible pitfalls in this estimate.

27. See Kawashima, "Wage Differentials Between Women and Men in Japan," p. 164.

28. Neither the Equal Pay Act nor Title VII prevents employers from paying earnings premiums for work experience or merit.

29. See Blau and Ferber, *The Economics of Women, Men and Work*, pp. 224–27. Barbara Bergmann found there was tremendous variability from one company to another in utilization of women in management, and concluded that companies faced very little pressure from the OFCC; those changes that were made, were largely voluntary. See Bergmann, *In Defense of Affirmative Action* (New York: Basic Books, 1996), chapter 2. Policies such as these have a greater effect on women's behavior than on employer behavior. In particular, if women believe that they may be treated more fairly as a result of the policies, they may be more willing to undertake nontraditional training and apply for nontraditional jobs and promotions.

30. A random survey of ninety-four compliance reviews of the headquarters of *Fortune* 1000 companies found that in 1990, women were 6.6 percent of all managers at the level of assistant vice president or higher.

31. See Linda N. Edwards, "The Status of Women in Japan: Has the Equal Employment Opportunity Law Made a Difference?" *Journal of Asian Economics*, 5 (2) (1994): 217–40; and Lam, *Women and Japanese Management*, chapter 5. The legislation does not rely on lawsuits to achieve its ends; indeed, cutting down on lawsuits by women against employers was one of the motivations for passing the law.

32. For example, between 1981 and 1987, Ministry of Labor surveys of employers' human resource practices showed a marked decline in the number of firms admitting direct discrimination against women in recruitment, conditions of employment, job assignment, and job rotation. However, there was little improvement with regard to promotion. Also, the percentage of firms that provided equal wages for women and men recruits at both the high school and the university level increased. In 1980, only 35.5 percent of firms said they provided equal wages for women and men university recruits. By 1987, that proportion was 78.9 percent. See Lam, *Women and Japanese Management*, pp. 123–128. Finally, after 1985, the percentage of women university and four-year college graduates who found employment increased, so that by 1990, the percentages of women and men were equal at 81 percent. See Edwards, "The Status of Women in Japan," p. 228.

33. Although this two-track system existed before the EEO law, the number of firms with such systems increased rapidly after the law went into effect. Josei Shokugyo Zaidan (Women's Vocational Institute), *Kosubetsu Koyo-kanri ni Kansuru Kenkyu-kai Hokokusho* (A Survey Report on Career Tracking) (Tokyo, 1990). Cited in Edwards, "The Status of Women in Japan," p. 228; and Lam, *Women and Japanese Management*, p. 129.

34. See Edwards, "The Status of Women in Japan," pp. 228–30; and Lam, *Women and Japanese Management*, pp. 128–33. Large Japanese companies ask women and men to choose, at the time of initial employment, which track they wish to be on. In a highly controversial article, Felice N. Schwartz suggested that American companies institutionalize a two-track system in the same way. See Schwartz, "Management Women and the New Facts of Life," *Harvard Business Review*, 67 (2) (January–February 1989): 65–76. For letters to the editor in response to Schwartz, see *Harvard Business Review*, 67 (3) (May–June 1989): 182–214.

35. See "Newly Opened Corporate Career Paths Prove Rocky," *Nikkei Weekly*, February 21, 1994, cited in Lincoln and Nakata, "The Transformation of the Japanese Employment System," p. 40.

36. See Kangmin Zeng, "The Dragon Gate: The Origin and Development of the University Entrance Examinations and the Peripheral Cultures in Japan, Korea and Taiwan" (Ph.D. dissertation, Stanford University, 1996), pp. 236–37. Figures are from the Japanese Ministry of Education, *Survey of the Extracurricular Activities of Children/Students* (in Japanese), 1985, and *Report on the Survey of Issues Related to the Academic Juku* (in Japanese), 1995.

37. See Zeng, "The Dragon Gate." Recently, the Japanese system of college entrance has become more complicated, with more avenues and different sets of requirements.

38. Recently, some colleges and universities have begun offering the possibility of early application and early admissions decisions. Students participating in these programs generally take the SAT earlier than the fall of their senior year.

39. Many private universities, including Stanford, give favorable consideration to children of alumni and alumnae as well as children of faculty members. In addition, admissions committees seek to "balance" their classes geographically and to assure that there are sufficient numbers of students with the requisite talents to play in the orchestra, play on competitive athletic teams, etc.

40. See Kimi Hara, "Challenges to Education for Girls and Women in Modern Japan: Past and Present," in Kumiko Fujimura-Fanselow and Atsuko Kameda (eds.), *Japanese Women: New Feminist Perspectives on the Past, Present and Future* (New York: The Feminist Press at City University of New York, 1995), p. 98.

41. For more details, see Education Material Investigating Committee, *The History of the Educational System After the Meiji Period* (Tokyo: Education Material Investigating Committee, 1939), vol. 5, p. 375.

42. See Masako Amano (ed.), *Joshi Koto Kyoiku no Zahyo* (Tokyo: Kono Publications, 1986).

43. See Hara, "Challenges to Education ...," p. 102.

44. However, part of the increase was simply a result of a change in definitions. After World War II, the government recognized many private coed and female schools as colleges and universities.

45. Kumiko Fujimura-Fanselow, "College Women Today: Options and Dilemmas," in Fujimura-Fanselow and Kameda (eds.), *Japanese Women: New Feminist Perspectives* (New York: The Feminist Press, 1995), p. 127.

46. Interestingly, in 1965, when junior colleges were largely male (60 percent), a more varied curriculum was offered. During the 1970s, when institutions of higher education mushroomed, junior colleges became institutions especially for women and the schools altered their curricula to fit the student population.

47. Quoted in Charlotte Williams Conable, *Women at Cornell: The Myth of Equal Education* (Ithaca, NY: Cornell University Press, 1977), p. 19.

48. See Frederick Rudolph, *The American College and University: A History* (New York: Vintage Books, 1962).

49. Conway argues that the reasons why women were admitted to Oberlin were as much economic (women students did the domestic work of the college) as they were ideological. See Jill Conway, "Perspectives on the History of Women's Education in the United States," *History of Education Quarterly*, 14 (spring 1974): 1–12.

50. See Mary Frank Fox, "Women and Higher Education: Gender Differences in the Status of Students and Scholars," in Jo Freeman (ed.), *Women: A Feminist Perspective*. Mountain View, CA: Mayfield, 1995), pp. 220–37.

51. See Rudolph, *The American College and University*; and Barbara Miller Solomon, *In the Company of Educated Women* (New Haven: Yale University Press, 1985).

52. Cornell University has several colleges that are private and several that are public.

53. Several of the men's colleges that had been founded much earlier created coordinate colleges for women as a way of avoiding coeducation. For example, Harvard created the Harvard Annex in the 1880s (renamed Radcliffe College in 1894), and Brown chartered Pembroke College in 1897. See Solomon, *In the Company of Educated Women*; and Polly W. Kaufman (ed.), *The Search for Equity: Women at Brown University: 1891–1991* (Providence, RI: Trustees of Brown University, 1991).

54. In terms of degrees awarded, 54 percent of bachelor's degrees, 54 percent of master's degrees, 39 percent of professional degrees, and 37 percent of doctorates are now awarded to women. National Center for Education Statistics, *Digest of Educational Statistics* (Washington, DC: U.S. Government Printing Office, 1993).

55. For more detailed information see *Kokuritsu Kyuiku Kenkyujo* (1974): 3, 827–32.

56. Although the large representation of Tokyo graduates in ministries was common knowledge, people were shocked that in some ministries, 70 to 80 percent of the employees were from Tokyo University. Many expressed the view that reducing the representation to 50 percent was not enough. If 50 percent of the employees were still to be graduates of Tokyo University, the desire to enter Tokyo University would only escalate.

57. *Shinbun*, October 17, 1997.

58. See Takenori Matsuura, *Shushoku* (Tokyo: Nihon Keizai Shinbun, 1978); and Kijiro Miyahara, "Intercollege Stratification: The Case of Male College Graduates in Japan," *Sociological Forum*, 3 (1) (1988): 25–43.

59. The question asked was What impact has your Todai (Stanford) education had on your life?

60. Seven of the most prestigious universities started before the beginning of the Revolutionary War (1775) as colleges to train clergy and teach young men in the colonies. See Rudolph, *The American College and University*.

61. In the spring of 1977, there were 9,900 applicants for admission to Stanford's first-year class. Of these, 2,520 were admitted. Of those admitted, 62 percent enrolled (1,553). Some of those who entered in the fall of 1977 took time out from their studies ("stopped out") during the following four years and therefore graduated after 1981. Some who graduated in 1981 had actually entered before 1977 and also had "stopped out."

62. Orin L. Elliot, *Stanford University: The First Twenty-five Years* (Stanford, CA.: Stanford University Press, 1937), p. 132.

63. This trend toward equality in numbers was echoed at other Western institutions, as the number of girls graduating from high school exceeded the number of boys. At the University of California, for example, the proportion of women students increased from 27 percent in 1891 to 44 percent in 1899.

64. Elliot, *Stanford University*, p. 134. Mrs. Stanford was right in suggesting that the public had misgivings about the level of female attendance at Stanford. Concerns had been raised in the press about the number of male students at the time of a series of Stanford athletic losses to the University of California. The *Portland Oregonian* suggested: "Another objection to the present status is the increase of power among the women. They are voting themselves into

all the offices and thereby rendering the institution less desirable to male students than it otherwise would be. A woman edits the Junior annual, another brings out the weekly paper, and still another leads the inter-collegiate debate. Thus there is an alarming tendency apparent toward reducing the University to the level of a 'woman's seminary' which Mrs. Stanford very much dreads." Ibid., p. 133.

65. Ibid., p. 136.

66. Edith R. Mirrielees, *The Story of a University* (New York: G. P. Putnam, 1959).

67. J. Pearce Mitchell, *Stanford University: 1916–41* (Stanford, CA.: Trustees of Stanford University, 1958).

68. Stanford University, *Campus Reports*, June 7, 1972, p. 1.

69. Ibid., September 20, 1972, p. 2.

70. Ibid., March 14, 1973, p. 1.

Chapter 2

1. Two different questionnaires were used. A subgroup of the class had participated during their undergraduate years in a study run by Herant Katchadourian. This subgroup received the same questionnaire as the others in the class, except that it had an additional section that asked some questions in order to follow up on the original study.

2. Because all respondents were anonymous, it was not possible to match their responses with Stanford's records on entering test scores, courses taken, grades, etc.

3. Stanford did not send a second survey to nonrespondents. Strober attempted to contact a random sample of 155 nonrespondents by telephone, to ask them a few brief questions, but was able to reach only 43 percent of them.

4. Even among men engineers, the group that some might predict would be less likely to return a survey of this sort, the proportion in the sample is almost exactly equal to the proportion in the class as a whole. The only group that is somewhat underrepresented in the sample is women in the humanities.

5. The total number of graduates from the class of 1981 at Todai was 3,989, of whom 263 (6.6 percent) were women. In order to get a larger sample of women, women graduates from the classes of 1980 and 1982 were also surveyed. For men, a random sample (one out of three from each faculty) was taken from the class of 1981. The number of graduates sampled was 2,068 (1,227 men and 841 women).

6. The response from the first survey sent out was only 430, 34 percent. To increase the response rate, nonrespondents for whom we had correct addresses were called. Of these, 276 said they would not respond to the survey. The remaining 554 received a second survey and 148 returned it, for a total of 578 surveys returned from the first and second rounds combined. Of these, twenty-three men and eleven women were not in the correct Todai class. Thus the final sample included 544 respondents, 179 women and 365 men.

7. Graduates from the faculty of law do not generally practice law. Many students major in law with no intention of becoming a lawyer.

8. Only among African Americans was there a gender difference; there were three African-American men in the sample (0.75 percent of all men in the sample) and ten African-American women (3 percent of all women in the sample).

9. Two men and two women living with partners had at least one child. Since we did not ask about sexual orientation in the survey, we do not know whether these graduates were in same-sex or opposite-sex partnerships.

10. There appear to be stronger norms in Japan than in the United States about when during the life cycle marriage and childbearing should take place. Mary Brinton shows that Japanese women are more likely than U.S. women to marry in their twenties and to have children when they are aged between twenty-five and thirty-four, and particularly between twenty-five and twenty-nine. See Mary Brinton, *Women and the Economic Miracle* (Berkeley: Univeristy of California Press, 1993), pp. 30–32.

11. Over time, the student body at Tokyo University has become progressively less "upper class." According to the Japanese Ministry of Education, in 1885, 48.1 percent of students at Todai were commoners, 51.7 percent were from the samurai class, and 0.2 percent were from the nobility. This represented a large change from 1878, when 25.5 percent were commoners, 73.9 percent were from the samurai class, and 0.6 percent were from the nobility. Cited in Kangmin Zeng, "The Dragon Gate" (Ph.D. dissertation, Stanford University, 1996), p. 39.

12. These data are useful for understanding the graduates in the sample, but should not be used to generalize to the population of graduates from the two institutions. It may well be that nonrespondents' social class differed significantly from that of respondents, since graduates who have been relatively unsuccessful may have been less willing to fill out the survey and return it.

13. It may also be that Japanese respondents felt it was "bad form" to report a high social class standing.

14. Using education level to measure social class mobility, stability of social class is also seen in the U.S. population as a whole. Among women and men in the United States who were high school sophomores in 1980 (a cohort about five years younger than the Stanford graduates), twelve years later, about 54 percent of those whose parents had only a high school degree also had only a high school degree. See Michael J. Mandel, "The Great Equalizer," *Business Week*, July 22, 1996, p. 74.

15. Within each of these faculties there are different departments that allow students to concentrate on their field of interest. Students generally stay in the faculty that they enter. The faculties listed are those the graduates belonged to in their senior year.

16. To enter the law faculty, one must first have been in Humanities 1; to enter the economics faculty, one must first have been in Humanities 2; students in the faculties of letters, education, and liberal arts were first in Humanities 3. In the sciences, Science 1 and 2 lead to the natural sciences and engineering, and Science 3 leads to the medical faculty.

17. The faculty of law is different from law schools in the United States. Students studying in the faculty of law do not necessarily go on to be lawyers. Many of them do not even take the bar exam. These graduates may enter government or take other kinds of white-collar jobs.

18. The distribution of faculties for the women closely resemble the results obtained by the 1985 survey of Todai alumnae. See Satsuki-Kai, *Female Graduates of Tokyo University: Life Report* (Tokyo: Sanshodo, 1989).
   The faculties of the Todai men were in many respects quite similar to those of men graduating from other colleges and universities in Japan at that time, although the proportion majoring in the social sciences was lower for Todai than for the rest (38.8 percent for the men from Todai, 47.9 percent for men nationwide). This is in part because the business fac-

ulty is included in the social science category for the country as a whole, but no Todai graduates were in a business faculty. Among all men graduating from four-year colleges and universities in Japan in 1980, 47.9 percent were in the social sciences, including business and law; 3.4 percent were in science and math; 7.4 percent were in the humanities; and 24.6 percent were in engineering. See Linda Edwards, "The Status of Women in Japan," *Journal of Asian Economics*, 5 (2) (1994): 224. It is interesting that the percentage of men engineering graduates in the Todai class, 25.3 percent, was virtually identical with the percentage nationwide, 24.6 percent. Todai men were more likely to be in science (7.6 percent) than their fellow male graduates nationwide (3.4 percent).

Among women, however, Todai graduates showed more difference from their counterparts at other universities. Todai women were less likely to major in education and the humanities than other women graduates at that time, and somewhat more likely to be in science, math, and engineering. Among all women graduates in 1980, 18.1 percent were in the faculty of education, compared with 9.0 percent of women Todai graduates (classes of 1980–82), and 35.9 percent of all women graduates were in the faculty of humanities, compared with 24.5 percent of Todai women graduates. Among all women graduates, 2.2 percent were in the faculty of science or math and 1.3 percent in engineering. Among Todai women graduates, 4.6 percent were in the faculties of science and math, and 4.6 percent in engineering.

19. Although the engineering school is separate from the school of humanities and sciences, students are admitted to the university as a whole, and are not asked to designate engineering (or anything else) as a major before they arrive.

20. Jaelim Oh, in her 1992 dissertation from Stanford University, "Gender Differences in Patterns of Changing College Major" (tables 2.14 and 2.15), calculated the transition probabilities between field of first declared major and field of conferred major for women and men Stanford graduates in the class of 1989. The transition probabilities were high (meaning that most students' conferred major was the same as their first declared major), and ranged from .92 in engineering to .78 in humanities. The only gender difference was in the field of human biology, where men were more likely to stay in the field than women.

21. The similarity by gender for social science as a whole, however, masks considerable differences by discipline. For example, among men, 60 percent of the social science majors were in economics, whereas for women, only 40 percent of the social science majors were in economics.

22. Oh, "Gender Differences in Patterns of Changing College Major," table 2.9, reported that for the class of 1989, 13 percent of the women, but only 5 percent of the men, majored in human biology.

23. For the class of 1989 at Stanford, among women 10 percent of the graduates majored in engineering; among men, 26 percent majored in that field. Ibid.

The distribution of Stanford graduates across majors was very different from other graduates getting bachelor's degrees in the United States in 1980–81. Almost 60 percent of bachelor's degrees for women and about 40 percent of bachelor's degrees for men in 1980–81 were awarded in subjects not available as undergraduate majors at Stanford. Agriculture, home economics, business, and education were among these majors.

If we compare only those Stanford graduates and all college and university graduates who majored in four fields (engineering, humanities, natural sciences and math, and social sciences), we find that the distributions across the four areas were very similar for the two groups of men. Among the women, however, Stanford women were much more likely to major in engineering and much less likely to major in the humanities, compared with all women bachelor's degree recipients. See U.S. Department of Education, *Digest of Educational Statistics* (Washington, DC: U.S. Government Printing Office, 1983). This pattern for Stanford women compared with all U.S. women is similar to the pattern for Todai women compared with all Japanese women. Compared with their counterparts in their own country, both Stanford and Todai women were more likely to major in engineering (a nontraditional field for women) and less likely to major in the humanities (the more traditional course of study for women).

24. The percentage that obtained an advanced degree was smaller than the percentage that enrolled in postbaccalaureate programs sometime during the prior nine years. Four-fifths of the men and 70 percent of the women had attended postbaccalaureate programs.

25. Among the Stanford respondents, ten men and eleven women (2.5 percent of the men and 3.3 percent of the women) indicated that at the time of the survey they were enrolled as full-time graduate students. In the Todai sample, five men and seven women (1.4 percent of the men and 3.9 percent of the women) were enrolled as full-time graduate students.

26. Although teachers do not earn a high salary, teaching is a stable profession for women in Japan. It allows women with family commitments better hours and longer holidays. The majority of high-school teachers are men, and women teachers are the majority in primary schools. Graduates from Tokyo University are welcomed by high-level private schools and as lecturers in *jukus* (preparatory schools for entrance examinations). Flower arrangement and handwriting teaching certificates allow women to open classes on their own. Although many women learn the arts as a prerequisite for marriage and refinement, these certificates also provide the insurance of a job when needed.

27. One of the part-time women homemakers had no children. The man who specified his occupation as homemaker had no children of his own but was raising his stepchild and was not employed.

28. These distinctions are clearly arbitrary. Many of the other women and men in the sample were also part-time homemakers. However, they did not designate their occupation as homemaker.

29. Determining who was a full-time homemaker was difficult, proving once again that people's lives are more complex than bureaucratic categories. The usual definition of a full-time homemaker is someone who is married, is not employed for pay (and therefore has no earned income), and is not seeking work. There were eight women in the Stanford sample who categorized themselves as homemakers whom we kept in that category even though they had earned income. Five of them earned $4,000 or less. Three had earned between $30,000 and $68,000 when they were employed but were currently on child care leave. Of the sixteen whom we removed from the homemaker category, two were attending school and the remainder had earnings greater than $4,000. In the Todai sample, all of the women who classified themselves as homemakers remained in that category for our analyses. Four of these women did not have children. In the Stanford sample, all of the homemakers had children.

30. Japanese women are much less likely than American women to be administrators or managers. In the late 1980s, women were 8.8 percent of workers in this category in Japan, but 39.8 percent in the United States. International Labour Organization, *Yearbook of Labor Statistics, 1990–91* (Geneva: ILO, 1991). In 1990, in companies with more than 1,000 employees, less than 1 percent of women were department heads (*bucho*), compared with 2.7 percent of men, and only 1.2 percent of women were group leaders (*kacho* and *kakaricho*), compared with 6.7 percent of men. See Clair Brown, Yoshifumi Nakata, Michael Reich, and Lloyd Ullman, *Work and Pay in the United States and Japan,* (New York: Oxford University Press, 1997), chapter 5.

31. It is well known that Stanford students do not go on to be professors to the same extent that graduates of other selective research universities do.

32. Comparisons of the index across the two samples should be made cautiously, since the occupational categories are not exactly the same, although the numbers of occupational categories are similar. For seven managerial occupations and twenty-four professional and technical occupations in Japan, Brinton calculated indices of segregation of 34.0 and 61.1, respectively. The index of segregation for the Todai graduates lies within this range. Similarly, Brinton calculated indices of segregation for the same groups of occupations in the United States that were 16.2 for managerial occupations and 54.3 for professional and technical occupations. The index of segregation for the Stanford graduates lies within this range. See Brinton, *Women and the Economic Miracle*, pp. 57–61.

33. From here on, the term "employed" includes those who are self-employed.

34. Some graduates provided information on hours but not on income. For these, we were able to designate whether they were full-time or part-time earners. Graduates who provided information on income but not on hours were listed as employed, but unclear as to whether full-time or part-time. Graduates who listed an occupation but provided data on neither income nor hours were listed as missing.

35. However, the labor force participation rate for Stanford women was in line with the U.S. rate for women twenty-five to thirty-four with four years of college (83.1 percent). The U.S. rate for those with five or more years of postsecondary education was 87.2 percent. See Daphne Spain and Susan M. Bianchi, *Balancing Act: Motherhood, Marriage, and Employment Among American Women* (New York: Russell Sage, 1996), p. 67.

36. See Japan Statistics Bureau, *Japan Statistical Yearbook* (Tokyo: JSB, 1993), table 3.2, p. 85.

37. In 1990, there were 30,485,000 women twenty-five to fifty-four working full-time and 7,584,000 women in that age group working part-time. See U.S. Department of Labor, Bureau of Labor Statistics, *Employment and Earnings*, January 1991, Table 7, p. 171. Among employed men twenty-five to fifty-four, 4 percent worked part-time.

38. Joyce P. Jacobsen and Laurence M. Levin, "Effects of Intermittent Labor Force Attachment on Women's Earnings," *Monthly Labor Review*, 118 (9) (September 1995): 14–19, estimate that for a woman who is a college graduate, a seven-year hiatus in employment results in an earnings penalty that is the equivalent of three years of lost earnings over the twenty years after she returns to the labor market. For Japanese women, the penalties for interrupted employment are even greater than for U.S. women, since it takes them altogether out of the running for the more lucrative positions.

39. It may be that some women who became full-time homemakers nonetheless received an important economic return from their investment in their education by being able to marry particularly well. Claudia Goldin, "Career and Family: College Women Look to the Past," in Francine Blau and Ronald Ehrenberg, eds., *Gender and Family Issues in the Workplace* (New York: Russell Sage, 1997), p. 41, found that because attending college increased the probability of marrying a college graduate, U.S. women college graduates who married in the 1950s had husbands who earned 40 percent more than the husbands of women who did not graduate from college. Perhaps the marriage premium that Goldin found for the average U.S. woman college graduate of the 1950s still existed for the Todai and Stanford women graduates of the early 1980s.

Chapter 3

1. There are some important wrinkles in this theory. Education is seen to raise productivity (and hence earnings) for one's entire work life. But not so for work experience, which is a

proxy for on-the-job training. A year of work experience in early career is seen as making a larger contribution to productivity than a year of experience later in life. That is, at some point there are considered to be diminishing returns to work experience.

2. For a review of these theories, see Myra H. Strober, "Human Capital Theory: Implications for HR Managers," in Daniel J. B. Mitchell and Mahmood A. Zaidi (eds.), *The Economics of Human Resource Management* (Oxford: Basil Blackwell, 1990), pp. 60–85.

3. See Lester C. Thurow, "Education and Economic Equality," *The Public Interest*, 28 (Summer 1972): 66–81; and Michael Spence, "Job Market Signalling," *Quarterly Journal of Economics*, 87 (1973): 355–74.

4. See James L. Medoff and Katharine G. Abraham, "Are Those Paid More Really More Productive: The Case of Experience," *Journal of Human Resources*, 16 (Spring 1981): 186–216; and their "Experience, Performance and Earnings," *Quarterly Journal of Economics*, 95 (December 1980): 703–36.

5. See Edward P. Lazear and Robert L. Moore, "Incentives, Productivity, and Labor Contracts," *Quarterly Journal of Economics*, 77 (May 1984): 275–95.

6. The idea that women choose fields that have a low penalty for dropping out of the work-force to raise a family has been put forth by Jacob Mincer and Solomon Polachek, "Family Investments in Human Capital: Earnings of Women," *Journal of Political Economy*, 82 (2) (March/April 1974): S76–S108. Harriet Zellner argued that because women expect to leave the labor force to raise children, they choose jobs with higher entry earnings even though these jobs may have less potential for advancement. See Zellner, "The Determinants of Occupational Segregation," in Cynthia B. Lloyd (ed.), *Sex Discrimination and the Division of Labor* (New York: Columbia University Press, 1975), pp. 125–45.

7. See Randall Filer, "The Role of Personality and Tastes in Determining Occupational Structure," *Industrial and Labor Relations Review*, 39 (April 1986): 412–24.

8. For a review of empirical findings that contradict the human capital speculations, see Paula England, George Farkas, Barbara Stanek Kilbourne, and Thomas Dou, "Explaining Occupational Sex Segregation and Wages: Findings from a Model with Fixed Effects," *American Sociological Review*, 62 (August 1988): 544–58.

9. See Gary S. Becker, "Human Capital, Effort and the Sexual Division of Labor," *Journal of Labor Economics*, 3 (January 1985): S33–S58.

10. See Denise D. Bielby and William T. Bielby," She Works Hard for the Money: Household Responsibilities and the Allocation of Work Effort," *American Journal of Sociology*, 93 (March 1988): 1031–59.

11. These issues are part of the debate on equal pay for work of comparable value (often called the comparable worth or the pay equity debate.) For a comprehensive discussion of the issues, see Robert T. Michael, Heidi I. Hartmann, and Brigid O'Farrell (eds.), *Pay Equity: Empirical Inquiries* (Washington, DC: National Academy Press, 1989).

12. See Gary Becker, *The Economics of Discrimination* (Chicago: University of Chicago Press, 1957). In fact, although Becker first brought the possibility of employer discrimination into the economics literature, he does not believe that employers discriminate. He argues that in the long run, economic competition in fact prevents employers from indulging their prejudices. Any nonprejudiced employer who hires more women at the lower wage would be able to reduce labor costs and charge lower prices. Such employers would force discriminating

employers to stop discriminating or go out of business. However, since discrimination does appear to persist, explanations to reconcile reality and theory are necessary. There are several possible reconciliations: either the economy is insufficiently competitive, or there are no nondiscriminating employers, or the economy has simply not yet reached the "long run."

13. See Edmund Phelps, "The Statistical Theory of Racism and Sexism," *American Economic Review*, 62 (September 1972): 659–61.

14. See Peter B. Doeringer and Michael J. Piore, *Internal Labor Markets and Manpower Analysis* (Lexington, MA: D. C. Heath, 1971).

15. See Paul Osterman, "White-Collar Internal Labor Markets," in Paul Osterman (ed.), *Internal Labor Markets* (Cambridge, MA: MIT Press, 1984), pp. 163–89.

16. See Doeringer and Piore, *Internal Labor Markets and Manpower Analysis*; Michael J. Piore, "Notes for a Theory of Labor Market Stratification," in Richard C. Edwards, Michael Reich, and David M. Gordon (eds.), *Labor Market Segmentation* (Lexington, MA: D. C. Heath, 1975), pp. 125–50; Richard C. Edwards, "The Social Relations of Production in the Firm and Labor Market Structure," in Edwards, Reich, and Gordon, *Labor Market Segmentation*, pp. 3–26; Richard C. Edwards, *Contested Terrain* (New York: Basic Books, 1979); David M. Gordon, Richard C. Edwards, and Michael Reich, *Segmented Work, Divided Workers: The Historical Transformation of Labor in the United States* (New York: Cambridge University Press, 1982).

17. Because the job market is segregated by race and education as well as gender, not all men get first choice of occupations. Rather, within race and educational categories, men are permitted to choose before women do.

18. See Myra H. Strober, "Toward a General Theory of Occupational Sex Segregation: The Case of Public School Teaching," in Barbara F. Reskin (ed.), *Sex Segregation in the Workplace: Trends, Explanations, Remedies* (Washington, DC: National Academy Press, 1984), pp. 144–56; Myra H. Strober and Carolyn Arnold, "The Dynamics of Occupational Segregation Among Banktellers," in Clair Brown and Joseph Pechman (eds.), *Gender in the Workplace* (Washington, DC: Brookings Institution, 1987), pp. 107–57.

19. See Myra H. Strober, "The Relative Attractiveness Theory of Occupational Segregation: The Case of Women in Medicine," in *Proceedings of the Annual Meetings of the Industrial and Labor Relations Research Association, Fall 1992*, pp. 42–50.

20. See chapter 2, note 32, on occupational segregation in the United States and Japan.

21. For Stanford graduates who were full-time employed, the median earnings for women were $45,000 and the median earnings for men were $56,000. The female/male earnings ratio based on these medians was 80 percent. For the Todai graduates, the median earnings for women were ¥5 million and the median for men was ¥6.5 million, yielding a female/male earnings ratio of 76.9 percent.

22. What is somewhat surprising is that in the United States, but not in Japan, the female/male earnings ratio was lower (*less* unequal) among college graduates than for the labor force as a whole (61 percent compared with 69 percent).

23. All of the Japanese earnings listed in the table include annual special earnings (such as summer and year-end bonuses) as well as scheduled and unscheduled contractual earnings.

24. There are no published data on total earnings for this group. Although there are published data for average monthly scheduled earnings for college- and university-educated women and men age 25–34, there are no published data for the other two components of earnings: unscheduled monthly contract earnings and annual special earnings.

Taking the published data on scheduled monthly contract earnings, we added estimates of unscheduled contract earnings and annual special earnings based on the percentages that unscheduled contract earnings and annual special earnings were of the total earnings of all college and university graduates.

Using monthly scheduled earnings alone as an estimate of earnings not only understates total earnings but also overstates the female/male earnings ratio (makes it look more equal than it is). Because men are more likely than women to have substantial bonuses and other special earnings, the gender difference in total earnings is larger than the gender difference in monthly contract earnings. For example, for all university and college graduates, men's annual special earnings added 36.2 percent to men's total contractual earnings, whereas women's special earnings added only 25.2 percent to women's total contractual earnings. As a result, for all university and college graduates, although the female/male earnings ratio of monthly contract earnings was 66 percent, the female/male earnings ratio for total earnings was only 63 percent.

The published data on scheduled monthly contract earnings are for university and college graduates 25–29 and 30–34, separately for women and men. We aggregated these by weighting each by the number of persons in each category. We then multiplied the men's scheduled contract earnings by 1.07927 to obtain total contract earnings and then by 1.362 to obtain total earnings including annual special earnings. For women, the multiplicative factors were 1.0793529 and 1.252, respectively. In all cases, these multiplicative factors were obtained from the published data on all college and university graduates.

25. To put these ratios in perspective, note that for the United States as a whole in 1989, mean earnings of men college and university graduates were about 1.8 times mean earnings of men high school graduates, and mean earnings of women college and university graduates were about 1.7 times the earnings of women high school graduates. U.S. Department of Commerce, Bureau of the Census, Current Population Reports, Consumer Income, Series P-60, *Money Income of Households, Families and Persons in the United States: 1988 and 1989* (Washington, DC: Bureau of the Census, 1991), table 24, pp. 102–03.

26. To put these comparisons into perspective, it is interesting to note that in Japan as a whole in 1990, men who were university and college graduates earned 1.27 times the earnings of men who were high school graduates, and women who were university and college graduates earned 1.39 times the earnings of women high school graduates. See Japanese Ministry of Labour, *Year Book of Labour Statistics, 1990* (Tokyo: The Ministry, 1990), table 95, p. 146. These ratios are smaller than those for the United States given in note 22. Yoshio Higuchi, "Higher Education and Income Distribution in Japan," Discussion Paper, Keio University, 1994, notes that since the late 1980s, unlike other industrialized countries, Japan has not witnessed an increase in the earnings differentials by education levels.

27. The difference in the Stanford women's and men's earnings distributions was at the extremes; the interquartile range was virtually the same ($36,000 for the full-time men and $31,000 for the full-time women).

28. For example, in 1989, the average number of hours worked in manufacturing was 38.5 in the United States and 42.9 in Japan. Bank of Japan, *International Comparative Statistics, 1990*, as cited in Takatoshi Ito, *The Japanese Economy* (Cambridge, MA: MIT Press, 1994), p. 229. In 1991, the average Japanese worker was employed for 2,044 hours a year, about 200 more than the average U.S. worker. "Hatarakisugi kara nukedasutameni" (Escaping from Overwork), *Asahi Shimbun*, December 29, 1991, p. 2, as cited in Kumiko Fujimura-Fanselow and Atsuko Kameda, "The Changing Portrait of Japanese Men," in Kumiko Fujimura-Fanselow and Atsuko Kameda (eds.), *Japanese Women: New Feminist Perspectives* (New York: The Feminist Press at the City University of New York, 1995), p. 229.

29. We appreciate Clair Brown's suggestion on this point.

30. We tried two alternative specifications of the earnings regressions. In the first, we substituted type of graduate degree for occupation. In both the Todai and Stanford samples, the regression "fit," as measured by the adjusted R-square, was better using the occupational dummies.

Among those who were employed full-time, in the Stanford samples and in the sample of Todai women, major or faculty was not a significant determinant of earnings. For Todai men, faculty was significantly related to earnings. We ran regressions with the log of earnings as the dependent variable and years of work experience, hours of employment, and a series of dummy variables representing major or faculty as the independent variables. The reference group was those in the natural sciences or mathematics. In the Stanford regressions for women and men, none of the dummy variables was significant and the adjusted R-squares were both 0.05. In the Todai regression for women, none of the dummy variables was significant and the adjusted R-square was 0.15. In the regression for Todai men, the adjusted R-square was relatively high, 0.24, and several dummy variables were significant. Todai men from the faculties of economics, law, and medicine had significantly higher earnings than those from natural sciences and mathematics, and those from education had significantly lower earnings.

31. In the Stanford regressions, we removed two "outliers" from the analyses, one woman and one man whose earnings were so high that they distorted the regression results. In the Todai regressions, we also removed two outliers, a woman who reported working 122 hours a week and a man whose income was exceedingly high.

32. Economists have used the natural logarithm of earnings as the dependent variable in earnings regressions since Jacob Mincer showed a better statistical fit with such regressions. See Jacob Mincer, *Schooling, Experience and Earnings* (New York: National Bureau of Economic Research, 1974).

33. Because the Todai term finishes about 11 weeks earlier in the year than the Stanford term, Todai graduates generally begin work 11 weeks earlier in the year than Stanford graduates. If graduates from both institutions had begun work immediately upon graduation and had worked continually until the survey date, Stanford graduates would have worked 13 months more than Todai graduates.

34. We are grateful to Lawrence Kahn for suggesting this specification.

35. See Yoko Kawashima, "Female Workers: An Overview of Past and Current Trends," in Kumiko Fujimura-Fanselow and Atsuko Kameda (eds.), *Japanese Women: New Feminist Perspectives* (New York: The Feminist Press at the City University of New York, 1995), p. 278.

36. In interpreting the coefficients on the occupational dummies, it is important to remember that among all Stanford men earners, the reference group is the 25 percent of the sample whose occupations are not listed; among all Stanford women earners, the reference group is the 37 percent of those whose occupations are not listed. Among full-time workers, the reference group for Stanford men is the 22 percent of the sample whose occupations are not listed, and for Stanford women, the 31 percent of the sample whose occupations are not listed. For the Todai samples, the reference groups were much larger than for the Stanford samples. Among all earners, the reference group for men was 58 percent of the sample, and for women it was 50 percent of the sample. Among full-time earners, the reference group for men was 51 percent of the sample, and for women it was 53 percent of the sample.

37. See Gary S. Becker, "Human Capital, Effort and the Sexual Division of Labor," *Journal of Labor Economics*, 3 (January 1985): S33–S58; and Victor Fuchs, "Women's Quest for Economic Equality," *Journal of Economic Perspectives*, 3 (January 1985): 25–41.

38. In U.S. studies, even after controlling for education and work experience, researchers find that women with children earn about 10 to 15 percent less than women without children, while married men, most of whom have children, earn about 10 to 15 percent *more* than other men. Based on 1991 data, regressions for young men and women that held constant experience, education, race, and marital status found that women with two or more children earned 11 percent less than other women, and men with two or more children earned 4 percent more than other men. See Jane Waldfogel, "Understanding the 'Family Gap' in Pay for Women and Children," *Journal of Economic Perspectives*, 12 (Winter 1998): 137–56.

39. In general for the United States, OLS regressions that include work experience measures do not find that the presence of children negatively affects mothers' earnings. However, Sanders Korenman and David Neumark argue that the presence of children may indirectly affect mothers' earnings through a reduction in work experience. "Marriage, Motherhood and Wages," *Journal of Human Resources*, 27 (Spring 1992): 233–55. In our study, this is not the case among full-time earners where, in both samples, men and women have virtually identical years of full-time work experience. However, in the Todai sample of all earners, women have about a year less of full-time work experience, and thus children may have indirectly affected women's earnings in that sample. Also, as we shall see in table 4.12, in some of the samples children negatively affect the hours their parents work, and that may indirectly negatively affect parents' earnings.

40. Todai men and women were much more likely than all Japanese men and women to be employed in a firm with more than 500 employees and to be employed by government. Two-thirds of Todai men and one-third of Todai women worked in a firm with more than 500 employees, compared with 26 percent of all men and 21 percent of all women. Seventeen percent of Todai men and 24 percent of Todai women worked for the government, compared with 11 percent of all men and 10 percent of all women. *Labor Force Survey*, 1990.

41. In economic terms, the higher capital/labor ratios increase marginal physical product, and the economies of scale increase marginal revenue product.

42. For a review of other theories on the relationship between employer size and earnings, see Kevin T. Reilly, "Human Capital and Information: The Employer Size–Wage Effect," *Journal of Human Resources*, 30 (Winter 1995): 3–4.

43. Graduates from social classes with high mean earnings also tended to have high mean nonwage income. However, because many graduates did not answer the question about nonwage income, we need to be careful in our interpretation of those data. In the Todai sample, so few answered the question that we provide no analysis of the data. Data on nonwage income for Stanford graduates are in table 3A.2. Note that graduates who responded that they had zero nonwage income are included in the calculation of mean nonwage income.

Among the Stanford men, those from the upper class had mean nonwage income of $66,667, two-thirds higher than the mean nonwage income for all Stanford men ($39,756). Stanford women from the lower middle class had mean nonwage income of $51,643, almost two-thirds higher than the mean nonwage income for all Stanford women ($31,550).

The distribution of nonwage income across the groups by social class origin was even more unequal than the distribution of earnings across these groups. Stanford men from the upper class had mean earnings that were almost 1.4 times higher than the mean earnings of all men. But the mean nonwage income for men from the upper class ($66,667) was about 1.7 times higher than the mean nonwage income for all Stanford men ($39,756).

Nonwage income may be a return on inherited or gifted assets and/or on assets purchased with one's own or one's spouse's income. In the case of the Stanford women from the lower middle class, it is much more likely that they purchased their assets than that they inherited them or received them as gifts. In the case of the Stanford men from the upper class, we simply do not know the proportion of nonwage income that came from inherited or gifted assets. However, the fact that both the men from the upper class and the women from the lower middle class had assets about two-thirds higher than the mean for their same-sex classmates, and incomes about 30–40 percent higher than their same-sex classmates, suggests that for the Stanford men, too, the assets producing the nonwage income may well have come from their own purchases rather than through inheritance or gift.

44. Japanese earnings for men in large companies are an excellent example of efficiency wage theory, as explained earlier in this chapter.

45. The earnings penalties were larger for having children than for being married. For example, for all workers, of the 0.2048 demographic differences in coefficients, 0.01254 was attributable to having children. For full-time earners, of the 0.1032 demographic difference, 0.0835 was attributable to having children.

Appendix to Chapter 3

1. See United Nations, Department for Economic and Social Information and Policy Analysis, Statistical Division, *Statistical Yearbook, 1993* (New York: United Nations, 1995), table 21, pp. 160 and 168.

2. Purchasing power parities tell us what it would cost to buy the food, clothing, shelter, medical care, transportation and communication services, and education and recreational services in the two countries. See Organization for Economic Cooperation and Development (OECD), Statistics Directorate, *Purchasing Power Parities and Real Expenditures, 1990*, vol. 2 (Geneva: OECD, 1991), table 1.8, p. 37.

3. For women, the Stanford/Todai ratios are about four percentage points higher using median rather than mean earnings ratios. For men, they are about six percentage points higher.

4. If the regression coefficients based on those who are employed do not generalize to the entire sample, there is said to be sample selection bias. Sample selection bias should not be confused with nonrespondent bias. Nonrespondent bias concerns generalizability to those who did not respond to the survey. Sample selection bias concerns generalizability to those who responded to the survey but were not included in the regression sample, either because they were not employed or because they failed to provide information about their earnings, work experience, or hours of employment.

5. Sigma is the square root of the variance of the error term in the generalized tobit model. Rho is the correlation of the error term in the probit regression and the error term in the generalized tobit model. Although Heckman's two-stage model is frequently used to correct regression coefficients for sample selection bias, there is a good deal of controversy about these estimates. See, for example, Julie A. Schaffner, "The Sensitivity of Wage Equation Estimates for a Developing Country to Changes in Sample Selection Mode Specification," Stanford University, 1995 (processed). We decided to use the generalized tobit model to examine possible sample selection bias because it provides more valid standard errors than the Heckman method.

6. For the Stanford women, the probit regression to predict full-time labor force participation (214 positive observations out of 306 total observations) included five variables, all of which were significant. The first four were negatively associated with full-time labor force

participation: a dummy variable for being married, a dummy variable for having children, a dummy variable for coming from the upper class, and a dummy variable for being a student. The fifth was positively related to being in the labor force: having a graduate degree. For predicting total labor force participation, both full-time and part-time (258 positive observations out of 301 total observations), we excluded the student dummy variable. Being a parent and coming from the upper class were significant and negative; having a graduate degree was significant and positive. Being married was not significant.

For the Todai women, to predict full-time labor force participation (71 positive observations out of a total of 138 total observations), we used two dummy variables, being married and having children. Having children was significant and negative; being married was not significant. To predict both full-time and part-time labor force participation, the only variable in the probit regression was a dummy variable for having a graduate degree, which was significant and positive.

7. In fact, the gender difference in means could be weighted by the female coefficients and the gender difference in coefficients could be weighted by the male means. However, its has become conventional to use the weighting system we have used.

8. Some economists agree that women and men may be differentially influenced by "society" in their choices about education, hours of employment, work experience, and occupation, but that such differential influence can be seen only as "societal" discrimination for which employers have no responsibility. Exactly how society and employers are to be distinguished is never made clear, but the point these economists make is that the particular employer for whom the man or woman works should be held blameless with respect to the gender difference in means.

9. For example, suppose employers discriminate and there are very few women in an occupation or firm. That will have an effect on women's choices to apply for employment in that occupation or firm. Women may think that since the likelihood of getting such employment is small, going through the application process is simply too costly. Or they may think that working in such an occupation or firm would be too costly in terms of either possible opprobrium from friends and family or actual harassment, or both.

10. Of course, motivation and assessment of ability may also be affected by employer discrimination. A woman's motivation may be sapped by an employment situation that involves sexual harassment; or individual excellence may be assessed in a discriminatory fashion by a discriminatory supervisor.

11. See Ronald L. Oaxaca and Michael R. Ransom, "Identification in Detailed Wage Decompositions," unpublished paper, department of Economics, University of Arizona (October 1995).

12. An illustration of the process of calculating the numbers in table 3A.1 follows. If we look at table 3.4, we see that Todai men in the full-time-earner regression were employed 52.1 hours per week (52.13468 hours per week, before rounding off), while Todai women in the full-time-earner regression were employed 47.2 hours per week (47.21127 hours per week before rounding off). Part of the reason why Todai men earned more than Todai women was that Todai men were employed, on average, 4.92341 hours per week more than Todai women.

At the same time, if we look at table 3.5, we see that for Todai men the coefficient on the hours of employment variable was 0.003 (0.00348881 before rounding off), while the coefficient for women was 0.01 (0.010341 before rounding off). Todai men's return on an hour of employment was less than Todai women's return by 0.00685219 percentage point. This difference in returns to an hour of work made a negative contribution to the gender difference in Todai earnings.

If we multiply the difference in mean hours of employment (4.92341) by the coefficient on hours in the men's regression, (0.00348881), we find that the gender difference in mean hours worked made a contribution of 0.0172 to the total gender difference in earnings. That number is in the bottom half of table 3A.1, in the Hours row of the column labeled "Means" for Todai II.

If we multiply the gender difference in coefficients on the hours variable (-0.00685219) by the women's mean hours of employment (47.21127), we get -0.3235, which may be found in the Hours row in the column labeled "Coefficients" under the Todai II decomposition.

Chapter 4

1. While it is possible that a few of the men and women in the two samples happen to be married to one another, it is important to remember that by and large, the mothers and fathers whose responses we are analyzing in this chapter are *not* married to one another. While men as well as women can be full-time homemakers and, in fact, one man in the Stanford sample was a full-time homemaker, men full-time homemakers are still quite rare. The discussion here relates only to women.

2. In order to make the Stanford and Todai data comparable, Stanford graduates who were living with a partner were not included in the analyses.

3. We use the terms "two-earner", "two-career", and "dual-earner" synonymously.

4. For further discussion of these theories, see Gary S. Becker, Elisabeth M. Landes, and Robert T. Michael, "An Economic Analysis of Marital Instability," *Journal of Political Economy* 85 (6) (December 1977): 1141–87; Paula England and George Farkas, *Households, Employment and Gender: A Social, Economic and Demographic View* (Hawthorne, NY: Aldine, 1986); and Frances K. Goldscheider and Linda J. Waite, *New Families, No Families?* (Berkeley: University of California Press, 1991).

5. Janice Steil and Karen Weltman, "Marital Inequality," *Sex Roles*, 24 (February 1991): 161–179.

6. In her consulting work, Myra has been told repeatedly by both managers and their bosses about the importance of staying later than one's immediate supervisor. Putting in face time is said to show commitment to the work organization.

7. The "rub" comes if there is a divorce and the woman can no longer share equally in the fruits of the career that has been favored.

8. And, of course, there is a vicious circle that operates here. Women do not gain access to the better jobs in part because they quit good jobs to follow their husbands. This makes it difficult for any particular woman to advance and also makes employers less willing to give the better jobs to married women, for fear that they will leave to further their husbands' careers. The more that women do not gain access to these jobs, the more their gaining access becomes less likely.

9. See Bina Agarwal, *A Field of One's Own* (Cambridge: Cambridge University Press, 1994) and "Bargaining and Gender Relations," *Feminist Economics*, 3 (1) (1997): 1–51.

10. See Wenda O'Reilly, "Where Equal Opportunity Fails" (Ph.D. diss., Stanford University, 1983). Also see Rhona Mahoney, *Kidding Ourselves* (New York: Basic Books, 1995).

11. Interestingly, none of the Stanford women living with a partner had ever turned down a career opportunity for her partner.

12. Given the type of employment that most Todai men have, it would be exceedingly difficult for them to limit their career for their spouse's sake. For Japanese men who work in the primary labor market (in large and medium firms and for the government), there would be an enormous penalty for turning down an employer's request to transfer. In the primary labor market, acceding to one's employer's "requests" for transfer is part of the price one pays for the benefit of lifetime employment.

13. Myra Dinnerstein, in her book on women's lives, describes the large differences between "career homemakers," those who make a commitment to full-time, long-term domesticity, and homemakers who consider their homemaking to be full-time but temporary. See *Women Between Two Worlds* (Philadelphia: Temple University Press, 1992).

14. On the prestige of Japanese homemakers, see Joy Hendry, "The Role of the Professional Housewife," in Janet Hunter, ed., *Japanese Women Working* (London: Routledge, 1993): "Housework and the care of children has undoubtedly always been a part of the working life of Japanese women, as it is part of the lives of most women, but in few parts of the world have these roles been granted the importance and status they have acquired in Japan" (p. 224). Mary Brinton, *Women and the Economic Miracle* (Berkeley: University of California Press, 1993), p. 94, points out that the largest association of Japanese women is the Shufuren, an association of housewives.

15. The following quotation will give American readers a flavor of the expectations for Japanese mothers: "Japanese mothers generally follow their children's schooling very closely, and while their children are young they are expected to help them prepare for school each day in a number of very detailed ways, from rehearsing with them the work that will be covered the next day in school so that they will do well in class, to being sure they have hankies pinned to their shirts, to equipping them with odds and ends the schools specifically request that they bring in for art and science projects—no easy job for working mothers!" Reiko Atsumi, "Dilemmas and Accommodations of Married Japanese Women in White-Collar Employment," *Bulletin of Concerned Asian Scholars*, 20 (3) (1988), repr. in Anthony Burik, ed., *Work in Japan: A Reader* (Oakland, CA: Japan Pacific Resource Center, 1991), p. 31.

16. We did not look at differences in the percentages of full-time homemakers and employed mothers who majored in engineering because the numbers in both groups were too small.

17. It may also be, of course, that coming from an upper-class family had taste and/or ideology effects, as well as economic effects, on the decision to become a homemaker. For example, it may be that women who came from the upper class were more likely to have mothers who were not employed and served as role models for them.

18. Only 5 full-time homemakers and 19 employed mothers provided information about their family's nonwage income.

19. Even if we wanted to test this hypothesis, we could not use data on upper-class origins to do so, since so few respondents came from the upper class.

20. It is quite interesting that the percentages of the two types of families that have relatives nearby is so similar. Perhaps as many homemaker families make a decision to live near parents, in-laws, or siblings for traditional family reasons as two-career families do for purposes of facilitating their employment.

21. Many of the cities and types of jobs cited here have been changed to protect confidentiality.

22. See Myra Marx Ferree, "Feminism and Family Research," in A. Booth, ed., *Contemporary Families* (Minneapolis, MN: National Council on Family Relations, 1991), pp. 103–21.

23. See Arlie Hochschild, *The Second Shift* (New York: Avon Books, 1991), Hochschild talks about the economy of gratitude, situations where employed women are so pleased that their husbands "let" them work that they are willing to do all of the housework in return for this favor.

24. In the Stanford sample, 42 percent of the men and 47 percent of the women had regular paid household help, the vast majority for only a few hours a week. In the Todai sample, only 3 percent of the men and 13 percent of the women had such help. It may be that some Todai graduates also had help with housework from their mother or mother-in-law, but we did not ask about this on the questionnaire.

25. Sampson Blair and Daniel Lichter ("Measuring the Division of Household Labor," *Journal of Family Issues*, 12 (1) [March 1991]: 91–113) also found that sharing housework is less equal after couples have children. In an interview study of 12 dual-earner couples, half of whom were parents, Wenda Brewster O'Reilly (Where Equal Opportunity Fails") also found that sharing tasks was greater for couples without children.

26. Married women with children spent 19.4 hours per week, and married women without children spent 15.2 hours per week, on housework. Married men with children spent 9.0 hours per week, and married men without children spent 7.6 hours per week, on housework. Joni Hersch, "The Impact of Nonmarket Work on Market Wages," *American Economic Review*, 81 (2) (May 1991): 158.

27. See Families and Work Institute, *Highlights of the National Study of the Changing Workforce* (New York: Families and Work Institute, 1993), pp. 48–49. While women had the overwhelming responsibility for cooking, cleaning, and shopping, men had the overwhelming responsibility for repairs. For paying bills, 58 percent of women said they did it and 50 percent of the men said their wives did it.

28. Japanese Prime Minister's Office, *International Comparative Survey on the Life and Attitudes of Women* (Tokyo: Prime Minister's Office, 1984), cited in Mari Osawa, "Corporate-Centered Society and Women's Labor in Japan Today," *U.S.–Japan Women's Journal, English Supplement*, 2 (1992): 27. This paper was originally published in Japanese under the title "Gendai Nihon shakai to josei rodo, kazoku, chiiki" (Contemporary Japanese Society and Women: Labor, Family, and Local Community), in Institute of Social Science, University of Tokyo, ed., *Gendai Nihon shakai, 6: Mondai no shoso* (Contemporary Japanese Society, 6: Multifarious Problems) (Tokyo: University of Tokyo Press, 1992). Housework tasks were defined as cleaning, laundry, shopping, preparing meals, cleaning up after meals and washing the dishes, and infant care.

29. Norman Stockman, Norman Bonney, and Sheng Xuewen, *Women's Work in East and West: The Dual Burden of Employment and Family Life* (Armonk, NY: M. E. Sharp, 1995).

30. Goldscheider and Waite (*New Families*, p. 133) also found that husbands of women who were employed more hours increased their sharing.

31. This finding was different from those in 1982 as cited in the Japanese Prime Minister's Office study (1984), where there was only a 10 percent difference in sharing between full-time homemakers and wives who worked full-time.

32. However, Stanford women who were employed full time had a higher rate of equal sharing (57.9 percent) than those in dual-earner couples (49.7 percent), and Todai women had virtually the same rate of equal sharing for those who were employed full-time (23.9 percent) and those in dual-earner couples (23.2 percent).

33. The rate of dissatisfaction among full-time-employed Stanford married women is much higher than the rate Barbara Bergmann calculated for the U.S. population as a whole. Bergmann found that 47 percent of wives who were employed full-time and did most of the housework said they would have liked more help from their husbands. Barbara Bergmann, *The Economic Emergence of Women* (New York: Basic Books, 1986), p. 268.

34. This is a much higher rate of dissatisfaction with traditional arrangements than is the case for Japanese women in general. A 1984 survey in Japan found that only 13 percent of employed wives thought that household tasks should be shared equally. See Mary Saso, *Women in the Japanese Workplace* (London: Hilary Shipman, 1990), p. 134.

35. The dependent variable was 1 if the graduate in the two-earner couple shared household tasks equally and 0 if he or she did not. Because many of the variables of interest were highly correlated with one another, we could not run a single regression to test our hypotheses. Thus, table 4.6 reports the results of four separate regressions. The table gives the relationship between a 1 dollar or 1 yen increase in earnings, a one percentage point increase in the ratio of wife's/husband's earnings, or a one hour increase in hours of employment and the probability that the couple would share financial responsibility.

36. It is important to recognize that in running these regressions, we have a very special test of bargaining power. We are looking at bargaining power only among couples where there are two earners and both have economic bargaining power, and are looking at the effects on sharing of relatively small differences in bargaining power. Wives and husbands who are not in the labor force at all, and who therefore have relatively little economic bargaining power (except insofar as they have nonwage income), are excluded from this analysis.

37. Goldscheider and Waite, *New Families*, pp. 137 and 133.

38. Catherine Ross, "Division of Labor at Home," *Social Forces*, 65 (3) (March 1987): 827.

39. Elizabeth Maret and Barbara Finlay, "The Distribution of Household Labor Among Women in Dual-Earner Families," *Journal of Marriage and the Family*, 46 (May 1984): 357–65.

40. Gary S. Becker, "Human Capital, Effort and the Sexual Division of Labor," *Journal of Labor Economics*, 3 (January 1985): S35.

41. Denise D. Bielby and William T. Bielby, "She Works Hard for the Money," *American Journal of Sociology*, 93 (5) (March 1988): 1031–59.

42. Kathy Cannings, "Family Commitments and Career Success: Earnings of Male and Female Managers," *Relations industrielles*, 46 (1) (1991): 141–56.

43. Hersch, "The Impact of Nonmarket Work on Market Wages," pp. 157–60.

44. Joni Hersch, "Male–Female Differences in Hourly Wages: The Role of Human Capital, Working Conditions, and Housework," *Industrial and Labor Relations Review*, 44 (4) (July 1991): 746–59.

45. Because we were interested in the effect of household tasks only on the earnings of those who were employed, we did not correct these regressions for sample selection bias.

46. The t-value on the coefficient on the household tasks arrangement for Stanford men in the full-time-earners regression is 0.127. In a regression for full-time Stanford men with no occupational dummy variables and no dummy variable for parental status (the only included variables being number of years of full-time work experience, number of years of part-time work experience, number of hours worked per week, and the dummy variable "does at least half of household tasks"), the dummy variable for household tasks had a coefficient of

−0.227, which was significant at the 1 percent level. For Stanford men in the all-earner sample, in a regression that included only work experience variables, hours worked variables, and the dummy for household tasks, the coefficient on the household tasks variable was −0.244, significant at the 1 percent level. For the Stanford women, the coefficient on the household task dummy was not significant in this alternative specification. For the Todai men and women, the coefficient on the household task dummy variable was not significant in this alternative specification, nor in a specification including the occupational dummies and the parental status dummy, but excluding the company size dummy variables.

47. Note that spouse's income in rows 1 and 2 of the table includes those with zero income, but the ratio of wife's to husband's income is calculated only for those with incomes >0.

48. The data for Stanford women, however, tell a different story. The average earnings of wives in traditional families were not lower than the average earnings of wives in other types of families.

59. It may be, however, that the high nonwage income came from the assets of the wife rather than the husband in these families.

50. The wives of Stanford men in egalitarian families earned more than the wives of Stanford men in other types of families. Perhaps this gave the wives bargaining power in negotiating for egalitarian arrangements. However, though Stanford women in egalitarian families were not the highest earners, they, too, managed to negotiate egalitarian arrangements. The highest-earning Stanford women with children were in traditional families. Clearly, what one wishes to bargain for, as well as one's bargaining power, is determined by more than one's income.

51. As an aside, it is notable that the average rates of employing household help are so much lower for the Todai sample than for the Stanford sample. Overall, 3 percent of Todai men and 13 percent of Todai women employed household help. The Todai rates ranged from 3 percent for men graduates with children in traditional and hybrid families to 19 percent for women graduates with children in hybrid families. The Stanford rates, on the other hand, ranged from 27 percent for women graduates without children in hybrid families to 57 percent in a number of types of families with children. Overall, 42 percent of Stanford men and 48 percent of Stanford women employed household help.

52. See Alan Booth and Lynn White, "Thinking About Divorce," *Journal of Marriage and the Family*, 42 (1980): 605–16; and Joan Huber and Glenna Spitze, "Considering Divorce," *American Journal of Sociology*, 86 (1980): 75–89.

53. Of course, these strategies were not necessarily consciously chosen by the graduates for the purpose of combining career and family. We are looking at the data and concluding from the graduates' behavior that they employed these strategies.

Appendix to Chapter 4

1. In Japan, about 80 percent of husbands hand over their paychecks to their wives and receive a certain amount of pocket money for themselves in return. Wives therefore have the responsibility of meeting their families' needs within the constraint of that paycheck plus any income they themselves earn. However, less than one-third of Japanese wives see themselves as having joint financial power or having sole financial power. See Mary Saso, *Women in the Japanese Workplace* (London: Hilary Shipman, 1990), p. 90.

2. Among Stanford graduates who were living together, 57.7 percent of the men and 78 percent of the women said they shared financial responsibility. Stanford married men had a

higher rate of sharing than Stanford men who lived with a partner, and Stanford married women had a lower rate of sharing than those who lived with a partner.

3. We also ran probit regressions looking at the effect of hours of employment, holding earnings constant. For women, the hours variable remained significant; for men, it remained insignificant.

4. Among those who lived together, 87 percent of the Stanford men and 61 percent of the Stanford women shared household management tasks.

5. Very few women (one in the Stanford sample and two in the Todai sample) reported that their husbands were mainly responsible for household management. However, 6 percent of the Stanford men and 11 percent of the Todai men said they were mainly responsible, putting them into the reverse-traditional category.

Chapter 5

1. About 3 percent of Todai women provided information on their income but not on their hours. They were designated as employed, but unclear as to whether full-time or part-time. Three percent of Stanford men and 4 percent of Todai men also were employed but in the unclear category. See chapter 2, note 34.

2. The data for the United States are from unpublished data from the March 1990 Current Population Survey made available to us by Howard Hayghe. The data for Japan are from Bernadette Lanciaux, "The Status of Women in Japan," in Janice Peterson and Doug Brown (eds.), *The Economic Status of Women Under Capitalism* (London: Edward Elgar, 1994), p. 162.

3. If we look at the employment rates only for mothers living with their husbands and having children under the age of 13, we find that they are not very different from the rates for mothers living with their husbands and having children under 18 (62 percent employed; 43 percent employed full-time and 19 percent employed part-time). The source of these data is the same as in note 2.

4. See Lanciaux, *The Economic Status of Women*, p. 162.

5. This question was asked of all of the graduates, but our analysis is confined to those who had children.

6. It is important to permit respondents to surveys to indicate multiple arrangements for child care because most parents do have multiple arrangements. In the United States, the National Study of the Changing Workforce, carried out in 1992, found that parents with children under five had 1.66 nonparental arrangements for their youngest child, while parents with children ages 5 to 12 had 2.04 nonparental arrangements. The range was from 1 to 12 arrangements per family. See Families and Work Institute, *Highlights of the National Study of the Changing Workforce* (New York: Families and Work Institute, 1993), p. 65.

7. Sandra Hofferth et al., *National Child Care Survey, 1990* (Washington, DC: The Urban Institute, 1991). That study also found that about 30 percent of all employed mothers with a child less than five used child care centers, and 20 percent used family day care homes.

8. Use of nursery schools among Todai women might have been even higher had the availability of such care arrangements not declined during the 1980s. See Alice Lam, *Women and Japanese Management* (London: Routledge, 1992), p. 230.

9. In the National Study of the Changing Workforce, 72 percent of employed parents with children under 13 indicated that they were very happy with the quality of their child care arrangements. See Families and Work Institute, *Highlights of the National Study*, p. 65.

10. Although the category includes those who did all of the child care as well as those who did more than half, in fact no Stanford fathers and no husbands of Stanford mothers did all the child care in hours of nonemployment.

11. In making the Stanford/Todai comparison, it is important to remember that Todai men may have underreported their hours of work and that in general, Todai men probably have longer commute times than Stanford men.

12. Such a bargaining power theory of course assumes that men do not want to do child care, but women want them to. This assumption is more likely to be universally correct concerning household chores than child care.

13. It is also interesting that the average household nonwage income in active fathers' families was less than half of that in nonactive fathers' families. However, since we don't know which spouse brought in the nonwage income, we cannot use that income to look at relative bargaining power.

14. We did not look at the relationship between being an active father and the ratio of wives'/husbands' earnings in the Todai sample, because the number of observations on the ratio was too small to be meaningful.

Chapter 6

1. Francine E. Gordon and Myra H. Strober, "Initial Observations on a Pioneer Cohort: 1974 Women MBAs," *Sloan Management Review*, 19 (2) (1978): 15–23.

2. Herbert L. Smith and Brian Powell, "Great Expectations: Variations in Income Expectations Among College Seniors," *Sociology of Education*, 63 (July 1990): 194–207.

3. We analyze all of the responses to these questions: from those who are part-time-employed, full-time-employed, and not employed.

4. The ratio of median expected earnings to median hoped-for earnings was 75 percent for Stanford and Todai men, 80 percent for Stanford women, and 85 percent for Todai women. Todai women are seen as even more optimistic than Todai men if ratios of expected to hoped-for earnings are based on means. The ratio of mean expected earnings to mean hoped-for earnings was 65 percent for Todai men and 89 percent for Todai women. The ratios for Stanford women and men were not very different when based on medians: 81 percent for Stanford men and 79 percent for Stanford women.

5. If we use the 1990 exchange rate of 144.79 to convert yen to dollars, we find that Stanford men and women had much higher earnings hopes than Todai men and women. In the comparisons based on the means, Todai men and women hoped for roughly half of what Stanford men and women hoped for. In the comparisons based on the medians, Todai men and women hoped for about 70 percent of what Stanford men and women hoped for.

6. If we calculate the ratio of median expected earnings to median hoped-for earnings, we find that for Stanford and Todai men it was 75 percent. For Stanford women it was 80 percent, and for Todai women it was 85 percent. This is another way of saying that men and women were somewhat closer in their earnings expectations than in their earnings hopes.

Again, using the 1990 exchange rate of 144.79, we can compare the earnings ratios for women and men across the two samples. For the medians, for both women and men, the Todai/Stanford ratios were quite similar to what they were for hoped-for earnings, about 70 percent. For the means, the Todai/Stanford ratio for the men was about 45 percent, and for the women about 55 percent.

7. Brenda Major and Ellen Konar, "An Investigation of Sex Differences in Pay Expectations and Their Possible Causes," *Academy of Management Journal*, 27 (4) (1984): 777–92.

8. Ann Machung, "Talking Career, Thinking Job: Gender Differences in Career and Family Expectations of Berkeley Seniors," *Feminist Studies*, 15 (1) (Spring 1989): 35–58. Interestingly, the gender differential for predicted earnings in their first jobs was much higher, 78 percent, and quite close to Stanford and Todai's earnings differential by gender 10 years out.

9. Myra H. Strober, "The MBA Degree: Same Passport to Success for Women and Men?" in Phyllis A. Wallace (ed.), *Women in the Workplace* (Boston: Auburn House, 1982), pp. 25–44.

10. It is possible that physicians systematically underestimate their future earnings. It is also possible that in 1990 they believed that with the changes in physician reimbursement practices, their earnings would not be increasing to the same extent as those of lawyers or managers. It would be interesting to see, in a follow-up study, whether they were correct in their predictions about their future earnings.

11. It is interesting that for Todai women, although being a professor is associated with a significant penalty for current earnings, it is associated with a significant premium for expected earnings.

12. The sample size for Todai women in the regression where we investigated the effect of homemaking on expected earnings was 87. The sample size for Stanford women was 242.

Chapter 7

1. We remind the reader of our caveat in chapter 1. Because the Stanford sample under-represents nonwhites, we make no claims about its experiences as a guide for future change for nonwhite families in the United States.

2. See Japan Ministry of Health and Welfare, *Vital Statistics 1989*. Cited in Kazuko Tanaka, "Work, Education and the Family," in Kumiko Fujimura-Fanselow and Atsuko Kameda (eds.), *Japanese Women: New Feminist Perspectives on the Past, Present, and Future* (New York: The Feminist Press at the City University of New York, 1995), p. 298.

3. In 1992, Myra was asked by the Tokyo Chamber of Commerce to consult with them on this matter. She was asked particularly about what policies designed to assist the combining of career and family have been successful in the United States.

4. This is a highly complicated matter, because these challenging and highly paid jobs are those that provide lifetime employment and operate under the *nenko* wage system. We examine it in further detail below, when we discuss employment flexibility.

5. See Barbara Bergmann, *In Defense of Affirmative Action* (New York: Basic Books, 1996). Affirmative action for women was strong in the United States during the 1970s, but has languished since the beginning of the 1980s. It is now caught up in the larger debate concerning affirmative action for race, and it seems doubtful that it will be resurrected with any meaningful clout anytime soon.

6. See Robert Michael, Heidi Hartmann, and Brigid O'Farrell, eds., *Pay Equity* (Washington, DC: National Academy Press, 1989). While some state governments and a few unions have successfully used comparable worth pay adjustments, they have not been used much in private industry. There is relatively little political pressure at this time to extend the use of comparable worth pay adjustments.

7. Assuming that women who move into men's occupations receive equal pay to that of men, either affirmative action or comparable worth can be successful in reducing the gender earnings gap.

8. One of Myra's U.S. students, hoping for a career in commercial real estate, said that as far as she was concerned, all she wanted from the woman's movement was the same freedom to have a heart attack that any man had.

9. For a flavor of the U.S. debate on whether women and men have different management styles, see Judy B. Rosener, "Ways Women Lead," *Harvard Business Review*, 68 (November–December 1990): 199–125, and the rebuttal by other scholars in the following issue.

10. For a full discussion of these issues see Barbara Bergmann, *The Economic Emergence of Women* (New York: Basic Books, 1986).

11. We don't mean to imply that the kind of earnings discrimination we found in the Stanford sample does not exist in Japan. In fact, we think it probably does; it was just not present in the Todai sample.

12. Part-time workers who are employed fewer hours expect to get less total income; but they don't want to earn less per hour of employment than full-time workers.

13. See Alice Lam, *Women and Japanese Management* (London: Routledge, 1992), pp. 222–23; and Ronald Dore, Jean Bounine-Cabale, and Kari Tapiola, *Japan at Work* (Paris: OECD, 1989), pp. 40–41.

14. In Japan, the Child Care Leave Law, allowing either parent to take up to one year of unpaid leave, was passed in 1991. In the United States, the Family Leave Act, passed in 1992, requires employers to provide up to 12 weeks of unpaid leave to new parents as well as to employees who need to take care of a sick family member or who are themselves sick.

15. For a discussion of the economics of child care in the United States, including concerns about quality, see David M. Blau (ed.), *The Economics of Child Care* (New York: Russell Sage, 1991); and Myra H. Strober, "The Economics of Child Care," in *The International Encyclopedia of Education* (Oxford: Pergamon Press, 1994); and Myra H. Strober, Suzanne Gerlach-Downie, and Kenneth E. Yeager, "Child Care Centers as Workplaces," *Feminist Economics*, 1 (May 1995): 93–120.

16. Japan's efforts to increase the availability of public child care as part of a plan to raise the fertility rate failed to match demand in big cities. Also, nurseries often close by 4:30 or 5:00, making it difficult for parents to work full-time and pick up their children on time.

17. Cited in Charles Douglas Lummis and Satomi Nakajima with Kumiko Fujimura-Fanselow and Atsuko Kameda, "Dialogue," in Fujimura-Fanselow and Kameda, eds., *Japanese Women: New Feminist Perspectives* (New York: The Feminist Press at the City University of New York, 1995), p. 244.

18. The first award of monetary damages in a sexual harassment suit occurred in 1992. In 1993, Doi Takako was the first woman to serve as speaker of the House of Representatives, and in 1994 Takahashi Hisako became the first woman Supreme Court judge. See

"Appendix," in Kumiko Fujimura-Fanselow and Atsuko Kameda, eds., *Japanese Women: New Feminist Perspectives* (New York: The Feminist Press at the City University of New York, 1995), pp. 413–14.

19. Masanori Yamaguchi, "Men on the Threshold of Change," in Kumiko Fujimura-Fanselow and Atsuko Kamdeda, eds., *Japanese Women: New Feminist Perspectives* (New York: The Feminist Press at the City University of New York, 1995), p. 249.

20. Ibid., p. 248.

21. Lummis, et al., "Dialogue," pp. 237–38.

References

Abraham, Katharine, and Farber, Henry. "Job Duration, Seniority and Earnings." *American Economic Review*, 77 (June 1987): 278–97.

Agarwal, Bina. "Bargaining and Gender Relations: Within and Beyond the Household." *Feminist Economics*, 3 (1) (1997).

———. *A Field of One's Own: Gender and Land Rights in South Asia*. Cambridge: Cambridge University Press, 1994.

Amano, Masako (ed.). *Joshi Koto Kyoiku no Zahyo*. Tokyo: Kono Publications, 1986.

Atsumi, Reiko. "Dilemmas and Accommodations of Married Japanese Women in White-Collar Employment." *Bulletin of Concerned Asian Scholars* 20 (3) (1988). Repr. in Anthony Burik (ed.), *Work in Japan: A Reader*, pp. 25–33. Oakland, CA: Japan Pacific Resource Center, 1991.

Becker, Gary S. *The Economics of Discrimination*. Chicago: University of Chicago Press, 1957.

———. *Human Capital: A Theoretical and Empirical Analysis with Special Reference to Education*. New York: National Bureau of Economic Research, 1964.

———. "Human Capital, Effort and the Sexual Division of Labor." *Journal of Labor Economics*, 3 (January 1985): S33–S58.

Becker, Gary S., Landes, Elisabeth M., and Michael, Robert T. "An Economic Analysis of Marital Instability." *Journal of Political Economy*, 85 (6) (December 1977): 1141–87.

Bergmann, Barbara R. *The Economic Emergence of Women*. New York: Basic Books, 1986.

———. *In Defense of Affirmative Action*. New York: Basic Books, 1996.

Bielby, Denise D., and Bielby, William T. "She Works Hard for the Money: Household Responsibilities and the Allocation of Work Effort." *American Journal of Sociology*, 93 (5) (March 1988): 1031–59.

Blair, Sampson Lee, and Lichter, Daniel T. "Measuring the Division of Household Labor: Gender Segregation of Housework Among American Couples." *Journal of Family Issues*, 12 (1) (March 1991): 91–113.

Blau, David M. (ed.). *The Economics of Child Care*. New York: Russell Sage, 1991.

Blau, Francine D., and Ferber, Marianne A. *The Economics of Women, Men and Work*. Englewood Cliffs, NJ: Prentice-Hall, 1992.

Blau, Francine D., and Kahn, Lawrence M. "The Gender Earnings Gap: Learning from International Comparisons." *American Economic Review*, 82 (May 1992): 533–38.

Booth, Alan, and White, Lynn. "Thinking About Divorce." *Journal of Marriage and the Family*, 42 (1980): 605–16.

Brinton, Mary C. *Women and the Economic Miracle: Gender and Work in Postwar Japan.* Berkeley: University of California Press, 1993.

Brown, Clair. Communication via E-mail. October 4, 1996.

Brown, Clair, Nakata, Yoshifumi, Reich, Michael and Ullman, Lerget. *Work and Pay in the United States and Japan.* New York: Oxford University Press, 1997.

Burik, Anthony (ed.). *Work in Japan: A Reader.* Oakland, CA: Japan Pacific Resource Center, 1991.

Cannings, Kathy. "Family Commitments and Career Success: Earnings of Male and Female Managers." *Relations Industrielles* 46 (1) (1991): 141–56.

Chan, Agnes M. K. "Combining Work and Family: Gender Comparisons of Graduates of Tokyo University Class of 1981." Ph.D. dissertation, Stanford University, 1994.

Conable, Charlotte Williams. *Women at Cornell: The Myth of Equal Education.* Ithaca, NY: Cornell University Press, 1977.

Conway, Jill. "Perspectives on the History of Women's Education in the United States." *History of Education Quarterly*, 14 (Spring 1974): 1–12.

Davis, Kingsley. "Wives and Work: A Theory of the Sex-Role Revolution and Its Consequences." In Sanford M. Dornbusch and Myra H. Strober (eds.), *Feminism, Children, and the New Families*, pp. 67–86. New York: Guilford Press, 1988.

Dinnerstein, Myra. *Women Between Two Worlds.* Philadelphia: Temple University Press, 1992.

Doeringer, Peter B., and Piore, Michael J. *Internal Labor Markets and Manpower Analysis.* Lexington, MA: D.C. Heath, 1971.

Dore, Ronald, Bounine-Cabale, Jean, and Tapiola, Kari. *Japan at Work: Markets, Management and Flexibility.* Paris: OECD, 1989.

Education Material Investigating Committee. *The History of the Educational System After the Meiji Period.* Tokyo: Education Material Investigating Committee, 1939. Vol. 5.

Edwards, Linda N. "The Status of Women in Japan: Has the Equal Employment Opportunity Law Made a Difference?" *Journal of Asian Economics*, 5 (2) (1994): 217–40.

Edwards, Richard C. *Contested Terrain.* New York: Basic Books, 1979.

———. "The Social Relations of Production in the Firm and Labor Market Structure." In Richard Edwards, Michael Reich, and David Gordon, (eds), *Labor Market Segmentation*, pp. 3–26. Lexington, MA: D. C. Heath, 1975.

Elliot, Orin L. *Stanford University: The First Twenty-Five Years.* Stanford, CA.: Stanford Press, 1937.

England, Paula, and Farkas, George. *Households, Employment and Gender: A Social, Economic and Demographic View.* Hawthorne, NY: Aldine, 1986.

England, Paula, Farkas, George, Kilbourne, Barbara Stanek, and Dou, Thomas. "Explaining Occupational Sex Segregation and Wages: Findings from a Model with Fixed Effects." *American Sociological Review*, 62 (August 1988): 544–58.

Families and Work Institute. *Highlights of the National Study of the Changing Workforce*. New York: Families and Work Institute, 1993.

Ferree, Myra Marx. "Feminism and Family Research." In A. Booth, (ed.), *Contemporary Families*, pp. 103–21. Minneapolis, MN: National Council on Family Relations, 1991.

Filer, Randall. "The Role of Personality and Tastes in Determining Occupational Structure." *Industrial and Labor Relations Review*, 39 (April 1986): 412–24.

Fox, Mary Frank. "Women and Higher Education: Gender Differences in the Status of Students and Scholars." In Jo Freeman (ed.), *Women: A Feminist Perspective*, pp. 220–37. Mountain View, CA: Mayfield, 1995.

Fuchs, Victor. "Women's Quest for Economic Equality." *Journal of Economic Perspectives* 3 (1) (Winter 1989): 25–41.

Fujimura-Fanselow, Kumiko. "College Women Today: Options and Dilemmas." In Kumiko Fujimura-Fanselow and Atsuko Kameda (eds.), *Japanese Women: New Feminist Perspectives on the Past, Present and Future*, pp. 125–54. New York: The Feminist Press at the City University of New York, 1995.

Fujimura-Fanselow, Kumiko, and Kameda, Atsuko, "The Changing Portrait of Japanese Men." In Kumiko Fujimura-Fanselow and Atsuko Kameda (eds.), *Japanese Women: New Feminist Perspectives on the Past, Present and Future*, pp. 229–30. New York: The Feminist Press at the City University of New York, 1995.

Goldin, Claudia. "Career and Family: College Women Look to the Past." In Francine D. Blau and Ronald G. Ehrenberg (eds.), *Gender and Family Issues in the Workplace*. New York: Russell Sage, 1997.

Goldscheider, Frances K., and Waite, Linda J. *New Families, No Families?* Berkeley: University of California Press, 1991.

Gordon, David M., Edwards, Richard C., and Reich, Michael. *Segmented Work, Divided Workers: The Historical Transformation of Labor in the United States*. New York: Cambridge University Press, 1982.

Gordon, Francine E., and Strober, Myra H. "Initial Observations on a Pioneer Cohort: 1974 Women MBAs." *Sloan Management Review*, 19: (2) (1978): 15–23.

Gross, Edward. "Plus Ca Change . . . ? The Sexual Structure of Occupations over Time." *Social Problems*, 16 (1) (Fall 1968): 198–208.

Hara, Kimi. "Challenges to Education for Girls and Women in Modern Japan: Past and Present." In Kumiko Fujimura-Fanselow and Atsuko Kameda (eds.), *Japanese Women: New Feminist Perspectives on the Past, Present and Future*, pp. 93–106. New York: The Feminist Press at the City University of New York, 1995.

Harvard Business Review, 67 (3) (May–June 1989): 182–214.

Hendry, Joy. "The Role of the Professional Housewife." In Janet Hunter (ed.), *Japanese Women Working*. London: Routledge, 1993.

Hersch, Joni. "The Impact of Nonmarket Work on Market Wages." *American Economic Review*, 81 (2) (May 1991): 157—60.

———. "Male–Female Differences in Hourly Wages: The Role of Human Capital, Working Conditions, and Housework." *Industrial and Labor Relations Review*, 44 (4) (July 1991): 746—59.

Higuchi, Yoshio. "Higher Education and Income Distribution in Japan." Discussion Paper, Keio University, 1994. ("Daigaku Kyouiku to Syotoku Bonpu." In Tsuneo Ishikawa (ed.) *Nihon no Syotoku to Tomi no Bunpu*. Tokyo: Tokyo University Press, 1994.

Hochschild, Arlie. *The Second Shift*. New York: Avon Books, 1991.

Hofferth, Sandra, et al. *National Child Care Survey, 1990*. Washington, DC: The Urban Institute, 1991.

Huber, Joan, and Spitze, Glenna, "Considering Divorce." *American Journal of Sociology*, 86 (1980): 75—89.

International Labour Organization (ILO). *Yearbook of Labor Statistics, 1990–91*. Geneva: International Labour Organization, 1991.

Ito, Takatoshi. *The Japanese Economy*. Cambridge, MA: MIT Press, 1994.

Jacobsen, Joyce P., and Levin, Laurence M. "Effects of Intermittent Labor Force Attachment on Women's Earnings." *Monthly Labor Review*, 118 (9) (September 1995): 14—19.

Japan Statistics Bureau, Prime Minister's Office. *Japan Statistical Yearbook, 1982*. Tokyo: Japan Statistics Bureau, 1982.

Japanese Ministry of Education. *Report on a Survey of the Issues Related to the Academic Juku*. Tokyo: Ministry of Education, 1995.

———. *Survey of the Extracurricular Activities of Children/Students*. Tokyo: Ministry of Education, 1985.

Japanese Ministry of Labour, Minister's Secretariat, Policy Planning and Research Department. *Yearbook of Labour Statistics, 1990*. Tokyo: Ministry of Labour, 1990.

Japanese Prime Minister's Office. *International Comparative Survey on the Life and Attitudes of Women, 1984*. Cited in Osawa Mari, "Corporate-Centered Society and Women's Labor in Japan Today." *U.S.–Japan Women's Journal, English Supplement*, 2 (1992): 27. Originally published in Japanese under the title "Gendai Nihon shakai to josei rodo, kazoku, chiiki" (Contemporary Japanese Society and Women: Labor, Family, and Local Community), in Institute of Social Science, University of Tokyo, ed., *Gendai Nihon shakai, 6: Mondai no shoso* (Contemporary Japanese Society, 6: Multifarious Problems). Tokyo: University of Tokyo Press, 1992.

Josei Shokugyo Zaidan (Women's Vocational Institute). *Kosubetsu Koyo-kanri ni Kansuru Kenkyu-kai Hokokusho* (A Survey Report on Career Tracking). Tokyo: Josei Shokugyo Zaidan; 1990. Cited in Linda Edwards, "The Status of Women in Japan," *Journal of Asian Economics*, 5 (2) (1994): 228; and Alice Lam, *Women and Japanese Management*, p. 129. London: Routledge, 1992.

Katchadourian, Herant, and Boli, John. *Cream of the Crop: The Impact of Elite Education in the Decade After College*. New York: Basic Books, 1994.

Kaufman, Polly W. (ed.). *The Search for Equity: Women at Brown University: 1891–1991*. Providence, RI: Trustees of Brown University, 1991.

Kawashima, Yoko, "Female Workers: An Overview of Past and Current Trends." In Kumiko Fujimura-Fanselow and Atsuko Kameda (eds.), *Japanese Women: New Feminist Perspectives on the Past, Present, and Future*, pp. 271–294. New York: The Feminist Press at the City University of New York, 1995.

————. "The Place and Role of Female Workers in the Japanese Labor Market." *Women's Studies International Forum*, 10 (6) (1987): 599–611.

————. "Wage Differentials Between Women and Men in Japan." Ph.D. dissertation, Stanford University, 1983.

Korenman, Sanders, and Neumark, David. "Marriage, Motherhood and Wages." *Journal of Human Resources*, 27 (2) (Spring 1992): 233–55.

Lam, Alice C. L. *Women and Japanese Management*. London: Routledge, 1992.

Lanciaux, Bernadette. "The Status of Women in Japan." In Janice Peterson and Doug Brown (eds.), *The Economic Status of Women Under Capitalism*, pp. 157–76. London: Edward Elgar, 1994.

Lazear, Edward P., and Moore, Robert L. "Incentives, Productivity, and Labor Contracts." *Quarterly Journal of Economics*, 77 (May 1984): 275–95.

Lincoln, James R., and Nakata, Yoshifumi. "The Transformation of the Japanese Employment System: Nature, Depth and Origins." *Work and Occupations*, 24 (1) (February 1997): 33–55.

Machung, Ann. "Talking Career, Thinking Job: Gender Differences in Career and Family Expectations of Berkeley Seniors." *Feminist Studies*, 15 (1) (Spring 1989): 35–58.

Mahony, Rhona. *Kidding Ourselves*. New York: Basic Books, 1995.

Major, Brenda, and Konar, Ellen. "An Investigation of Sex Differences in Pay Expectations and Their Possible Causes." *Academy of Management Journal*, 27 (4) (1984): 777–92.

Mandel, Michael J. "The Great Equalizer." *Business Week*, July 22, 1996, pp. 74–75.

Maret, Elizabeth, and Finlay, Barbara. "The Distribution of Household Labor Among Women in Dual-Earner Families." *Journal of Marriage and the Family*, 46 (May 1984): 357–65.

Matsura, Takenori. *Shushoku*. Tokyo: Nihon Keizai Shinbun, 1978.

Medoff, James L., and Abraham, Katharine G. "Are Those Paid More Really More Productive: The Case of Experience." *Journal of Human Resources*, 16 (Spring 1981): 186–216.

————. "Experience, Performance and Earnings." *Quarterly Journal of Economics*, 95 (December 1980): 703–36.

Michael, Robert T., Hartmann, Heidi I., and O'Farrell, Brigid (eds.). *Pay Equity: Empirical Inquiries*. Washington, DC: National Academy Press, 1989.

Mincer, Jacob. *Schooling, Experience and Earnings*. New York: National Bureau of Economic Research, 1974.

Mincer, Jacob, and Polachek, Solomon. "Family Investments in Human Capital: Earnings of Women." *Journal of Political Economy* 82 (March/April 1974): S76–S108.

Mirrielees, Edith R. *The Story of a University*. New York: G. P. Putnam, 1959.

Mitchell, J. Pearce. *Stanford University: 1916–41*. Stanford, CA.: Trustees of Stanford University, 1958.

Miyahara, Kijiro. "Intercollege Stratification: The Case of Male College Graduates in Japan." *Sociological Forum*, 3 (1) (1988): 25–43.

National Center for Education Statistics. *Digest of Educational Statistics*. Washington DC: U.S. Government Printing Office, 1993.

"Newly Opened Corporate Career Paths Prove Rocky." *Nikkei Weekly*, February 21, 1994.

Oaxaca, Ronald L., and Ransom, Michael R. "Identification in Detailed Wage Decompositions." Unpublished Paper, Department of Economics, University of Arizona, October 1995.

Oh, Jaelim. "Gender Differences in Patterns of Changing College Major." Ph.D. dissertation, Stanford University, 1992.

O'Reilly, Wenda Brewster. "Where Equal Opportunity Fails: Corporate Men and Women in Dual-Career Families". Ph.D. dissertation, Stanford University, 1983.

Organization for Economic Cooperation and Development (OECD), Statistics Directorate. *Purchasing Power Parities and Real Expenditures, 1990*. Vol. 2. Geneva: OECD, 1992.

Osawa, Mari. "Corporate-Centered Society and Women's Labor in Japan Today." *U.S.–Japan Women's Journal, English Supplement* 2 (1992): 3–35.

Osterman, Paul. "White-Collar Internal Labor Markets." In Paul Osterman (ed.), *Internal Labor Markets*, pp. 163–89. Cambridge, MA: MIT Press, 1984.

Papanek, Hannah. "Men, Women and Work: Reflections on the Two-Person Career." *American Journal of Sociology*, 78 (1973): 852–72.

Phelps, Edmund. "The Statistical Theory of Racism and Sexism." *American Economic Review*, 62 (September 1972): 659–61.

Piore, Michael J. "Notes for a Theory of Labor Market Stratification." In Richard C. Edwards, Michael Reich, and David M. Gordon (eds.), *Labor Market Segmentation*, pp. 125–50. Lexington, MA: D. C. Heath, 1975.

Reilly, Kevin T. "Human Capital and Information: The Employer Size–Wage Effect." *Journal of Human Resources*, 30 (1) (Winter 1995): 1–18.

Reskin, Barbara F., and Hartmann, Heidi I. (eds.). *Women's Work, Men's Work: Sex Segregation on the Job*. Washington, DC: National Academy Press, 1986.

Rosener, Judy B. "Ways Women Lead." *Harvard Business Review*, 68 (November–December 1990): 119–25.

Ross, Catherine E. "The Division of Labor at Home." *Social Forces*, 65 (3) (March 1987): 816–33.

Rudolph, Frederick. *The American College and University: A History*. New York: Vintage Books, 1962.

Saso, Mary. *Women in the Japanese Workplace*. London: Hilary Shipman, 1990.

Satsuki-Kai. *Female Graduates of Tokyo University: Life Report*. Tokyo: Sanshodo, 1989.

Schaffner, Julie A. "The Sensitivity of Wage Equation Estimates for a Developing Country to Changes in Sample Selection Mode of Specification." Stanford University, 1995. (Processed.)

Schwartz, Felice N. "Management Women and the New Facts of Life." *Harvard Business Review*, 67 (2) (January 1989): 65–76.

Smith, Herbert L., and Powell, Brian. "Great Expectations: Variations in Income Expectations Among College Seniors." *Sociology of Education*, 63 (July 1990): 194–207.

Solomon, Barbara Miller. *In the Company of Educated Women*. New Haven: Yale University Press, 1985.

Sorifu (Office of the Prime Minister). *Fujin no Genjo to Shisaku*. Tokyo: Office of the Prime Minister, 1989.

Spain, Daphne, and Bianchi, Suzanne M. *Balancing Act: Motherhood, Marriage, and Employment Among American Women*. New York: Russell Sage, 1996.

Spence, Michael. "Job Market Signaling." *Quarterly Journal of Economics*, 87 (August 1973): 355–74.

Stanford University. *Campus Reports*, June 7, 1972.

———. *Campus Reports*, September 20, 1972.

———. *Campus Reports*, March 14, 1973.

Steil, Janice, and Weltman, Karen. "Marital Inequality: The Importance of Resources, Personal Attributes and Social Norms on Career Valuing and the Allocation of Domestic Responsibilities." *Sex Roles*, 24 (3–4) (February 1991): 161–79.

Stockman, Norman, Bonney, Norman, and Xuewen, Sheng. *Women's Work in East and West: The Dual Burden of Employment and Family Life*. Armonk, NY: M. E. Sharp, 1995.

Strober, Myra H. "Commentary on Chapter 2." In Francine D. Blau and Ronald G. Ehrenberg (eds.), *Gender and Family Issues in the Workplace*, pp. 61–64. New York: Russell Sage, 1997.

———. "The Economics of Child Care." In *The International Encyclopedia of Education*, pp. 344–48. Oxford: Pergamon Press, 1994.

———. "Gender and Occupational Segregation." In *The International Encyclopedia of Education*, pp. 248–52. Oxford: Pergamon Press, 1994.

———. "Human Capital Theory: Implications for HR Managers." In Daniel J. B. Mitchell and Mahmood A. Zaidi (eds.), *The Economics of Human Resource Management*, pp. 60–85. Oxford: Basil Blackwell, 1990.

———. "The MBA Degree: Same Passport to Success for Women and Men?" In Phyllis A. Wallace (ed.), *Women in the Workplace*, pp. 25–44. Boston: Auburn House, 1982.

———. "The Relative Attractiveness Theory of Occupational Segregation: The Case of Women in Medicine." *Proceedings of the Annual Meetings of the Industrial and Labor Relations Research Association*, pp. 42–50. 1992.

———. "Toward a General Theory of Occupational Sex Segregation: The Case of Public School Teaching." In Barbara F. Reskin (ed.), *Sex Segregation in the Workplace: Trends, Explanations, Remedies*, pp. 144–56. Washington, DC: National Academy Press, 1984.

————. "Valuing the Invisible Work of Women." Cambridge, MA: Radcliffe Public Policy Institute, 1998.

Strober, Myra H., and Arnold, Carolyn. "The Dynamics of Occupational Segregation Among Banktellers." In Clair Brown and Joseph Pechman (eds.), *Gender in the Workplace*, pp. 107–57. Washington, DC: Brookings Institution, 1987.

Strober, Myra H., Gerlach-Downie, Suzanne, and Yeager, Kenneth E. "Child Care Centers as Workplaces." *Feminist Economics*, 1 (May 1995): 93–120.

Tanaka, Kazuko. "Work, Education and the Family." In Kumiko Fujimura-Fanselow and Atsuko Kameda (eds.), *Japanese Women: New Feminist Perspectives on the Past, Present and Future*, pp. 295–308. New York: The Feminist Press at the City University of New York, 1995.

Thurow, Lester C. "Education and Economic Inequality." *The Public Interest*, 28 (Summer 1972): 66–81.

United Nations, Department for Economic and Social Information and Policy Analysis, Statistical Division. *Statistical Yearbook, 1993.* New York: United Nations, 1995.

U.S. Department of Commerce, Bureau of the Census. *Current Population Reports, Consumer Income, Series P-60,* "Money Income of Households, Families and Persons in the United States: 1988 and 1989," table 24, pp. 102–03. Washington, DC: U.S. Government Printing Office, July 1991.

U.S. Department of Education. *Digest of Educational Statistics.* Washington, DC: U.S. Government Printing Office, 1983.

U.S. Department of Labor, Bureau of Labor Statistics. *Employment and Earnings* (January 1991).

Waldfogel, Jane. "Understanding the 'Family Gap' in Pay for Women and Children." *Journal of Economic Perspectives*, 12 (1) (Winter 1988): 137–56.

Webster's New Twentieth Century Dictionary, Unabridged. 2nd ed. William Collins, 1979.

Yoshida, Aya. "The Social Life and Consciousness of Female Students of Tokyo University." *Higher Education in the Present*, no. 259 (1985): 52–57. (In Japanese.)

Zellner, Harriet. "The Determinants of Occupational Segregation." In Cynthia B. Lloyd (ed.), *Sex Discrimination and the Division of Labor*, pp. 125–45. New York: Columbia University Press, 1975.

Zeng, Kangmin. "The Dragon Gate: The Origin and Development of the University Entrance Examinations and the Peripheral Cultures in Japan, Korea and Taiwan." Ph.D. dissertation, Stanford University, 1996.

Index